THE REVELATION OF
Jesus Christ

A Commentary for the People

David C. Crenshaw

ISBN 978-1-0980-3330-9 (paperback)
ISBN 978-1-0980-3331-6 (digital)

Christian Faith Publishing, Inc.
832 Park Avenue
Meadville, PA 16335
www.christianfaithpublishing.com

Printed in the United States of America

Contents

Introduction

Early in my pastoral career, I read a book by one of my seminary professors, Dr. Jay Adams. The book was titled *The Time Is at Hand*. The title was taken from verse 3 of the Revelation, chapter 1. In this small but powerful book, Dr. Adams argues against the popular view of premillennial dispensationalism and biblically destroys that position. He also maintains the events of all but the last two chapters of Revelation have already happened. This is called the "orthodox preterist position." When I first read this book, I was really surprised. I thought my former professor had "gone off the deep end," theologically speaking. I had not previously been exposed to the preterist view of Revelation. *Preterism* comes from a Latin root, which means "past," and the orthodox preterist view holds that the events in the first twenty chapters of Revelation are already past. They are referring to the destruction of the Jewish age in AD 70.

At the time, I thought the view of Revelation presented by William Hendrickson in his commentary *More Than Conquerors* was the most biblical view. He presents Revelation as seven cycles of church history. I had even used Dr. Hendrickson's book as the basis for a Sunday school class I taught at a small church I had served while in seminary.

Several years later, while I was pastoring a church in Bakersfield, California, my congregation challenged me to teach through the book of the Revelation. In preparation for teaching that class, I read all of the Old Testament references. (My understanding is that Revelation has more references from the Old Testament than any other book in the Bible.) As I read them in context, I found many of them dealt with God's prophecy of the destruction of the Jewish temple at Jerusalem in AD 70. Others dealt with the judgment of God upon the Jewish leadership for their disobedience of Him. As I continued to study, I became more and more convinced that Dr. Adams had been right after all.

I then read a book by Kenneth Gentry, *666, The Beast of Revelation*, which deals with the dating of the book of Revelation. This book presents very strong evidence that John's letter was written before the destruction of the Jewish temple. Although many authors have maintained Revelation was written after the destruction of the temple in AD 70, Gentry's arguments convinced me that Revelation was a letter of comfort written to Jewish Christians in the first century. These Christians were about to undergo terrible persecution by the Jewish leadership and the Roman government. I came to believe Revelation predicted not the terrible destruction of the world of the future but the destruction of the temple, the destruction of the Jewish system of false worship and the Roman government, the false church and the false state.

There are very many learned men who hold a different view of the Revelation than do I. Therefore, I am not adamant that my view is the only or most correct view. My purpose in writing this book is not necessarily to convince you that my position is correct. The purpose is to encourage you to read God's Word, the Bible, and let His Spirit reveal His truth to you.

Before we begin, there are several definitions that you need to understand, especially if you have not been exposed to them before.

First are the major "eschatological" positions. Eschatology has to do with the study of the end-times—what is going to happen at the end of history.

The most popular position, at least since the beginning of the twentieth century, is the *premillennial dispensational*—people who hold this view believe that Jesus will return prior to the millennium (the one thousand years mentioned in Revelation 20). This is the view which Dr. Adams addressed and thoroughly refuted in his book, *The Time Is at Hand.*

Another popular position is the *postmillennial.* Those who hold this view generally believe that Christ is coming back after (post) the one thousand years of Revelation 20. Most also, generally, though not always, believe the world will become more and more Christian and that Christ will return to a basically Christian world.

The third major position is the *amillennial.* The Greek letter *a* placed before a word means "not." Therefore, technically, *a*millennial means "no millennium." Most amillennialists, however, do believe there is a thousand-year period (it is, after all, in Scripture), but it is usually understood as a "church age" of indefinite length (Christ will come back when He comes back).

"What is the definition of *apocalypse?*"

The popular understanding of the word *apocalypse* is that it deals with the end-times, what is going to happen at the end of the world.

However, the Greek word *apocalypse* actually means "revelation." In other words, the very title of the book means that something is being revealed. The first sentence of John's letter tells us that it is the *apocalupsis* of Jesus Christ—literally, "the Revelation of (or about) Jesus Christ."

All of the Bible is, in fact, a revelation of or about Jesus Christ. In John 5:39, Jesus tells the Pharisees (who were the Bible scholars of the day),

> You search the Scriptures because you think
> that in them you have eternal life; it is these that
> testify about Me.

We must remember, the only scriptures they had were what we refer to as the Old Testament.

After looking at the first three verses of the Revelation, to better understand how the Old Testament reveals Jesus Christ, we will return to Daniel 9:22–27. Analysis of this passage will enable us to determine the meaning of the "abomination of desolation," referred to in Matthew 24. We will also see that Matthew 24 addresses the same issues as the Revelation and the same period of time as Daniel 9. In Matthew 24, I intend to show that Jesus is not talking about

7

the end of the future world but the destruction of the Jewish temple, marking the end of the Jewish system or "age." He is not teaching about "the last days" (of history) but the last days of the Jewish economy, the false religious system of the Jews, and the beginning of the New Covenant era of the church.

We will then study the rest of Revelation, chapter 1, which explains Who Christ is. Next, we will look at the seven churches to which John was writing. Then we will continue with an overview of the rest of the book. This commentary will not deal with every event in the Revelation. It will deal more extensively with those events which are confusing to modern church people because of the lack of understanding of the Old Testament symbolism in the Revelation.

One thing to remember as you read is that this is not a normal commentary. That means I have not used extensive footnotes or endnotes. I also have not dealt extensively with many of the more obscure teachings in the Revelation. My purpose in writing this commentary is to introduce the average layperson to a broad overview of the Revelation. It is written in what I hope will be a way that is understandable to those without a seminary education and without the benefit of a knowledge of Greek and Hebrew (Aramaic).

Unless otherwise noted, all Bible quotations in this commentary are from the New American Standard Bible (NASB) Updated.

CHAPTER 1

Revelation 1:1–3

> The revelation of Jesus Christ which God gave Him to show to His bond-servants, the things which must shortly take place; and He sent and communicated it by His angel to His bondservant John... (Revelation 1:1)

Notice the book begins with, "The revelation (Greek, *apocalupsis*) of Jesus Christ." The Greek word which we understand to mean "of" is ambiguous. It could be *about* Jesus Christ or *from* Jesus Christ—as a source. Two things we know for certain are that *it has to do with Jesus Christ*, and *it ultimately comes from God*. It is what the theologians call "special revelation." It is truth revealed by God to Him (that is, Jesus Christ) to show to man. The word we translate *show* is "to point out or to make known." In the phrase "God gave to Him to communicate to His bond-servants," the word *communicate* in the Greek is actually "to sign."

The very first thing we learn is that the Revelation is from God and that it is something for His bond-servants to know. God gave it to man to make something known "to His bond-servants" (that is, to those who serve Jesus Christ as Lord). Therefore, as Christians, the Revelation is a book we can understand.

The revelation of Jesus Christ which God gave to Him to show to His bond-servants, the things which must shortly take place.

In this verse, does *shortly* mean "thousands of years" or a "few minutes/days/years"? Both *shortly* in verse 1 and *the time is near* in verse 3 repeat at the end of the book in chapter 22. The "things which must shortly take place" is repeated in verse 6, and "for the time is near" or, as Dr. Adams titled his book, *The Time is at Hand*, is repeated in verse 10. This suggests the Revelation is obviously a prophecy about events that were to occur very shortly after they were prophesied. Most commentators believe the book was written about AD 96, after the destruction of the temple. However, the book itself speaks of the temple as still in operation. Therefore, I believe it must have been written prior to AD 70. If, indeed, the book is a prophecy of the destruction of the temple in AD 70, and the temple had not yet been destroyed, the book was probably written sometime between AD 63 and 68.

Must shortly take place, and He sent and communicated it through His angel to His bond-servant John…

Communicated it is literally, in Greek, "signed it." The letter was written in terms of signs and symbols. As a blunt pastor friend used to say, "When we read Revelation, we shouldn't expect to see a literal red-winged dragon flying around the sky with a slutty broad on its back." Rather the dragon and the whore of Babylon are symbols or signs that point to something else.

I believe modern Christians do not understand Revelation because they do not understand the Old Testament symbolism and the historical situations of that time. Every Christian in the time of John would have understood the symbols. We do not understand the symbols because we do not understand the Jewish religious system and the temple worship as set forth in the Old Testament. Therefore, it is difficult for us to understand and "to know" what the prophecy was about.

> Who bore witness to the word of God and
> to the testimony of Jesus Christ, even to all that
> he saw. (Revelation 1:2)

In his vision, John actually witnessed everything he was told to write. Thus, in Revelation, he is witnessing to the Word of God, which is the testimony of Jesus Christ.

> Blessed is he who reads and those who hear
> the words of the prophecy, and heed the things
> which are written in it; for the time is near.
> (Revelation 1:3)

Reads is a special word in Greek. It means "reading publicly in worship." This is why some translations like the English Standard Version (ESV) say "reads aloud." John is specifically writing about reading the prophecy of the Revelation in a public worship context. He states the person reading the words of prophecy will be blessed as well as the ones hearing it. It is tragic that in churches today, pastors and congregations alike neither read nor hear the words of this marvelous letter from God to His church. Therefore, they do not receive the promised blessing.

Blessed are "those who hear the words of the prophecy, and heed the things which are written in it."

This is important. If Revelation was written about something far in the distant future, how could the people heed the words of the prophecy? *Heed* means "to do or to keep." Therefore, how could they do or keep something that did not pertain to them? They must have been able to hear, to understand, and to heed the prophecy in relevance to their own period of time.

So far, we have learned that the book is something revealed and it is to bear witness to or from Jesus Christ. It is to be read in public worship and is to be heard and kept or heeded. Thus, it cannot be far futuristic. It is a prophecy of things which were "shortly" to happen, and I believe this indicates the prophecy was fulfilled in the destruction of the temple in AD 70.

Additionally, we should always remember the context of any text is all-important. John is not writing the Revelation *to* us in the twenty-first century. He is writing to the people of the first century, particularly "to the seven churches in Asia" (Revelation 1:4). While scripture is always written *for* us in that we can learn from it, it is not always written specifically to us.

Someone might ask, "Do we know what the historical interpretations of the book of Revelation are? What has been the view of the church in ages past?"

In church history, Revelation has been interpreted mostly in a postmillennial or amillennial sense. Many early commentators interpreted the book as mostly symbolic. They believed that Christ would come back when Christ chooses to come back. The historical view of Revelation had nothing to do with the premillennial dispensational ideas we see in the church today. Those views did not even exist in the church until the mid-1800s. They originated with a vision that a young girl had in 1830 in Scotland. This vision influenced John Nelson Darby, an Anglican pastor who left the Church of England and founded the Plymouth Brethren. His views subsequently influenced C. I. Scofield who worked these ideas into the "Scofield Reference Bible," which he also published. As a result of this popular work, the premillennial dispensational view exploded in the American Christian world.

B. B. Warfield was a conservative Presbyterian pastor and professor at Princeton Theological Seminary in the early 1900s and a defender of the inerrancy of scripture. He wrote that Revelation is understandable if we know our Bible. I believe he is correct and that today, we do not adequately know our Bible. As Jesus Christ said to the Pharisees,

> You search the Scriptures because you think
> that in them you have eternal life; it is these that
> testify about Me. (John 5:39)

Since the Pharisees had only the Old Testament scriptures, in order to learn more about Jesus Christ, we need to learn more about the Old Testament.

Warfield also wrote,

> No one who knows his Bible need despair about knowing this book (Revelation), of reading this book with profit. Above all, he who can understand our Lord's great discourse concerning the last things (Matthew 24), cannot fail to understand the Apocalypse, which is founded on that discourse and scarcely advances beyond it.

I strongly believe that Warfield is right and that we cannot understand Revelation without an understanding of Daniel 9 and Matthew 24. Therefore, before proceeding with our study of Revelation, we need to study Daniel, chapter 9. We will be covering in detail the last three verses, 24–27, focusing particularly on verse 27.

CHAPTER 2

Daniel's Seventy Weeks

Seventy weeks have been decreed for your people and your holy city, to finish the transgression, to make an end of sin, to make atonement for iniquity, to bring in everlasting righteousness, to seal up vision and prophecy, and to anoint the most holy *place*. (Daniel 9:24)

This begins the section where many people have great difficulty understanding the prophecy of Daniel. The Hebrews did not have a word for *week*. The specific word used literally means "seven."

In Daniel 9:25, the angel Gabriel tells Daniel,

So you are to know and discern *that* from the issuing of a decree to restore and rebuild Jerusalem until Messiah the Prince *there will be* seven weeks and sixty-two weeks; it will be built again, with plaza and moat, even in times of distress.

What Gabriel literally said to Daniel is "seven *sevens* and sixty-two *sevens* have been decreed." Many theologians have attempted to determine what Gabriel meant by this statement. In an attempt to relate the prophecy to the time period from the decree of Cyrus

(Ezra, chapter 1) to restore Jerusalem and the coming of the Messiah, many understand Gabriel to be speaking of a time period of seventy weeks *of years*. In other words, Gabriel was saying to Daniel that from the decree of Cyrus to the coming of Jesus would be a period of 490 years (seven times seventy). However, if we interpret the seventy sevens as seventy weeks or seventy weeks of years, it becomes impossible to accurately know the dates involved. Nothing works out correctly on a calendar. While the dates do not work, we can know that Gabriel does say that seventy sevens have been decreed by God to do several things, six or seven things depending on how the Hebrew is translated.

When scholars look at these verses and the things mentioned, it is acknowledged by most of them that Gabriel is talking about Jesus Christ. He is the One Who came "to finish rebellion, to seal up sin, to make atonement for iniquities, to bring in everlasting righteousness (the One Who) came to seal up vision and prophecy." In this verse, "to seal up," as it is used here, does not mean to seal in the sense of closing off but to fulfill. Gabriel is saying the Old Testament prophecies were about Jesus and that they were going to be fulfilled in Him.

Jesus consistently taught the Pharisees the truth of Scripture. Remember, the Pharisees were Bible scholars who could quote large portions of the Old Testament scriptures from memory. For example, a story is told of a rabbi who went to a small synagogue which did not have a scroll of the book of Esther from which he was going to speak, so he sat down and wrote out the entire book from memory. Remembering that Jesus said to these Pharisees, "You search the Scriptures to learn of eternal life, but they testify *of Me*" (John 5:39), when reading a passage in the Old Testament, you should ask yourself, "What does this teach me about Jesus?"

In translating the phrase "to anoint the most holy *place*" in verse 24, Bible scholars are indicating by the italicized word (*place*) that the word is not in the original language. The word has been inserted by the translators to make the sentence flow more smoothly. The original wording at this point is literally, "to anoint the holy holies." The "holy of holies" was the name of the inner sanctum or the inner compartment of the tabernacle or temple of God. The temple built by Solomon and the tabernacle used by Israel in the wilderness were both built the same way. They were built according to the plan that God had shown Moses at Mt. Sinai.

Surrounding the tabernacle was a curtain with an opening for a gate that always faced to the east. When entering the tabernacle area, the first object encountered was the bronze altar of sacrifice. This was because there had to be a blood sacrifice before anyone could proceed to a closer communion with God.

Behind the altar of sacrifice was the laver, or basin. It was, in fact, a baptismal font. The priests were required to cleanse or baptize themselves before proceeding any further toward God. In the center of the complex, surrounded by the curtains, was the actual tabernacle, which had two compartments. The outer compartment, which was called the Holy Place, was entered from the east through another curtain with a gate or opening. Inside the Holy Place were several articles of furniture. The first, on the right side (north), was a table covered in gold. This was the table of the Presence, or the table of the Showbread. On the table were twelve loaves of unleavened bread (one for each of the tribes of Israel) and bowls for a drink offering (wine). Each week the priests would put out new loaves. Then they would eat the old bread and drink the wine. On the other side of the room was a golden lampstand to light the way. The tabernacle was covered with three different coverings which kept the area dark, even during the daylight hours. There was also an incense (golden) altar that was placed before the curtain separating the Holy Place from the Holy of Holies. The incense on the golden altar was always kept burning. We will learn later from Revelation that the smoke of the incense from the golden altar represents the prayers of the saints, and those prayers, like the smoke of the incense, are always before God.

The curtain that separated the Holy Place from the Holy of Holies was embroidered with the figures of the cherubim (the word is plural) with a flaming sword. This reminded the people of Israel that they were cut off from direct access to God. Behind this curtain, in the Holy of Holies, was the Ark of the Covenant, made of "incorruptible" wood completely covered in gold. The top of the Ark was covered by the "Mercy Seat," and above it were the outstretched wings of the cherubim. There, between the wings of the cherubim, dwelled the Shekinah Glory Cloud of God Himself.

Gabriel tells Daniel that seventy sevens have been decreed for these things to be completed and that the most holy holies was to be anointed. I believe Daniel and true believers of the time understood this symbolism. They realized that the Holy of Holies represented the Messiah, Jesus Himself. *Messiah* in Hebrew means the same as *Christos* in Greek. Both words mean "anointed." Christ is the Anointed One, the Coming One, promised by the prophets.

> So you are to know and discern *that* from the issuing of a decree to restore and rebuild Jerusalem until Messiah the Prince *there will be* seven weeks and sixty-two weeks; it will be built again, with plaza and moat, even in times of distress. (Daniel 9:25)

The decree of which Gabriel speaks is reported in Ezra, chapter 1:1–3. During the first year of King Cyrus, the king issued a decree stating that all Jews who wanted to return to Jerusalem could do so. The decree also stated that all the people of his kingdom must help the Jews rebuild the temple and help restore and rebuild Jerusalem. It is quite evident that Gabriel is referring here to Jesus. Virtually no one questions that Christ is the one referred to in the phrase "until Messiah the Prince."

Gabriel tells Daniel,

> There will be 7 sevens and 62 sevens, it [the temple] will be built again…even in times of distress.

Numerous kinds of distresses were occurring during the rebuilding of Jerusalem. The book of Nehemiah describes the deceit and harassment and the difficulties surrounding the Jews as they were rebuilding the temple.

> Then after the sixty-two weeks (sevens) the Messiah will be cut off and have nothing, and the people of the prince who is to come will destroy the city and the sanctuary. And its end *will come* with a flood; even to the end there will be war; desolations are determined. (Daniel 9:26)

Here is where the difficulty begins. Very clearly, "Messiah the Prince" mentioned in verse 25 is Jesus Christ. The question is, "Who are the people of the prince who is to come (who will destroy the city and the sanctuary)?" Who is this prince who is to come? In Hebrew, it is literally, "the Prince, the Coming One." I believe this is also referring to Jesus. But notice that most translations do not capitalize the word prince in verse 26.

When Jesus first started his ministry, John the Baptizer was preaching as the forerunner of "the Coming One." John sent his disciples to Jesus, and they asked Him, "Are you the Coming One?" In the Greek translation of the Hebrew version of Daniel 9, you will find that the Hebrew phrase "the prince who is to come" is translated by the Greek phrase, "the Prince, the Coming One." Therefore, I believe the passage is referring to Jesus.

If this is true, then whose people came to destroy the temple? It was the people of Christ. But who actually destroyed the temple? The Romans! Does this mean the Romans were the people of Jesus? Yes, because everyone is under God's control. God was in charge. God destroyed the temple because He had repeatedly prophesied in the Old Testament that if His people did not obey Him, if they did not completely surrender to Him, He would destroy them.

> And he will make a firm covenant with the many for one week, but in the middle of the week he will put a stop to sacrifice and grain offering. (Daniel 9:27)

Again, we need to ask, "Who is the *he* referred to?" I believe that the pronoun *he* refers to "the Coming One," "the Prince Who is to come," and should be capitalized.

The translation "and he will make a firm covenant" implies this person will do something that has not yet been done. But in Hebrew, the text literally is, "he will confirm the covenant." This gives a completely different meaning. Likewise, in the Greek Old Testament, the text reads, "he will confirm the covenant." And in Romans 15:8, Paul says (speaking of Jesus Christ), "[He] has been made a servant to the circumcision on behalf of the truth of God to confirm the promises given to the fathers." In other words, Jesus Christ was sent to confirm the covenantal promises of God.

Several different translations exist because even theologians have yielded to the idea that "the prince who is to come" (notice that *prince* is in small letters) is the sinful one, the minion of Satan. This is because they have accepted the popular futurist premillennial dispensational interpretation of Daniel 9:27 rather than looking at what God's Word actually says.

> But in the middle of the week he will put a
> stop to sacrifice and grain offering.

Remember that in Hebrew, there is no word for *week*. The word is literally seven. The text states that in the middle of the seven the Prince Who is to come "will put a stop to sacrifice and grain offering." What did Jesus Christ come to do? He came to fulfill the law, to fulfill the sacrificial system. Everything in that sacrificial system pointed to Jesus Christ, just as He said. The New Testament letter to the Hebrews confirms that He was the fulfillment of the sacrificial system. He was the ultimate sacrifice. He came to put a stop to sacrifice and grain offering because He was the one to whom the whole of the sacrificial system pointed.

What is the middle of seven? It is three and one half. How long did Jesus minister before His sacrificial death? He served for three and one half years. Jesus Christ came and was sacrificed for your sin and for my sin. He was cut off in the middle of the seven. Yet the unbelievers among the Jews not only murdered the Messiah but continued the sacrificial system, which was a shadow and a type pointing to the ultimate sacrifice of the Lamb of God, Jesus Christ. Since the Jews continued to sacrifice animals after the ultimate sacrifice of His Son, do you think God might have been a little bit upset? I do! He was so upset that He destroyed the temple and its sacrificial system.

Many Christians who hold to the premillennial dispensational point of view and who read Ezekiel and the marvelous prophecy of the rebuilding of the temple are working tirelessly to keep Israel from the Arabs. In concert with the Jews, they believe it is necessary to tear down the Mosque on the Dome of the Rock, rebuild the temple, and reinstitute the sacrificial system before Jesus returns. How do you think God would feel about that? I do not think He would be very pleased if they started sacrificing bulls, and goats, and lambs after He sent His Son to be the final sacrifice.

The Hebrew version of the ending of Daniel 9:27 reads, "He shall cause to cease the sacrifice and the oblation and for overspreading of abomination he shall make it desolate."

The Hebrew indicates the "Prince, the Coming One" shall make desolate the temple. In the New American Standard Bible (NASB), the verse is translated "he will put a stop to sacrifice and grain offering; and on the wing [the word translated *wing* in NASB may also be translated *pinnacle*] of abominations *will come* one who makes desolate." The word in Hebrew is *meshomem*, which is translated "make it desolate." It is actually a participle that means "the one making desolate." Who is that? It is the Coming One, Jesus Christ, the Prince. He is the one making desolate; He is making the *temple* desolate.

The NASB translates the last part of verse 27:

> Even until the complete destruction is
> poured out on the one who makes desolate.

When looking at the Hebrew version here, the text actually uses the same root word (for *desolate*), but this time it is not a participle. It is in a different form (*shomem*), a noun that means "the desolate *thing*." Now it begins to make perfect sense. The One Who is to come will make desolate and will pour out destruction upon the desolate thing; the temple that is still being used for sacrifices even though Christ has fulfilled the sacrificial system.

Therefore, I believe Daniel 9 is a prophecy of the destruction of the temple in AD 70. God destroyed the temple and Jerusalem because the Jews continued the sacrificial system after Jesus had fulfilled it and had borne our sins upon the cross.

CHAPTER 3

Matthew 24

Now let us turn to Matthew 24 and see how it relates to the understanding of Revelation.

"¹And Jesus came out from the temple and was going away when his disciples came up to point out the temple buildings to him. ²And He answered and said to them, "Do you not see all these things? Truly I say to you, not one stone here shall be left upon another, which will not be torn down." ³And as he was sitting on the Mount of Olives, the disciples came to him privately, saying, "Tell us, when will these things be, and what *will be* the sign of Your coming, and of the end of the age?" ⁴And Jesus answered and said to them, "See to it that no one misleads you. ⁵For many will come in my name, saying 'I am the Christ,' and will mislead many. ⁶And you will be hearing of wars and rumors of wars; see that you are not frightened, for *those things* must take place, but *that* is not yet the end. ⁷For nation will rise against nation and kingdom against kingdom, and in various places there will be famines and earthquakes. ⁸But all these things are *merely* the beginning of birth pangs. [9]Then they will deliver you to tribulation, and will kill you, and you will be hated by all nations on account of my name. [10]And at that time many will fall away and will deliver up one another and hate one another. [11]And many false prophets will arise, and will mislead many. [12]And because lawlessness is increased, most people's love will grow cold. [13]But the one who endures to the end, he shall be saved. [14]And this gospel of the kingdom shall be preached in the whole world for a witness to all the nations, and then the end shall come. [15]"Therefore when you see the ABOMINATION OF DESOLATION which was spoken of through Daniel the prophet, standing in the holy place (let the reader understand), [16]then let those who are in Judea flee to the mountains; [17]let him who is on the housetop not go down to get the things out that are in his house; [18]and let him who is in the field not turn back to get his cloak. [19]"But woe to those who are with child and to those who nurse babes in those days! [20]"But pray that your flight may not be in the winter, or on a Sabbath; [21]for then there will be a great tribulation, such as has not occurred since the beginning of the world until now, nor ever shall. [22]"And unless those days had been cut short, no life would have been saved; but for the sake of the elect those days shall be cut short. [23]"Then if anyone says to you, 'Behold, here is the Christ,' or 'There *He is*,' do not believe *him*. [24]"For false Christs and false prophets will arise and will show great signs and wonders, so as to mislead, if possible, even the elect. [25]Behold, I have told you in advance. [26]If therefore they say to you, 'Behold, He is in the wilderness,' do not go forth, *or*, 'Behold, He is in the inner rooms,'

24

do not believe *them*. [27]"For just as the lightning comes from the east, and flashes even to the west, so shall the coming of the Son of Man be. [28]"Wherever the corpse is, there the vultures will gather. [29]"But immediately after the tribulation of those days THE SUN WILL BE DARKENED, AND THE MOON WILL NOT GIVE ITS LIGHT, AND THE STARS WILL FALL from the sky, and the powers of the heavens will be shaken, [30]and then the sign of the Son of Man will appear in the sky, and then all the tribes of the earth will mourn, and they will see the Son of Man coming on the clouds of the sky with power and great glory. [31]"And He will send forth His angels with A GREAT TRUMPET and THEY WILL GATHER TOGETHER His elect from the four winds, from one end of the sky to the other. [32]"Now learn the parable from the fig tree: when its branch has already become tender, and puts forth its leaves, you know that summer is near; [33]even so you too, when you see all these things, recognize that He is near, *right* at the door. [34]"Truly I say to you, this generation will not pass away until all these things take place. [35]"Heaven and earth will pass away, but My words shall not pass away." (Matthew 24:1–35)

The key to understanding this passage is to understand the real question(s) being asked of Jesus. *Parousia* is a Greek word that means "the appearing, the coming, the appearance." Whenever the New Testament speaks about "the coming" of the Son of Man or "the appearance" of the Son of Man, the word normally is *parousia*. In verse 3, the disciples ask, "What will be the sign of your coming [parousia]?"

In 1878, J. Stuart Russell, a Puritan, wrote a book titled *The Parousia*. Russell took every verse in the New Testament where that Greek word appeared and looked closely at each of them in context.

His thesis (with which I do not agree as he was considered a heretic) stated that each verse addressing the coming of Jesus Christ in the New Testament is not speaking about the coming of Jesus Christ at the end of the world but is dealing with the coming of Jesus Christ and His destruction of the temple in AD 70. One of the interesting things Russell did in his book was to lay out Matthew, Mark, and Luke in parallel so that they could be easily compared.

One of the problems with the interpretation of Matthew 24 is that we are so immersed in the current popular culture (a futurist interpretation) that we read this chapter through the eyes of today's cultural influence. Thus, as we look at Luke and Mark, we read them in light of Matthew, and we miss what is really there.

Here is what I mean.

Jesus says in verse 14 of Matthew 24,

> This gospel of the kingdom shall be preached in the whole world for a witness to all the nations, and then the end shall come.

Has anyone actually seen "the gospel of the kingdom...preached in the whole world for a witness to all the nations...?" Most people would quickly answer, "No!" In fact, many mission agencies in the Christian world have it written into their charters that there is an urgency to take the Gospel to countries that have not heard it in order to bring about the return of Jesus Christ.

Let's see what the Bible itself has to say.

In Colossians 1:5–6, Paul says,

> Because of the hope laid up for you in heaven, of which you previously heard in the word of truth, the gospel, which has come to you, *just as in all the world* also it is constantly bearing fruit and increasing, even as *it has been doing* in you also since the day you heard *of it* and understood the grace of God in truth [emphasis added].

Colossians 1:23 reads,

> The gospel…which was proclaimed *in all creation under heaven* [emphasis added].

What is the Gospel that Paul is speaking of here? He is writing about the truth that there is a God and He is the only One in whom we have any hope. Paul tells us that *in his day*, the truth was being preached in all the world (Colossians 1:5–6) and that the Gospel had been proclaimed (*past tense*) "in all creation under heaven." How does someone who has never read the New Testament or heard the Gospel know about God? First of all, Paul says in Romans 1 that everything essential about God—His power, His beauty, His glory—has been revealed in the Creation. But men have suppressed the truth and exchanged it for the lie of Satan that the Word of God cannot be trusted.

In Matthew 24, verse 2, Jesus gives a prophecy. He says,

> Do you not see all these things? Truly I say to you, not one stone here shall be left upon another, which will not be torn down.

To better understand why this verse is important, one needs to consider the seven wonders of the ancient world: their magnificent beauty and their phenomenal engineering feats. Although the temple was not one of the seven ancient wonders, it probably could have been considered one. The temple in Jerusalem was astounding! There were huge blocks of stone that had been carved out and placed there to build the walls of the temple itself and the retaining walls. As the disciples left the temple, they would have seen gold filigree laid in the blocks and jewels adorning the exterior of the building. It was an absolute marvel of beauty and engineering! It was the pride of the Jews and they were justified in being proud.

The parallel passages in Mark and Luke put it this way.

> And as He was going out of the temple, one of His disciples said to Him, "Teacher, behold

what wonderful stones and what wonderful buildings!" (Mark 13:1)

And while some were talking about the temple, that it was adorned with beautiful stones and votive gifts [Jesus] said... (Luke 21:5)

The disciples focused on the temple itself and not on what it represented. When Jesus said, "See these stones? I tell you the truth, not one stone here shall remain upon another," they were stunned and asked the obvious question, "What do you mean Lord?" The four disciples (Peter, James, John, and Andrew—see Mark 13:3) came to Jesus later that day as He was sitting on the Mount of Olives. In Matthew 24:3, they asked, "Tell us, when will these things be, and what will be the sign of Your coming, and of the end of the age?" What are the disciples concerned about? What are they asking about? The key here is, are they asking three different questions about three different things, or are they asking three questions about the same concern, or are they really asking only one question? The distinction here is very important. If they were asking three different questions—when will the temple be torn down, what is the sign of your coming, and what about the end of the world—then we have to look at Matthew 24 for answers to these same three questions.

Now, look at the parallel passage in Mark 13. In verse 1, one of the disciples, we are not told which one, remarks on the wonder of the temple. Jesus said to him (one of His disciples),

Do you see these great buildings? Not one stone shall be left upon another which will not be torn down.

And as he was sitting on the Mount of Olives opposite the temple, Peter and James and John and Andrew were questioning him privately, "Tell us, when will these things be, and what *will be* the sign when all these things are going to be fulfilled?"

What does verse 2 say? Exactly the same thing as Matthew 24:2. In verse 3, the Gospel of Mark tells us which disciples were asking the questions. In verse 4, it is very clear that they are asking a two-part question about the same matter: *When* are these things going to happen? And *what is the sign* that these things are going to happen? Although they were asking a two-part question, it was actually only one question. Clearly, in context, they were asking about the destruction of the temple.

We see the same thing in Luke 21:7.

> And they questioned him, saying, "Teacher, when therefore will these things be? And what *will be* the sign when these things are about to take place?"

Once again, what are they really asking Him? They are asking about the destruction of the temple! That really has nothing to do with the end of the world, does it? Absolutely not!

The context then is extremely important. Remember, one of the most important things in understanding any Bible passage is context, context, context! What the disciples understood was that Jesus was going to come and destroy the temple, but not in the sense of ushering in the end of the world. However, we tend to confuse the two. Why? Because we have heard repeatedly that Matthew 24 is talking about the end of the world. So when we read Matthew 24, we naturally read it in terms of Jesus coming back at the end of the world. It is time to get back to the original understanding. So far, we have established that what the disciples are really asking Jesus is, when will the destruction of the temple occur, and what will be the signs of this happening so that we can be prepared?

In Matthew 24, Jesus answered and said to them (the disciples Peter, James, John and Andrew as quoted in Mark 13:3),

> See to it that no one misleads *you*... And *you* will be hearing of wars and rumors of wars; see that *you* are not frightened...then they will

deliver *you* to tribulation and will kill *you*, and *you* will be hated by all nations…therefore when *you* see ABOMINATION OF DESOLATION…pray that *your* flight may not be in the winter… Then if anyone says to *you* behold here is the Christ, or there *He is*, do not believe *him*… Behold I have told *you* in advance. (Emphasis added.)

Who is Jesus speaking to? He is speaking to the four disciples, not some unknown people two thousand (or more) years into the future. Jesus is talking to His disciples, and He is telling *them* something is going to happen to *them*. They are asking the question, "Lord, when is the temple going to be torn down and what is the sign of when the temple is to be torn down?" What do we see as we read through Jesus's answer? You, you, you—*you* (disciples) can understand, when *you* (disciples) see all these things happen, etc. That is the context.

Therefore, we have established that Jesus was not talking about the far-distant future of more than two thousand years. Nor was He speaking of the end of the world. Instead, He was speaking of the destruction of the temple, the end of the Jewish age.

We have also shown by comparing Matthew, Mark, and Luke that the disciples were not asking three questions: (1) When is the temple going to be torn down? (2) When are You coming back? And (3) What is the sign of the end of the age (or, as we say it, the end of the world)? They were really asking one two-part question: "When is the temple going to be destroyed, and what is the sign that it is going to happen?"

What does it mean then in Matthew 24:3 when the disciples say, "What *will be* the sign of Your coming (Your *parousia*) and of the end of the age? What is the end of the age? It is the Old Testament age, the Jewish economy. Jesus is referring to the Jewish way of doing things. He is not referring to "the age" in the sense of the time of the end of the world, but rather the end of the Jewish age, the Old Testament age.

There is a vast majority of people, even today, that pour millions of dollars into Israel, to support the state of Israel. Why? Because they believe it is "the Holy Land." They truly believe that the prophecy of Ezekiel says that a literal new temple must be rebuilt on Mount Zion before God can return. What is the problem with this? There is currently a Muslim mosque there, the Mosque of the Dome of the Rock! An ungodly building now stands there! And many believe it must be torn down and the temple rebuilt.

But what is the problem with rebuilding the temple and reinitiating the sacrificial system? Jesus! Jesus shed His blood as a fulfillment of the entire Old Testament sacrificial system. The book of Hebrews tells us the sacrifices of the temple did not accomplish the salvation of anyone. It was only the sacrifice of the Great High Priest Himself (Jesus) that accomplished everything to which God was pointing. So why in the world would God allow sacrifices to continue when His Son died on the cross as the fulfillment of all those sacrifices? Is it any wonder God destroyed the temple? Absolutely not! However, God graciously waited for forty years—one entire generation—until He fulfilled the prophecy of Jesus in Matthew 24.

CHAPTER 4

Further Historical Evidence

Consider the fact that Jesus says in verses 6 and 7 of Matthew 24,

> And you will be hearing of wars and rumors of wars; see that you are not frightened, for *those things* must take place, but *that* is not yet the end. For nation will rise against nation and kingdom against kingdom, and in various places there will be famines and earthquakes.

Does this not relate to our present time?

First, remember that Jesus is speaking to the four disciples, Peter, James, John, and Andrew. Second, we need to realize that we have been conditioned by popular teaching to believe these things are presently taking place. In *The Parousia*, J. Stuart Russell presents a different picture by quoting extensively from ancient writings, in particular writings by Josephus, a Jewish historian. Russell quotes him in regard to Matthew 24.

> It is impossible to read this section and fail to perceive its distinct reference to the period between our Lord's crucifixion and the destruction of Jerusalem. Every word is spoken to the disciples and to them alone. To imagine that the

'you' in this address applies not to the disciples to whom Christ was speaking, but to someone unknown and yet nonexistent in a far distant age is so preposterous a supposition as to not deserve serious notice. That our Lord's words were fully verified during the interval between his crucifixion and the end of the age we have the most ample testimony. False christs and false prophets began to make their appearance at a very early period of the Christian era and continued to infest the land down to the very close of Jewish history. In the procuratorship of Pilate, AD 36 (3 [sic] years after the death of Christ), one such appeared in Samaria and deluded great multitudes. There was another in the procuratorship of Cuspius Fatus, AD 45, during the government of Felix, AD 53–60. Josephus tells us that the country was full of robbers, magicians, false prophets, false messiahs and imposters who deluded the people with promises of great events.

Josephus, the Jewish historian, writes in *The Antiquities* that all these events were happening at the same time. Although he was of Jewish extraction and was writing about the Jews, he was a collaborator with the Romans. It must be noted that Josephus was not a Christian. He is not building up the Christians in any way, but he writes that all these events were occurring. Russell continues,

The same authority (Josephus) informs us that civil commotions and international feuds were rife in those days. Especially between the Jews and their neighbors. In Alexandria, in Seleucia, in Syria, in Babylonia, there were violent tumults between Jews and the Greeks, between Jews and the Syrians inhabiting the same cities. Every city is divided into two camps, says

Josephus, the Jews and the others.(Josephus goes on and gives examples of cities divided into two camps.) In the reign of Caligula, great apprehensions were entertained in Judea at war with the Romans, in consequence of that tyrant's proposal to place his statue in the temple."

Consider the following functions of the temple in Jerusalem:

a. It was the pinnacle of the Jewish faith
b. It was the place of the altar of sacrifice that allowed one to atone for sins and to repent of those sins
c. It was the place where God's Ark of the Covenant had been, and where God himself had dwelled

Now the Roman emperor Caligula (considered by both himself and the Romans to be a god) wanted to place his statue in the temple in Jerusalem, thus elevating himself to be equivalent with God. Is it any wonder the Jewish people got upset?

Russell continues quoting Josephus,

In the reign of the emperor Claudius, AD 41–54, there were four seasons of great scarcity (remember, Jesus said there was going to be famine). In the fourth year of his reign, the famine in Judea was so severe that the price of food became enormous and great numbers perished. Earthquakes occurred in each of the reigns of Caligula and Claudius (he gives a footnote where those things are documented). Such calamities the Lord gave his disciples to understand would precede the end. But they were not its immediate antecedence, they were the beginning of birth pangs. But the end is not yet.

In American Christianity, people have a type of cultural myopia, a cultural nearsightedness. Most people today do not have the benefit of knowing history. They constantly think in terms of their own immediate culture, without bothering to learn what was actually occurring during the time immediately after Christ, in the time when the apostles were writing. When we do look at history, we see that there were wars and rumors of wars. In fact, there was incredible upheaval. False prophets and false messiahs appeared, proclaiming, "I am the Christ." There were major earthquakes and major famines. However, Jesus said all these things were merely the beginning of birth pangs.

CHAPTER 5

The Great Tribulation and the Abomination of Desolation

Jesus continues in verse 15–21 of Matthew 24.

> Therefore when you see the ABOMINATION OF DESOLATION which was spoken of through Daniel the prophet, standing in the holy place (let the reader understand), then let those who are in Judea flee to the mountains; let him who is on the housetop not go down to get the things out that are in his house; and let him who is in the field not turn back to get his cloak. But woe to those who are with child and to those who nurse babes in those days! But pray that your flight (you disciples) may not be in the winter, or on a Sabbath; for then there will be a great tribulation, such as had not occurred since the beginning of the world until now, nor ever shall.

In verse 21, we find the term the "Great Tribulation." A prominent teaching in the church today is that the Great Tribulation has yet to occur. Most Christians support this idea because they have been taught that such tragedies or terrible events have not happened in the past. Yet if we read the historical evidence about some of the terrible things that went on during that particular period of time, we would understand differently.

Looking at Matthew 24:15–22, Mark 13:14–20, and Luke 21:20–24 laid out in parallel form, you will note that Mark 13:14 reads,

> But when you see the ABOMINATION OF DESOLATION standing where it should not be (let the reader understand), then let those who are in Judea flee to the mountains.

In Luke 21:20, Jesus is quoted as saying,

> But when you see Jerusalem surrounded by armies, then know that the desolation thereof is near [literal translation]. Then let those who are in Judea flee to the mountains.

What is the "ABOMINATION OF DESOLATION" spoken of in Mark? Remember what group of people Jesus is addressing. He is speaking to the same four disciples Peter, James, John, and Andrew. What group is Jesus describing? He is speaking about the Jewish people, the apostate Jews, the unbelieving Jews. And what land or country is Jesus talking about? He is speaking about Israel. Again, He is answering the question of the disciples about the time of the destruction of the temple in Jerusalem. He is saying all these things are going to come upon Israel.

What does Luke tell us about the "ABOMINATION OF DESOLATION"?

Luke 21:20 states,

> But when you see Jerusalem surrounded by *armies*, then recognize that her desolation is at hand.

Many people have seen movies such as *Ben Hur* and *The Robe*. We know from historical evidence (and as depicted in the movies) that the Roman legions carried a banner or standard before each of their legions. That banner or standard was topped with an eagle. What was the significance of the eagle to the Roman army? The eagle was one of the gods of the Roman army. Therefore, they were carrying the banner of one of their gods before them. That being the case, what do you think the Jews would call Roman standards in the temple in Jerusalem? They would have seen it as an abomination, the "abomination of desolation." The temple was being desolated by other gods. I believe this is the event to which Jesus is referring.

Jesus says in Matthew 24:21, "for then." When is the *then* to which Jesus is referring? Is it sometime in our future? No, it is when the siege of Jerusalem takes place. Jesus is saying, "During the siege of Jerusalem, when you four disciples see the Roman army surrounding the temple" *then* there "will be a great tribulation, such as has not occurred since the beginning of the world until now, nor ever shall."

Is Jesus talking about something that is going to happen in our future? No. He is speaking about something that was going to happen to the people of Israel during the time of the four apostles.

Step back for just a moment and think about the circumstances. When the Roman army invaded the land of Judea, what did the Jews do? They sought refuge in Jerusalem. We think of Jerusalem as a fairly small city, but in those days, it was much larger than we might imagine. What was the population of Jerusalem while it was under siege by the Roman army? There were over two million people! According to Josephus, about two million people were killed during that two-year siege. That means more than two million people were in a relatively small city with very little food and very little water for two years.

You might ask, "Was this really the greatest tribulation that ever occurred in history?" Bear in mind, there are several other places in the scriptures that use the same type of hyperbolic language. The same phrase is applied to other events in biblical history, implying that nothing actually happened to such a degree, nor will anything this bad ever happen again. This language is used to convey the idea of something unbelievably horrible! It does not necessarily mean the very worst in all of history in every conceivable sense, but rather that it ranks in the very worst kind of category.

A second point to consider is this. What is the worst crime that has ever occurred? The death of Jesus Christ; the crucifixion of the Messiah, the Son of God! That event deserved the greatest tribulation, the greatest outpouring of the wrath of God.

Thirdly, not only were there two million people killed in Jerusalem, but more millions were killed in the country of Judea during the Jewish wars in AD 66–70, which lasted three and one half years.

Read what Josephus has to say regarding this time.

> Now of those that perished by famine in the city, the number was prodigious. And the miseries they underwent were unspeakable, for if so much as a shadow of any kind of food did anywhere appear, a war was commenced presently and the dearest friends fell to fighting with one another about it, snatching from each other the most miserable supports of life. Nor would men believe that those who were dying had no food, but the robbers would search them when they were expiring (people are dying, and others are going through their robes and searching their body to see if they were faking death and to see if they had any food on them). Lest anyone should have concealed food in their bosoms and counterfeited dying, many of these robbers gaped for want and ran about stumbling and staggering along like mad dogs, reeling against the doors of houses like drunken men. They would also in the great distress they were in, rush into the very same house 2–3 times in one and the same day. (They did not even remember what houses they had been in.) Moreover their hunger was so intol-

erable, that it obliged them to chew everything, while they gathered such things as the most sordid animals would not touch and endured to eat them. Nor did they at length abstain from girdles and shoes and the very leather which belonged to their shields, they pulled off and gnawed. The very wisps of old hay became food to some, and some gathered up fibers and sold a very small weight of them for 4 drachma. (These people were ripping the leather off their shields and eating their shoes because the famine was so severe.) But why do I describe the shameless impudence that the famine brought on men and their eating inanimate things? But I am going to relate a matter of fact, the like that which no history relates either among the Greeks or barbarians. (Remember, Josephus is a Jewish historian, not a Christian. He is writing about things that he saw; people he interviewed during this period of time.) It is horrible to speak of it and incredible when heard. I have indeed unwillingly admitted this calamity of ours and I might not seem to deliver what is so portentous to posterity but I have innumerable witnesses to it in my own age. And besides my country would have had little reason to thank me for suppressing the miseries that this woman underwent at this time.

There was a certain woman that dwelt beyond Jordan, her name was Mary. Her father was Eleazer...what food she contrived to save had also been carried off by the rapacious guards who came every day running in to her house for that purpose. But this poor woman came into very great passion and by the frequent reproaches and imprecations she cast at these villains, she had provoked them to anger against her. But none of them either out of the indignation she had raised against her self or out of the commiseration of her case would take away her life. And if she found any food, she perceived her labors were for others and not for herself. It had now become impossible for her to find any way to find any more food, while the famine pierced through her very bowels and marrow but also her passion was fired to a degree beyond the famine itself. She then attempted a most unnatural thing and snatching up her son who was a child sucking at her breast she said, "Oh you miserable infant. For whom shall I preserve you in this war? For famine, for this Sedition? As to the war with the Romans, if they preserve our lives we will be slaves. This famine will also destroy us." She slew her son and roasted him and ate one-half of him and kept the other half by her concealed.

Upon this the Seditious came in presently and smelling the horrible scent of this food they threatened her that they would cut her throat immediately if she did not share them what food she had gotten ready. She replied that she had saved a very fine portion of it for them and uncovered what was left of her son. Hereupon they were seized with a horror and amazement of mind and stood astonished at the sight when she said to them, "This is mine own son and what hath been done was mine own doing. Come, eat of this food for I have eaten of it myself." They were sickened and they left. Upon which the whole city was full of this horrid action immediately and while everybody laid this miserable case before their own eyes they trembled, as if this unheard of action had been done by themselves. So those that were thus distressed by the famine

were very desirous to die and those already dead
were esteemed happy because they had not lived
long enough either to hear or see such miseries.

In reality, we tend to think in terms of our own culture, our own time. We do not think in terms of what was actually happening when two million people were locked in a very small area for two years. They killed and ate each other, even members of their own families. They sold scraps of straw for food and gnawed the very leather from their shields.

A large percentage of the population of Palestine and virtually all of Jerusalem were destroyed. According to Josephus, as quoted by David Chilton, in his book *Paradise Restored*, 2.1 million people were killed in Jerusalem over the two-year period of the siege. Bodies were literally heaped in the streets. People would climb over these heaps of bodies searching for food on the corpses.

We think in terms of the tribulation having not yet occurred, because we do not understand the horrors of the siege of Jerusalem and all the gruesome and frightful events that were experienced and witnessed by the people.

CHAPTER 6

The Sign of the Son of Man

Jesus continues His prophecy in verse 29 of Matthew 24.

> But immediately after the tribulation of
> those days THE SUN WILL BE DARKENED, AND THE
> MOON WILL NOT GIVE ITS LIGHT, AND THE STARS
> WILL FALL from the sky, and the powers of the
> heavens will be shaken, and the sign of the Son
> of Man will appear in the sky, and then all the
> tribes of the earth will mourn, and they will see
> the SON OF MAN COMING ON THE CLOUDS OF THE
> SKY with great power and great glory. And he will
> send forth his angels with A GREAT TRUMPET AND
> THEY WILL GATHER TOGETHER his elect from the
> four winds, from one end of the sky to the other.
> (Matthew 24:29–31)

When many people read those verses, they immediately think
in terms of the future. Who has seen the sun darken? Who has seen
the moon not give its light? Who has seen the stars fall from the sky?
Has that ever happened? Yes! It has happened (in a biblical sense),
and that is what we need to understand. When most people read
those words today, they are so caught up in the popular conception

of Revelation as futuristic that they think in terms of Matthew 24 as also being futuristic when, in fact, the events Jesus speaks of have already happened.

The Old Testament gives us the clue.

> The oracle concerning Babylon which Isaiah the son of Amoz saw. [This is a prophecy that God gave the prophet Isaiah about Babylon.] For the stars of heaven and their constellations will not flash forth their light; The sun will be dark when it rises, and the moon will not shed its light. (Isaiah 13:1, 10)

God is prophesying about the fall of Babylon. That nation had overstepped her bounds. Despite the fact that she was under God's command to come in and destroy Jerusalem, she had gone overboard, and she was thinking that she was doing it herself. So God is saying, "I am going to condemn Babylon, and here is the sign that Babylon will be destroyed."

> Behold, I am going to stir up the Medes against them.

We know from history that the Babylonians were conquered by the Medo-Persian Empire. So we know that this oracle about Babylon has already occurred. Therefore, when Isaiah is saying, "For the stars of heaven and their constellations will not flash forth their light," he is not speaking about actual physical events. He is talking about the terribleness of the destruction that is going to occur when the Babylonian Empire falls. Jesus is using the same kind of language when He quotes pretty much verbatim from Isaiah. The disciples of Jesus, who understood Isaiah, who knew those verses, would understand that He was speaking about the incredible destruction and judgment of God.

We see the same kind of language used in Ezekiel.

In Ezekiel 32:2 God says to Ezekiel,

> Son of man, take up a lamentation over
> Pharaoh king of Egypt…

Here God is prophesying through the prophet Ezekiel about the destruction of Egypt. Again, the context is that Egypt had been an ally of Israel; the Egyptians too had overstepped their bounds and because they were prideful, because they thought they had done all this on their own strength, God is prophesying that He will bring down Egypt.

> I will cover the heavens, and darken their stars; I will cover the sun with a cloud, And the moon shall not give its light. All the shining lights in the heavens I will darken over you And will set darkness on your land.

Incredible words describing events that sound like something that has not yet happened. Notice, however, verse 11,

> The sword of the king of Babylon shall come upon you.

We know from history the Babylonian Empire actually conquered the Egyptian Empire. They brought them down, and they have never again risen. God goes on to say, "You'll never again have a prince." Indeed, Egypt never came back to its former glory. Here again, Ezekiel is using the exact same kind of language that Isaiah had used and that Jesus is using in Matthew 24. It is not futuristic at all. It is something that has already happened in the past.

So what is Jesus speaking about when He says, "But immediately after the tribulation of those days THE SUN WILL BE DARKENED, AND THE MOON WILL NOT GIVE ITS LIGHT, AND THE STARS WILL FALL from the sky"? Is He speaking about something in the far distant future? No, absolutely not. What is He talking about? When we look at the biblical context of the prophecies in Ezekiel and Isaiah and notice that Jesus is using the same kind of language, we can understand that He is speaking about the terribleness of the destruction and judgment that He is going to bring upon Jerusalem. Remember, the disciples had asked the question, "When will the temple be destroyed, and what will be the sign?" Jesus is answering them, and He says,

> And the sign of the Son of Man will appear in the sky, and then all the tribes of the earth will mourn, and they will see the SON OF MAN COMING ON THE CLOUDS OF THE SKY with great power and great glory.

Now has the sign of the Son of Man coming on the clouds appeared in the sky yet? Yes!

We do not understand this because we fail to understand the language of the Old Testament and the flow of Matthew 24. Notice when we read, "then...the sign of the Son of Man will appear in the sky," when is the *then*? In the context of the passage, the sign is coming at the end of the age, the Jewish age. Remember, Jesus is answering the question, "When will the temple be destroyed?" When? "Immediately *after* the tribulation." When will all these terrible things happen? Then "the sign of the Son of Man will appear in the sky." The New American Standard translates "and then all the tribes of the earth will mourn."

That is really an unfortunate translation. In the Greek of Matthew 24:30, it says the tribes of the *land* will mourn. In fact, it is almost a direct quote from Zechariah 12:12 that, in the time of the desolation of the temple, the *tribes* of the land will mourn. So if we translate it the tribes of the land, it means the tribes of Israel, the tribes of the Holy Land. Whereas, if the verse is translated, the tribes of the earth, it means the whole world. That makes a huge difference in the way we understand the passage. But what Jesus is really speaking about here is the tribes of Israel. He is saying that the whole of the Holy Land will mourn. Why? Because the land is being destroyed, Jerusalem is being destroyed, and the temple itself is being destroyed. The temple was the heart of the Jewish religion, where God Himself dwelt. They were mourning because of God's incredible wrath against them. Jesus is not speaking about something in which the whole world is going to be involved.

The first part of Matthew 24:30 is also a poor translation. The New International Version (NIV) says, "At that time the sign of the Son of Man will appear in the sky." That is not what the Greek literally reads. The Greek states very clearly, "And then shall appear the sign of the Son of Man in heaven." In other words, the destruction of Israel is the sign that indicates that Jesus is, indeed, the Son of Man Who is now reigning in heaven, in fulfillment of Daniel 7:13–14. That is the whole point of the statement. It is not speaking about the sign of the Son of Man coming in the sky at the end of the world. The destruction of Jerusalem and the destruction of the temple is the sign that the Son of Man is now reigning in heaven and bringing judgment upon Jerusalem for their continued animal sacrifices. Even though Jesus Christ is the ultimate, once-and-for-all sacrifice, the Jews rejected Jesus as the Messiah and continued the sacrificial system after His crucifixion, which is why God (in fact, Jesus Himself) is bringing judgment upon them.

Who is it that Jesus says will see the sign of the Son of Man coming on the clouds of the sky with great power and great glory? The tribes of the land: "then all the tribes of the land will mourn." If you turn to Matthew 26:62, Jesus is enduring one of the illegal kangaroo court trials before the high priest. This occurred early in the morning after the evening in which He was betrayed (Jesus went through six trials before dawn, all of them in violation of both Roman and Jewish law, all of them kangaroo courts, all of them illegal). Three of the trials were before the Jews, and three were before the Romans. Jesus is questioned by the Jewish high priest, even though under Old Testament law, the high priest was not allowed to question the accused.

> Then the high priest stood up and said to
> Jesus, "Do You make no answer? What is it that
> these men are testifying against You?" But Jesus

kept silent. And the high priest said to Him, "I adjure You by the living God, that You tell us whether You are the Christ, the Son of God." And Jesus said to him, "You have said it *yourself*, nevertheless I tell you [high priest], hereafter you [high priest] shall see the son of man sitting at the right hand of power, and coming on the clouds of heaven.

I would submit to you that if Jesus said that *that* high priest would see the sign of the Son of Man coming in the clouds, that either that high priest is still alive today, or the sign of the Son of Man coming on the clouds has already happened. The event is past tense. That is very, very clear.

Jesus goes on to tell the four disciples in Matthew 24:32–36.

Now learn the parable from the fig tree: when its branch has already become tender and puts forth its leaves, you know that summer is near; evenso, you too, when you see all these things, recognize that He is near, right at the door. Truly I say to you, this generation will not pass away until all these things take place. Heaven and earth will pass away, but My words will not pass away. But of that day and hour no one knows, not even the angels of heaven, nor the Son, but the Father alone.

I know that you have heard people in Christian circles talking about the fact that even though we may not know the day or the hour, we can still know the approximate time that Jesus is coming. Why? Because Jesus says, "Learn the parable from the fig tree…you know that summer is near." What is the contemporary understanding of that parable in regard to a futuristic interpretation? Look for the signs. You can understand, you can know when Jesus is right around the corner. But hold on! WHO is Jesus speaking to in the context of

Matthew 24? He is speaking to His disciples. Remember the context: they had asked Him, "When will the temple be destroyed?" He's speaking to the four of them. So when He says in verse 33, "Even so you [disciples] too, when you [disciples] see all these things, recognize that He is near, at the door. Truly I say to you [disciples] this generation will not pass away until all these things take place."

The New International Version (NIV) has a footnote here that says, "or race." In fact, some translations actually say, "This race will not pass away." But there is a real problem with that. The reason people put in "race" is because they presuppose Revelation and Matthew 24 must be future. Obviously, all these things have not happened yet (according to that view). So obviously, Jesus could not have meant "this generation living right now." Therefore, He must be talking about the Jewish race, and obviously they have not yet passed away.

But if you go through the Gospels and do a word study on the Greek word *genea*, or *generation*, you will find that it *never* refers to anything except "this present generation." Dr. Jay Adams, who is a Greek scholar and reads the Greek fluently, demonstrated conclusively in his book *The Time is at Hand* that *generation* always refers to "this present generation." For example,

> But the Pharisees and the lawyers rejected
> God's purpose for themselves, not having been
> baptized by John. [Jesus says] To what then shall
> I compare the men of this generation, and what
> are they like? (Luke 7:30)

No one thinks Jesus is speaking about the Jewish race here. There is no footnote even hinting it might be race. The word clearly means this present generation. Another example, Jesus said to His disciples in Luke 17:22–25,

> The days shall come when you will long to
> see one of the days of the Son of Man, and you
> will not see it... For just as the lightning, when
> it flashes out of one part of the sky, shines to the

> other part of the sky, so will the Son of Man be
> in His day. But first He must suffer many things
> and be rejected by this generation.

Again, there is no footnote. Everyone knows the word *genera-tion* here means "this present generation" and that Jesus was rejected by that generation. It was the Jews of His day that were in view here.

> For whoever is ashamed of Me and My
> words in this adulterous and sinful generation,
> the Son of Man will also be ashamed of him
> when He comes in the glory of His Father with
> the holy angels. (Mark 8:38)

Again, the New American Standard (NASB) has no footnote here. The translators understand that it is "this present generation" that is in view. By the way, the principle here also refers to us. If *we* are ashamed of the Son of Man, then He will be ashamed of us. The principle applies to us, but the context is that Jesus is speaking to the people of that day.

> For all the prophets and the Law prophe-
> sied until John [John the Baptizer]. "But to what
> shall I compare this generation? It is like children
> sitting in the market places, who call out to the
> other *children*. (Matthew 11:13, 16)

That generation living then heard the words of John the Baptizer teaching that Jesus is coming, and they absolutely refused to understand it. Again, there is no footnote here. The translators understand that Jesus was speaking about "this present generation."

So why is it that in Matthew 24, there is a footnote that says, "race"? Why is this the only place in the whole New Testament where *genea* is translated "race" instead of "generation"? It is in order to force the passage to fit a preconceived futuristic interpretation. If you translate the word *genea* properly as generation, what does that tell us about all these things that Jesus has just said? It tells us they have already happened! Perhaps the most telling example of all is:

> Truly I say to you, all these things shall come
> upon this generation. (Matthew 23:36)

Here Jesus is condemning the Pharisees, prophesying their imminent judgment. Then immediately afterward, He condemns their temple and pronounces its imminent judgment. He uses the same exact words, but many modern translators want to translate Matthew 24:26 differently. Why? It is because they have an unbiblical, futuristic bias.

CHAPTER 7

The Coming of the Son of Man

Let's continue on with Matthew 24:32–42:

> Now learn the parable from the fig tree:
> when its branch has already become tender, and
> puts forth its leaves, you will know that summer
> is near; even so you [disciples] too, when you see
> all these things, recognize that he is near, *right* at
> the door. Truly I say to you [disciples], this gen-
> eration will not pass away until all these things
> take place. Heaven and earth will pass away, but
> my words shall not pass away. But of that day
> and hour no one knows, not even the angels of
> heaven, nor the Son, but the Father alone. For
> the coming of the Son of Man will be just like
> the days of Noah. For as in those days which were
> before the flood they were eating and drinking,
> they were marrying and giving in marriage, until
> the day that Noah entered the ark, and they did
> not understand until the flood came and took
> them all away; so shall the coming of the Son
> of Man be. Then there shall be two men in the
> field; one will be taken, and one will be left. Two
> women *will be* grinding at the mill; one will be

taken, and one will be left. Therefore be on the alert, for you [disciples] do not know which day your Lord is coming.

What is Jesus speaking of here? It certainly sounds like Judgment Day! The end of the world! That is our cultural conditioning, but remember: "context, context, context!" What is the context here? Jesus is still answering the question of His disciples. Why then is it that in verse 33 when He says, "even so you too, when you see all these things, recognize [the word is literally *know*] that He [the Son of Man] is near," do we think He is suddenly talking about we who are living two thousand years later? That is the number one popular teaching today, that Jesus is talking about the end of the world.

But what is the context? Jesus is still talking to His disciples. Jesus is still answering their question about when the temple is going to be destroyed. There is nothing in the flow of Matthew 24 that changes that. Look at the parallel passage in Luke 17:22–37:

> And He [Jesus] said to the disciples, "The days shall come when you [disciples] will long to see one of the days of the Son of Man, and you [disciples] will not see it. And they will say to you [disciples], "Look there! Look here!" Do not go away, and do not run after them. For just as the lightning, when it flashes out of one part of the sky, shines to the other part of the sky, so will the Son of Man be in His day. But first He must suffer many things and be rejected by this generation."

We have noted that the word we translate as *generation*, in the whole New Testament, always means "this present generation" and that it cannot possibly, in Matthew 24 and Luke 17, mean "this race," which is how some people are forced to interpret it because of a futuristic bias. So Jesus is setting the context here as "this generation."

> And just as it happened in the days of Noah,
> so it shall be also in the days of the Son of Man.

Here again, Luke is using exactly the same words as Matthew.

> They were eating, they were drinking, they were marrying, they were being given in marriage, until the day that Noah entered the ark, and the flood came and destroyed them all. It was the same as happened in the days of Lot: they were eating, they were drinking, they were buying, they were selling, they were planting, they were building; but on the day that Lot went out from Sodom it rained fire and brimstone from heaven and destroyed them all.

What is Luke and Matthew writing about? When Jesus speaks about the days of Noah and the days of Lot, what is He talking about? He is speaking of the judgment of God! He is speaking of the suddenness of that judgment. In the context of Matthew 24, He is describing the judgment of God upon the Jewish people. In the case of Noah and Lot, God's judgment was upon ungodly people. Jesus is talking about the suddenness of His *parousia*, that appearing of the Son of Man in judgment. It is not something that comes with many warnings.

Why do people want to know when Christ is coming back? So they can get ready! The knowledge of when He will return presupposes that you can do what you want to do until just before He comes! But Jesus is telling His disciples, you are not going to have that opportunity. When judgment comes without warning, it is too late. In Noah's day, when the raindrops started falling, it was too late. In Lot's day, when the fire came down out of heaven, it was too late. Jesus is saying the same thing is about to occur at the destruction of the temple.

> Remember Lot's wife. Whoever seeks to
> keep his life shall lose it, and whoever loses *his
> life* shall preserve it. I tell you, on that night
> there will be two men in one bed; one will be
> taken, and the other will be left. [Sounds just like
> Matthew, doesn't it?] And answering [the disci-
> ples] said to him, "Where, Lord?" And he said
> to them, "Where the body *is*, there also will the
> eagles be gathered."

What is Jesus telling the disciples about the place where this is
going to happen? It is "where the body is, there the eagles will be gathered." The New American Standard translates the word *vultures*, but
it can also be translated *eagles*. What is Jesus speaking about? I believe
He is describing the Roman army. Remember that the Roman army
carried standards or banners before every unit. On the front of every
standard was the eagle, which symbolized the god of the army. The
eagle was the god of the Roman army. It was swift, it was powerful,
and it was invincible! It was their god. That is why Jesus speaks about
the abomination of desolation as armies surrounding Jerusalem.
It is not that Jesus is talking about vultures gathering over a dead
body. In context, He is speaking figuratively about the destruction
of Jerusalem—the Roman army feasting upon the dead body of the
apostate Jewish nation from which He has removed the life of His
Spirit and Presence (which is now indwelling the new temple of every
Christian).

If we return to Matthew 24: 40–44, what does Jesus mean when
He states "one will be taken"?

Jesus is speaking about "the elect." He is talking about the
fact that in Jewish families one might be saved and one might not.
Remember that Jesus is talking about the context of judgment here.

> For the coming of the Son of Man will be
> just like the days of Noah.

They did not know what was going to happen until Noah entered the ark and God closed the door.

> And they did not understand until the flood came and took them all away... Then there shall be two men in the field...

When is the *then* in the context of Matthew 24? This may be beginning to sound monotonous, but it is when the temple will be destroyed. That is what Jesus is saying. He is not speaking about the end of the world. He is saying that when the temple is destroyed

> *Then* there shall be two men in the field; one will be taken, and one will be left. Two women *will be* grinding at the mill; one will be taken, and one will be left. Therefore be on the alert, for you [disciples] do not know which day your Lord is coming. But be sure of this, that if the head of the house had known at what time of the night the thief was coming, he would have been on the alert and would not have allowed his house to be broken into. For this reason you [disciples] be ready too; for the Son of Man is coming at an hour when you [disciples] do not think *he will.*

What has Jesus told the disciples in these verses? "You [disciples] be ready. I am going to come back, you do not and cannot know when. If you think you know, you are wrong. I am going to come back at a time when you do not think." What is the principle that we can apply in our lives? Jesus is coming again. We know that from other Scriptures. There is no doubt about that. He is coming in judgment, and we cannot know when. If we think we know, we are wrong.

Notice, too, that this particular passage says "coming," not "coming back." There are many kinds of "comings" referred to in the Bible. It is not just at the end of time that God comes in judgment.

He came in judgment when Adam and Eve sinned in the Garden. He comes in judgment against nations. He comes to judge our hearts when we gather for worship. And He comes in judgment at death, either to take us to be with Him eternally or to suffer the eternal torments of hell. That specifically applies to every one of us. Since none of us knows when that will be, we should always be ready and prepared to "meet our Maker, our gracious Lord and Savior" when He comes for us individually.

In verses 42 and 44, Jesus is not talking about the end of the world. He is speaking about the destruction of the temple. He is speaking about the suddenness of His coming in judgment upon the ungodly Jews. How does that apply to you and me? There is a coming in judgment upon people. Look at the newspapers, at the teacher and little girls killed in the Jonesboro, Arkansas, school shooting. How did they know when the killer set off the fire alarm their lives were about to end? They did not. You see, that is the message we have to get across to people. You do not know when you are going to meet God. You might leave your home today and be hit by a truck at the stop sign. God forbid that would happen. But we do not know God's timetable. That is why it is so important for our unbelieving friends to understand their need for salvation. When you listen to people talk, listen in the context of, "How can I bring Jesus into this conversation? How can I bring up salvation in this conversation?" Because it is so important to say to people, "You don't know when God is coming, and you must be ready."

In this particular part of Matthew 24, it is very clear that there were to be no signs of Jerusalem's imminent judgment. Of course, this runs counter to what many people talk about as "the signs of the times" in Matthew 24:4 and following. But even there, if you look carefully at the words of Jesus, He is saying, "Even though these things are signs of the imminent destruction of the temple, they are not signs of the end of the world. Do not be fooled and led astray by earthquakes and famines and wars and rumors of war. These are merely signs of the end of the Jewish age.

Jesus clearly teaches in verse 8:

> But all these things are *merely* the beginning
> of birth pangs.

They are the beginning of the birth of what? The church. Even as the old Jewish era passes away, the new church era comes onto the scene as Christianity explodes into the world.

CHAPTER 8

What about the Rapture?

What is the end of time really like? Most people today think of Matthew 24 as speaking about the end of time, about the end of the world. A time when two men are working in the field and suddenly one will be gone. You may hear a song about this or see bumper stickers that say, "In case of rapture, this car will be driverless." Where do these ideas of a secret rapture come from? They come from a futurist interpretation of Matthew 24:40, which says,

> Then there shall be two men in the field;
> one will be taken and one will be left.

But the key question is, "What is the passage really describing?" Not "Is it popular?" but "Is it true?" In this section, we will look at four verses and try to figure out whether or not the popular view of "the Rapture" is biblical.

In 1 Corinthians 15, Paul is dealing with the question of the resurrection. There was a question in the church at Corinth about whether or not there really was a resurrection. Paul argues that if Jesus was, in fact, resurrected, then there must necessarily be a resurrection. If Jesus was not resurrected, then "we are of all men most to be pitied." (verse 19). That is because we are basing our lives on a lie, the promise of a resurrection that did not occur and will not occur. In the book by Frank Morison titled *Who Moved the Stone?* the author (a British journalist) began writing the book in order to disprove the resurrection and in the process of his investigation became a Christian. What were his findings? Based on the historical evidence, the resurrection of Jesus Christ is the most documented *fact* in all of history. Paul was dealing with that same question in his day, and he is saying the same thing early in the chapter. Paul argues that you should look at the evidence, and you will know that Jesus was, in fact, resurrected. Then toward the end of the chapter he writes:

> Now I say this, brethren, that flesh and blood cannot inherit the kingdom of God; nor does corruption inherit incorruption. Behold, I tell you a mystery; we shall not all sleep, but we shall all be changed, in a moment, in the twinkling of an eye, at the last trumpet; for the trumpet will sound and the dead will be raised incorruptible, and we shall be changed. For the corruption must put on the incorruption, and this mortal must put on immortality. But when this corruptible will have put on the incorruptible, and this mortal will have put on immortality, then will come about the saying that is written, "Death is swallowed up in victory." (1 Corinthians 15:50–54)

Paul is saying that, in our sinful flesh, we cannot come before God. We are corruptible—corruption because we are in a world that has been corrupted by sin. We must put off the old man completely. That is the process of sanctification which God the Spirit is working in us on a day-by-day basis. Since God has made us new, we must put on the new man. We are, in His reality, complete. At our salvation, we are truly changed. We are no longer natural; we are spiritual (in God's reality). But in our reality, we tend to slip back and forth between the sinful and the spiritual (up and down like the stock market). This is the process that the Bible calls "sanctification." In our reality, we are becoming more and more like the reality God sees (or knows). Now, when the trumpet sounds, we will be changed completely into God's reality. The reality of God will then become our reality. That is what Paul is writing about in 1 Corinthians 15. In this body we cannot be with God. We must all be changed (those whom God has saved) even those who are alive; we shall all be changed in an instant, "in the twinkling of an eye," and we will then be with God for eternity.

Another passage most people think is pertaining to the end of the world is 2 Thessalonians chapters 1 and 2.

> Therefore, we ourselves speak proudly of you among the churches of God for your perseverance and faith in the midst of all your persecutions and afflictions which you endure. [Notice the Thessalonians were being persecuted and afflicted.] *This is* a plain indication of God's righteous judgment so that you may be considered worthy of the kingdom of God, for which indeed you are suffering. [Notice again they, the Thessalonians, are being purified through suffering.] For after all it is *only* just for God to repay with affliction those who afflict you, and *to give* relief to you who are afflicted and to us as well [Paul is saying here there will come a time when God will turn the tables and afflict the persons afflicting the Thessalonians and He will reward those of them who are suffering now. The question is "When will that be?"] when the Lord Jesus shall be revealed from heaven with His mighty angels in flaming fire, dealing out retribution to those who do not know God and to those who do not obey the gospel of our Lord Jesus. And these will pay the penalty of eternal destruction, away from the presence of the Lord and from the glory of His power, when He comes to be glorified in His saints on that day, and to be marveled at among all who have believed—for our

testimony to you was believed. (2 Thessalonians 1:4–10)

What is Paul speaking about? Look at verse 7. Paul is saying it is expected soon. In the context he is saying this is going to happen very quickly, giving relief to those who were being afflicted and to Paul and his companions as well. Notice, he is including himself in this event. Let's continue on in chapter 2:

> Now we request you, brethren, with regard to the coming [the *parousia*] of our Lord Jesus Christ, and our gathering together to him, that you may not be quickly shaken from your composure or be disturbed either by a spirit or a message or a letter as if from us, to the effect that the day of the Lord has come. Let no one in any way deceive you, for *it will not come* unless the apostasy comes first, and the man of lawlessness is revealed, the son of destruction, who opposes and exalts himself above every so-called god or object of worship, so that he takes his seat in the temple of God, displaying himself as being God. (2 Thessalonians 2:1–6)

I have read all kinds of interpretations of these verses, saying that this apostasy is still future in our day and that this man of lawlessness or man of sin has not yet appeared, that this is the Antichrist who is going to appear sometime in the future and he will take his seat in the temple. That is why people believe the temple in Jerusalem has to be rebuilt and the sacrificial system reinstituted. How else can this person seat himself in the temple and declare himself to be God? But is that what the Bible really says? Look at verse 5.

> Do YOU not remember that while I was still with YOU, I was telling YOU these things? And YOU know what restrains him NOW, so

that in his time he may be revealed. (Emphasis added.)

Is the man of lawlessness future in Paul's time? No. Paul is clearly saying, "YOU, Thessalonians know what is restraining the man of lawlessness NOW." The Bible is clear; the man of lawlessness was contemporary to Paul's time. He says, "Don't you remember I was telling you about him?" So it obviously makes a lot more sense to say that the temple was still standing at this point and that the man of lawlessness was going to seat himself in that present temple and declare himself to be God. Therefore, this passage cannot be about the end of the world. It pertains to something that occurred in Paul's day.

> And YOU know what restrains him NOW, so that in his time he may be revealed. For the mystery of lawlessness is ALREADY at work; [when is the mystery of lawlessness at work? It is already at work during the time Paul wrote the letter; not some two thousand years into the future] only he who NOW restrains will do so until he is taken out of the way. and then that lawless one will be revealed whom the Lord will slay with the breath of His mouth and bring to an end by the appearance of His coming; the one whose coming is in accord with the activity of Satan, with all power and signs and false wonders, and with all the deception of wickedness for those who perish, because they did not receive the love of the truth so as to be saved. (Emphasis added.)

Paul is writing here about the Lord coming in judgment upon the temple, which is still future at the time Paul is writing to the Thessalonians. So again, here is a passage that many in our day believe is addressing something in the future because they do not understand what has really been written.

I am sure some will want to know, "Who is the lawless one?" There are several different interpretations of that. Some scholars think it was an apostate high priest. Some commentators think it was Nero. He wanted to put a statue of himself in the temple. There are other interpretations. Frankly, I do not think there is enough information in the passage to conclusively pin it down to a specific person. But there is enough information here to pin it down to a specific *time*. That was the time of Paul.

Let us move on then to 1 Thessalonians 4:13–17, where Paul addresses the rapture.

> But we do not want you to be uninformed,
> brethren, about those who are asleep, that you
> may not grieve, as do the rest who have no hope.
> (1 Thessalonians 4:13)

The contemporary situation was that in the church in Thessalonica, people were expecting the Lord to return at any moment. They were also saying that if someone had already died, then that person was not going to be with the Lord. For those who had died already, it was too late. Paul is saying, "No, you don't understand!" He is dealing with this particular theological question in the church at Thessalonica. He says,

> For if we believe that Jesus died and rose
> again, even so God will bring with Him those
> who have fallen asleep in Jesus.

Paul is saying that if someone is a Christian and falls asleep (dies), then, when Jesus returns, they are going to return with him.

> For this we say to you by the word of the
> Lord, that we who are alive, and remain until the

coming of the Lord, shall not precede those who
have fallen asleep.

Paul is saying there is no difference between Christians who
have died and those still alive. There is no hierarchy.

> For the Lord Himself will descend from
> heaven with a shout, with the voice of *the* arch-
> angel, and with the trumpet of God; and the
> dead in Christ shall rise first. Then we who are
> alive and remain shall be caught up together with
> them in the clouds to meet the Lord in the air,
> and thus we shall always be with the Lord.

Paul is writing that when the trumpet sounds on the Last Day,
when Christ returns, those who have died in Christ will come with
Him. Those who are alive at that time will be changed and will be
caught up together with them. Thus, we will all be together and
always be with the Lord.

> Therefore comfort one another with these
> words. (Look forward to that reality which is
> God's.)

This is the only place in the Bible that talks about any kind of
"rapture." But it is not speaking about a rapture as is generally understood in the church today, a sneaky sort of silent rapture where one
person will be taken and another will be left. Notice how noisy it is here.

> The Lord Himself will descend from heaven
> with a shout, with the voice of *the* archangel, and
> with the trumpet of God.

When Jesus returns on the Last Day, it will not be in secret.
Everyone will know He has returned. On that day there will be judgment for the wicked and reward for the righteous.

You see, the key in studying Scripture is to always look for time clues. The time clues here tell us that this event (the rapture) will occur when the general resurrection of the dead and the living occurs. Even though it does not tell us when this will happen, it tells us what will happen. We must look elsewhere in the Bible to find out when that is going to happen. For example, John is very clear on when the general resurrection will occur. In several places in the gospel of John, he uses the phrase "the Last Day," which specifically refers to the end of time. He uses this phrase over and over. Another time clue in 1 Thessalonians 4 is the phrase "and so we will be with the Lord God" at that point in time. Paul is speaking about the eternal state when all Christians will be with Christ.

In John 5:24 Jesus says,

> Truly, truly, I say to you, he who hears My word, and believes Him who sent Me, has eternal life, and does not come into judgment, but has passed out of death into life and does not come into judgment.

Notice it is not "will have," rather Jesus says the one who believes *has* eternal life—right now. Ephesians 2:6 tells us that in God's reality, we are seated at the right hand of the Father right now *in Jesus Christ*. Of course, we still see our sanctification being worked out, but in the reality of God things are different.

This is another point that needs to be strongly addressed. Many Christians talk about having to stand before the judgment throne of God. No Christian will stand before the throne of God in order to be judged in regard to our salvation. That issue is addressed in the chapter on "the great white throne judgment." We will stand before the throne of God but not in judgment. We will stand there as trophies of the grace of God so everyone will understand that we are in heaven for one reason and one reason only—the perfect righteousness of Jesus Christ alone. It is the non-Christian, the ungodly, who will stand there in judgment, and in that case, everyone will clearly understand that they will be going to hell as the just reward of their own sinfulness.

Jesus says those who believe in Him do not

> Come into judgment, but [have] passed out of death into life. Truly, truly, I say to you, an hour is coming [not just a day] and now is, when the dead shall hear the voice of the Son of God; and those who hear shall live. For just as the Father has life in Himself, even so He gave to the Son also to have life in Himself; and He gave Him authority to execute judgment, because He is the Son of Man. Do not marvel at this; for an hour [notice he repeats it again] is coming [but this time he does not say "and now is" because it is future, at the Last Day], in which all who are in the tombs shall hear His voice and shall come forth; those who did the good to a resurrection of life, those who committed the evil to a resurrection of judgment. (John 5:24–29)

Notice that Jesus Himself says that there is no thousand years between the resurrection of the righteous and the resurrection of the wicked. It happens not only on the same day, but also at the same hour.

CHAPTER 9

The Son of Man Revealed

Before looking at Revelation 1:4, carefully consider the following questions. What would you do if a door opened and the incarnate Jesus Christ walked in? Would you humbly bow down with your face to the floor? Would you shout with joy and jubilation? Would you have countless questions to ask Him? People have many differing ideas about what they would do if Jesus were to appear before them. Let's read through the passage and see what happens here.

> John to the seven churches that are in Asia: Grace to you and peace from Him who is and who was and who is to come; and from the seven Spirits who are before His throne; and from Jesus Christ, the faithful witness, the first-born of the dead, and the ruler of the kings of the earth. To Him who loves us, and released us from our sins by His blood, and He has made us *to be* a kingdom, priests to His God and Father; to Him *be* the glory and the dominion forever and ever. Amen. (Revelation 1:4–6)

Notice that John is describing Jesus as the Prophet, Priest, and King. He is the faithful witness (a prophet), the first born of the dead (which is His priestly function), and the ruler of the kings of the earth (which is His kingly function). John then describes what Jesus does: He loves us, and He has "released us from our sins by" the shedding of His own blood. He created us to be a kingdom (to rule with Him); He made us priests (to serve God and Christ); and He designed us to function as prophets (to be witnesses by telling others about Jesus Christ and the Word of God). These descriptions are immediately followed by a doxology: "To Him be the glory and the dominion forever and ever. Amen." This also appears in Paul's writings. The doxologies reflect how both writers were overcome with the magnificent glory of what they are writing about.

BEHOLD, HE IS COMING WITH THE CLOUDS, and every eye will see Him, even those who pierced Him; and all the tribes of the earth will mourn over Him. Even so, Amen. "I am the Alpha and the Omega," says the Lord God, "who is and who was and who is to come, the Almighty." I, John, your brother and fellow partaker in the tribulation and kingdom and perseverance *which are* in Jesus, was on the island called Patmos, because of the word of God and the testimony of Jesus. I was in the Spirit on the Lord's day, and I heard behind me a loud voice like *the sound* of a trumpet, saying, "Write in a book what you see, and send *it* to the seven churches: to Ephesus and to Smyrna and to Pergamum and to Thyatira and to Sardis and to Philadelphia and to Laodicea." And I turned to see the voice that was speaking with me. And having turned I saw seven golden lampstands; and in the middle of the lampstands *I saw* one like a son of man, clothed in a robe reaching to the feet, and girded across His breast with a golden girdle. And His head and His hair were white like white wool, like snow; and His eyes were like a flame of fire; and His feet *were* like burnished bronze, when it has been caused to glow in a furnace, and His voice *was* like the sound of many waters. and in His right hand He held seven stars; and out of His mouth came a sharp two-edged sword; and His face was like the sun shining in its strength. And when I saw Him, I fell at His feet as a dead man. And He laid His right hand upon me, saying, "Do not be afraid; I am the first and the last, and the living One; and I was dead, and behold, I am alive forevermore, and I have the keys of death and of Hades. Write therefore the things which you have seen, and the things which are, and the things which shall take place after these things. As for the mystery of the seven stars which you saw in My right hand, and the seven golden lampstands: the seven stars are the angels of the seven churches, and the seven lampstands are the seven churches." (Revelation 1:7–20)

After reading the passage above, reconsider your thoughts of what you might do if you were to see Christ in reality. Just as John did you would fall face down on the ground. Most believers have an image of Jesus as the wonderful, gentle shepherd opening His arms to the sheep. And yes, He certainly is that. However, believers also fail to realize that He is also *the* living and awesome and incredible God. Whenever people in Scripture see God as He really is, in His holiness and His glory, falling to the ground in reverence is their immediate response.

And when I saw Him, I fell at His feet as a dead man.

In Daniel 10, the prophet reacts in a very similar way.

In those days I, Daniel, had been mourn-ing for three entire weeks. I did not eat any tasty food, nor did meat or wine enter my mouth... And on the twenty-fourth day of the first month, while I was by the bank of the great river, that is, the Tigris, I lifted my eyes and looked, and behold, there was a certain man dressed in linen, whose waist was girded with *a belt of* pure gold of Uphas. His body also was like beryl, his face had the appearance of lightning, his eyes were like flaming torches, his arms and feet like the gleam of polished bronze, and the sound of his words like the sound of a tumult.... But I heard the sound of his words; and as soon as I heard the sound of his words, I fell into a deep sleep on my face, with my face to the ground. (Daniel 10:2–9)

In the Old Testament, when the angelic visitors appeared before Abraham, he realized who they were, and he fell face-down on the ground. These scenes remind us that God is the Creator and we are simply His creatures. Since God is our Heavenly Father, we will be able to say "Abba, Father." The term *Abba* has been defined in many sermons as meaning "daddy." However, this term has a different connotation in the Greek. It actually implies that the Father is the exalted head of the family. Although believers all have access to Him, they must remember who God really is. When John sees the vision of Christ and recognizes this is God, he falls down on his face in spontaneous reverence for God.

Let's take another look at verse 9:

I, John, your brother and fellow partaker in the tribulation and kingdom and perseverance in Jesus...

What is thought-provoking about this verse in light of the modern teaching on Revelation? Does John say that "the tribulation" is going to come some day in the future? No. He states that he himself is a "fellow partaker in the tribulation." He is writing of the tribulation in the present tense and not as an occurrence in the distant future. What does John say about "the kingdom?" Will "the kingdom" come when Christ returns and reigns for a thousand years? No. Again John uses the present tense.

Many have studied in Daniel 2:32–35 about the dream of Nebuchadnezzar. Daniel reveals to the king that his dream was of a great statue with,

> The head of that statue *was made* of fine gold, its breast and its arms of silver, its belly and its thighs of bronze, its legs of iron, its feet partly of iron and partly of clay. "You continued looking until a stone was cut out without hands, and it struck the statue on its feet of iron and clay and crushed them. Then the iron, the clay, the bronze, the silver and the gold were crushed all at the same time and became like chaff from the summer threshing floors; and the wind carried them away so that not a trace of them was found. But the stone that struck the statue became a great mountain and filled the whole earth."

In Daniel's interpretation of the dream, he reveals that the statue represented various worldly kingdoms. The stone which was cut without hands came and destroyed the statue. The stone then grew and grew becoming a kingdom that filled the entire earth. What does the text say about when that happened? When did that kingdom come into being? Notice that the feet of the statue were made of clay and iron and most commentators understand this represents Rome. Thus, the kingdom came into existence during the time of the Roman Empire. This is exactly what John understands in his writings. When Jesus Christ was crucified, resurrected, and ascended to the right hand of the Father (during the time of Rome), His kingdom came into being. Granted, as God Almighty, Jesus Christ has been King from eternity. But in a very special way, the church and His kingdom came into being during the time of Rome. It is an eternal kingdom that will fill the earth and will never pass away, and John understands this.

> I, John, your brother and fellow partaker in the tribulation and kingdom and perseverance in Jesus, was on the island called Patmos, because of the word of God and the testimony of Jesus.

Why was John on Patmos? His witnessing for Christ, His telling people about Jesus Christ had led to his exile to the island of Patmos. He was there "because of the word of God and the testimony of Jesus."

> I heard behind me a loud voice like of a trumpet.

Repeatedly in Scripture, we read this kind of description. In Genesis chapter 3, after the fall of Adam and Eve, their eyes were opened, and they knew they had sinned. They realized they were naked because their sin was not "covered," or atoned for. Genesis 3:8 reads,

> And they heard the sound of YHWH God walking in the garden in the cool of the day... [the Hebrew word translated as cool is actually the same word as wind or spirit] and the man and his wife hid themselves from the presence of YHWH God among the trees of the garden.

Why did Adam and Eve hide from God? They knew they had sinned, but why, if God was just out walking in the cool of the garden, were they hiding? Think of the thunderous, roaring sound of a tornado. Adam and Eve were hearing such a sound of great magnitude—the incredible, awesome, trumpet, roaring wind sound of God coming in judgment! Of course, they were afraid! God was not just out for a stroll in the garden. God was coming to judge them for their sin. That is why they were afraid when they heard that incredible roaring sound.

Similarly, when the Hebrews were gathered around Mt. Sinai as God was speaking, they told Moses to go speak to God and they said, "Let not God speak to us, lest we die." This is precisely what Adam and Eve heard and what John was hearing when he says, "I heard behind me a loud voice like of a trumpet." This is the sound of God coming in judgment. It is not a beautiful, melodious tune as heard from a windup music box. It is the sound of the awesomeness of God as He comes in judgment.

Next John sees a vision of the resurrected Christ saying,

> Write in a book what you see, and send to
> the seven churches: to Ephesus and to Smyrna
> and to Pergamum and to Thyatira and to Sardis
> and to Philadelphia and to Laodicea.

In the rest of the book of Revelation, John records what Jesus Christ told him to write. But to whom does John address these writings? Clearly, John is addressing his writings directly to the seven churches. The Revelation is not written primarily to the people in the twentieth-century church, which is the strong assumption of many in the modern church. In principle, however, it is written *for* present-day believers. In other words, we can study the Revelation and derive principles from it that apply to our lives. However, John states clearly that it is written specifically *to* the seven churches that existed during his time, and it was written for a particular purpose. A map of the area clearly shows that the geographical locations of Ephesus, Smyrna, Pergamum, Thyatira, Sardis, Philadelphia, and Laodicea form a large circle. As a seaport, Ephesus was the originating point of a trade road that went to each of the other six churches. Thus, when Jesus says, "Write this letter to the seven churches," He is sending it out to every church within this area. This was a typical practice in those days. Letters from John and Paul as well as the other apostles would be sent from church to church, where they would be read aloud to the congregation. These were the Holy Scriptures and the people in the congregations fully understood that these were the words of God.

John continues,

> And I turned to see the voice that was speaking with me. And having turned I saw seven golden lampstands; and in the middle of the lampstands *I saw* one like a son of man, clothed in a robe reaching to the feet, and girded across His breast with a golden girdle.

No one argues that this is truly a vision of Jesus Christ. However, what do the seven lampstands represent and what is the significance that He is standing in the middle of the lampstands? It means that Jesus is present with each of the seven churches. He has not separated Himself from the church. He is the imminent God, Immanuel, Who is always with His church. Jesus is continually among His people, as He told His disciples, "And lo, I will be with you always." This is a beautiful picture of God always being among His people. Glance back at the Old Testament. How did the Hebrews lay out their camp in the desert? What was centrally located in the middle of their encampment? It was the tabernacle, where, in the Holy of Holies, the Shekinah Glory-Cloud, the presence of God Himself, dwelled. Even in the Old Testament God was saying to His people, "I am God and I am going to be incarnate; I am going to be among My people." God does not leave His people alone to struggle for themselves. He is always here among His beloved church.

The clothing that John describes Jesus wearing is somewhat strange to the eyes of the modern person. He is "clothed in a robe reaching to the feet, and girded across His breast with a golden girdle." The high priest of the Old Testament dressed in a similar robe. In the Greek version of the Old Testament, the word John uses for *robe* is the same word used for the "robe of the high priest." He was dressed in a long robe of fine linen with a pouch adorned with twelve jewels that extended across the chest. The pouch was attached by gold chains to a jewel on each shoulder of the high priest. He also wore a turban that held a crown which said, "Holy to YHWH." What did the high priest look like as he functioned in the temple wearing precious jewels, gold, and fine linen? With the candlelight and firelight sparkling from the jewels and flashing from the gold, His appearance would have been spectacular. He represented the power and authority of Christ. In a small way, the high priest was an earthly picture of Jesus, which is what John is seeing here and what Daniel saw in his vision. The power of His light and truth as depicted in this incredible and awesome incarnation of God is undoubtedly blinding to man. Thus, in response, each of these godly men fell to the ground.

And His voice like the sound of many waters.

Again, there is this incredible, rushing water, trumpet, wind sound.

And in His right hand He held seven stars; and out of His mouth came a sharp two-edged sword.

This sword is not small. The Greek word used reveals that this was a Thracian sword. That type of sword was actually worn on the shoulder, as it would not fit at the waist. Because of its length it would drag on the ground. It resembled the broadsword of the medieval knights in armor. It required two hands to maneuver it. Does Christ really have a large sword emerging from His mouth? No. This image symbolizes the Word of God. Hebrews 4:12 tells us,

The word of God is living and active and sharper than any two-edged sword...and able to judge the thoughts and intentions of the heart.

Scripture is the standard by which God judges His people. As seen later in Revelation, it is the Word of God that gains the final victory. It is not how hard the believer works. Neither is it the number of doors on which we knock or the number of people the believer tells about Jesus Christ. It is the Word of God that is all-important. When Jesus was tempted in the desert, He did not respond with magic or miracles. Instead, He responded,

It is written…

Keep in mind that Jesus quoted verses from the Old Testament. There was no New Testament. Jesus was in the midst of creating it.

Believers need to respond in the same way, quoting Scripture that is appropriate to the situation. This is the reason it is so important to regularly read the Word of God. This is the reason the believer should study Scripture. To be able to respond with accuracy and timeliness requires knowledge and confidence. Then when you are confronted with something you know is not biblical, you can respond appropriately. As the Word of God says,

It is written that…

But how can the believer do this without studying the Word and memorizing it?

John writes,

> And when I saw Him, I fell at His feet as a dead man. And He laid His right hand upon me, saying, "Do not be afraid; I am the first and the last…"

Many people have difficulty understanding the Trinity. For example, they have a problem with the fact that Jesus prays to God the Father. Thus, some say "How can He be God if He prays to God?" But notice when Jesus says, "I am the first and the last." He is, in fact, saying, "I am Yahweh." In Isaiah 44:6, God (Yahweh) says, "I am the first and the last." There is absolutely no doubt about who Jesus really is if one understands that it was God Who first said, "I am the first and the last." But now Jesus is saying, "I am the first and the last." Which is it? There cannot be two beings who are both the "first and last." Thus, Jesus is saying very clearly that He is Yahweh of the Old Testament, the God Almighty.

Notice the symbology here—Jesus is described as "someone like a son of man" which is a very clear reference to the Messiah of Daniel 7. He is then immediately described, using the same terminology, as the Ancient of Days in Daniel 7. Therefore, Jesus must be a person of the divine Trinity, God the Father, God the Son, and God the Holy Spirit. What is symbolized here in Revelation is the divine Messiah. Note also that what is seen here is a picture of the Son of Man reigning in heaven. This is the reality to which the destruction of Jerusalem points. As Jesus says in Matthew 24:30,

> At that time will appear the sign of the Son
> of Man [reigning] in heaven…

Jesus tells John,

> Do not be afraid; I am the first and the last,
> and the living One; and I was dead, and behold,
> I am alive forevermore.

How can it be stated more clearly than this? Some people argue about whether or not Jesus Christ actually died on the cross. One theory, the "swoon theory," states that He "swooned on the cross." He simply fainted, lost consciousness, and when placed in the tomb, the coolness of the tomb revived Him, bringing Him "back to life." Other theories state that Jesus neither died nor did He actually rise from the dead. But the fact that this is Jesus Christ speaking, and that He states, in the Greek, "I became dead," presents us with a dilemma. There are only two choices: either Jesus died and was resurrected from the dead, or Jesus is a liar.

> I am alive forevermore, and I have the keys
> of death and of Hades.

Scripture clearly states that Jesus is God. At the same time, Jesus is fully man—He died and rose again and is alive forevermore. Because of His victory on the cross, He is the only one who holds the keys to death and Hades. Their works do not get people into heaven. Quite the contrary! Doing works in order to gain entrance into heaven is what actually leads one to hell. It is only through Jesus Christ that one gains entry into heaven. It is not what we do, but what we believe that is important. Trusting in Christ alone for salvation is all that matters. As Jesus says, He alone has the keys to death and Hades.

Jesus says to John,

> Write therefore the things which you have
> seen, and the things which are, and the things
> which shall take place after these things.

He is telling John that some of the things he should write concern the past, some of the things concern the present, and some will occur in the future. A large number of people view the book of Revelation as being divided into those categories. Chapter 1:9–18 refers to events in the past. Chapter 1:19–3:22 refers to present events in the seven churches. The remaining verses refer to events that are still future. Although this is one way of dividing the book, this author does do not agree with the perspective that a majority of the Revelation is still future to contemporary times. But His Word clearly indicates that Jesus is telling John to record events from the past, events of the present (contemporary to the time of John), and events that are still future to the time of John.

> As for the mystery of the seven stars which
> you saw in My right hand, and the seven golden
> lampstands: the seven stars are the angels of the
> seven churches, and the seven lampstands are the
> seven churches.

Notice that Jesus speaks of the mystery of the seven stars. The definition of the word *mysterion* in the New Testament does not have the same meaning as the English word used today. Rather, it denotes something that was previously unknown and has now been revealed. This is precisely what Jesus is doing in this passage. He is revealing the mystery. The seven stars and seven lampstands are the seven angels and the seven churches. Does this imply that every church has an angel? Are there angels watching over the churches of today? The Greek word *angelos* means "messenger" (either human or angelic), and it is also used in reference to the "messenger of the Word," which is the pastor of a church.

Notice in chapter 2, Jesus says, "To the angel of the church in Ephesus write," and then in verse 2, He says, "I know your deeds." Spiritual angels would not be doing the types of things that the *angelos* of these churches are doing. Therefore, it should be clear that Jesus is speaking specifically to the pastors of the churches. Continuing in verse 2, when He says,

> I know your deeds and your toil and perseverance, and that you cannot endure evil men, and you put to the test those who call themselves apostles...

It is made clear that Jesus is speaking about a human being who is contemporary with the church. Jesus must, therefore, be speaking of the pastor of the church.

God's judgment of a given church comes through the pastor of the church. This type of "federal headship" is seen throughout the Bible. In the Old Testament when Israel was divided into the Northern Kingdom (Israel) and the Southern Kingdom (Judea), there were no good kings ruling in the north, and only a few good kings ruling in the south. When the kings walked in obedience to God, the people were good and faithful. However, when the kings disobeyed the commands of God, the people were vile and sinful. Similarly, this idea of "federal headship" is at work in the church today. The pastor leads the congregation into either righteousness or sinfulness.

"Judgment starts with the house of God" (1 Peter 4:17), with its leaders. The congregation has the right and responsibility to confront their pastor(s) with the truths of the Bible. Should they hear inaccurate or false teachings, all brothers and sisters in Christ have a responsibility to confront or correct each other if they hear or see something that conflicts with the Word of God.

CHAPTER 10

The Churches of Revelation
The Church in Ephesus

To the angel of the church in Ephesus write: The One who holds the seven stars in His right hand, the One who walks among the seven golden lampstands, says this: I know your deeds and your toil and perseverance, and that you cannot endure evil men, and you put to the test those who call themselves apostles, and they are not, and you found them *to be* false; and you have perseverance and have endured for My name's sake, and have not grown weary. But I have *this* against you, that you have left your first love. Remember therefore from where you have fallen, and repent and do the deeds you did at first; or else I am coming to you, and will remove your lampstand out of its place—unless you repent. Yet this you do have, that you hate the deeds of the Nicolaitans, which I also hate. He who has an ear, let him hear what the Spirit says to the churches. To him who overcomes, I will grant to eat of the tree of life, which is in the Paradise of God. (Revelation 2:1–7)

As we read through the seven letters to the seven churches, we see that each of the letters is written in a consistent style or pattern. Each one begins with "To the angel of the church in…"—in this case, "Ephesus." Who is the letter from? In each case, we see there is a reference to some part of the vision of Jesus Christ in chapter 1. Note here in chapter 2, verse 1:

> The One who holds the seven stars in His right hand…

And in verse 8,

> And to the angel of the church in Smyrna write: The first and the last, who was dead, and has come to life…

And in verse 12,

> And to the angel of the church in Pergamum write: The One who has the sharp two-edged sword…

And in verse 18,

> And to the angel of the church in Thyatira write: The Son of God, who has eyes like a flame of fire, and His feet are like burnished bronze…

John is writing according to a very consistent pattern.

One might ask, "Is this then simply a collection of letters?" Did John just make a copy of what he wrote to the churches? Or did he write this information as if it were written in letters?

It appears that the Revelation is, in fact, letters written to the particular churches, but together they form something greater than the sum of the parts. Some theologians think they might have been individual letters that were included in one document, which is the book of the Revelation. Although we cannot be positive, I think that is highly unlikely. It is important to note that although each of the letters was addressed to the pastor of an individual church, they were also intended for use by all of the churches. You will notice in each of the letters:

> He who has an ear, let him hear what the
> Spirit says to the churches.

Note the word *churches*. In every case it is plural—the information in each letter is intended for every church. We also see that in the letters of Paul. They were addressed to particular churches, addressing specific incidents, but the information was for all the churches (not just then, but for all time).

What was Ephesus like? Sometimes we tend to think of ancient biblical cities as small, mud hut kinds of primitive places. We think of our cities of San Francisco or New York with millions of people, but we think biblical cities were all small. But in fact, Ephesus was a large city with a population of about 250,000. It had a tremendous harbor. It was *the* trade center for that part of the world. It was one of the most important cities in Asia. It was a center of the provincial Roman government. One of the things that the Romans did was to make particular cities like "county seats" with control over the surrounding area for the Roman government.

From the harbor, there was an immense tree-lined boulevard that was thirty-five feet wide. Our normal roads are about sixteen feet wide, so this road was like a four-lane highway. It was also lined with magnificent marble columns. As you went up the road toward the center of the city, there was an enormous building in the middle that was the temple of Artemis (also known as Diana). This temple was the focus of life in the city of Ephesus. The temple was 425 feet long, 220 feet wide, and 60 feet high. It was huge. It was almost twice as large as the

Parthenon in Greece. The temple had been built once and burned to the ground; it was then rebuilt. It had 127 columns of marble, 36 of them were covered with gold and encrusted with jewels. It was an incredible wonder. In the temple, there was a statue of the goddess that had been carved out of a meteorite that had fallen to earth. Therefore, it was said that Artemis came from the heavens. She was a fertility goddess. Her statue had seven breasts that symbolized her fertility.

The temple of Artemis was not only a worship area; it was also the area bank. The citizens would deposit their money, jewels, and valuables in the temple for safekeeping. So it was a really important place, the focus of secular and religious life in Ephesus.

There was also a theater in the city which seated around twenty-five thousand. You can see the partially restored ruins of this theater today. It was an amphitheater built into a hollowed-out portion of a hill with benches all around it and a stage at the bottom. Events and concerts are still held in this theater today.

Ephesus was located right across from the tip of Achaia (Greece as we know it) on the Aegean Sea. It would be a part of present-day Turkey. It no longer has a harbor though. The ruins of the city of Ephesus are now about six miles inland, because the river filled the harbor with silt. Over the years the people kept dredging it, but finally gave up and the harbor filled in.

Jesus says in Revelation 2:1,

> To the angel of the church in Ephesus write.

Remember that *angel* refers to the pastor of the church. If it is an angel of heaven, why would Christ tell John to write a letter to a heavenly creature? Additionally, why would Jesus say,

> I know your deeds and your toil and perseverance, and that you cannot endure evil men, and you put to the test those who call themselves apostles, and they are not, and you found them to be false; and you have perseverance and have endured for My name's sake, and have not grown

90

> weary. But I have this against you, that you have
> left your first love. Remember therefore from
> where you have fallen.

Jesus is obviously speaking about a real person. In fact, in the Greek, the *you* is singular. He is not speaking to all of the congregation of the church; He is speaking to the leader of the church. And He says, "I know what you have been doing."

The people that were calling themselves apostles, whom Jesus is speaking about here, were actually false prophets. Remember that as Jesus had warned, there would be many people who would claim to be prophets of God. They would say, "Listen to us. Don't read the word, listen to us." As Paul says to the Ephesian elders in Acts 20:28,

> Be on guard for yourselves and for all the
> flock, among which the Holy Spirit has made
> you overseers to shepherd the church of God
> which He purchased with His own blood. I know
> that after my departure savage wolves will come
> in among you, not sparing the flock; and from
> among your own selves men will arise speaking
> perverse things, to draw away the disciples after
> them. Therefore be on the alert...

Who is Paul speaking about? These were not people from the outside who were condemning the church. They were not secular people. They were people within the church who were saying, "We are the real prophets; listen to what we have to say." In 1 John 2:18, John writes, "Even now, many antichrists have arisen." Where does he say they came from? "They came out from among us." The Antichrist is not something totally outside the church. The false apostles whom Jesus is speaking about in Revelation, chapter 2 are people within the church, who are subverting the church with false teaching.

> I know your deeds and your toil and perse-
> verance, and that you cannot endure evil men,

and you put to the test those who call themselves
apostles, and they are not, and you found them
to be false.

What kind of test is Jesus speaking about here? He is speaking of
the test of Scripture! The pastor had tested the false prophets against
Scripture and had found them to be false. If someone shows up at
your church claiming to be an apostle sent by God, how would you
know whether that person is or is not an apostle? Jesus is saying to the
pastor of the church in Ephesus, "I know you have put these people to
the test of Scripture." One of the interesting things about my denom-
ination, the Presbyterian Church in America (PCA), is that when a
new pastor arrives, even a PCA pastor from another Presbytery, one
of the first things the new Presbytery does is sit him down with the
Candidates and Credentials Committee and spend anywhere from
two to four hours asking him about Scripture and how he interprets
it. Does he understand Scripture the way we understand Scripture,
the way the Westminster Confession of Faith sets forth the Scripture,
the way we believe it teaches the truth? We want to be certain this
person will be teaching the truths of Scripture to those under his care.

And you have perseverance and have
endured for My name's sake, and have not grown
weary. But I have this against you, that you have
left your first love.

Jesus has just commended the pastor for strictly observing doctrine. We know from other writings that the people of Ephesus were
very strict on doctrine. But they forgot to be gracious in love. You
will find that same situation in many modern churches. They are
very strict on doctrine, but they have forgotten that the idea of love
is central to the teachings of Christ. Remember that in John 13, Jesus
tells His disciples, verse 34:

A new commandment I give you: Love one
another. As I have loved you, so you must love

> one another. All men will know that you are My
> disciples if you love one another.

Jesus continues His address to the pastor.

> Remember therefore from where you have
> fallen, and repent and do the deeds you did at
> first; or else I am coming to you, and will remove
> your lampstand out of its place—unless you
> repent.

There is no church at Ephesus today. Although they were once a flourishing church, very precise in their teaching of the Word, at some point they apparently failed to follow the teachings of Christ, and Jesus did, in fact, remove that church. Note that only Ephesus and Laodicea—the first and last churches Jesus mentions—are threatened with destruction.

> Yet this you do have, that you hate the deeds
> of the Nicolaitans, which I also hate.

The Greek word *nico* means "victory." The Greek word *laos* means "people." Thus *Nicolas* means "victory over the people." Interestingly enough, Jesus says to the church in Pergamum in Revelation 2:14,

> But I have a few things against you, because
> you have there some who hold the teaching
> of Balaam, who kept teaching Balak to put a
> stumbling block before the sons of Israel, to eat
> things sacrificed to idols, and to commit *acts of
> immorality.*

In Hebrew, the name *Balaam* means "victory over the people." In other words, these were two individuals who were apparently doing the same thing. To gain victory over Christians, they were lying to them in the spirit of Balaam and Nicholas. They taught them "to eat things sacrificed to idols, and to commit *acts of* immorality."

In those days, the pagan worship service consisted of sacrifice to their god(s), followed by a meal where the worshipper ate part of the sacrifice. If you were involved with cults such as that of Artemis (Diana), you could also go in and have sex (communion) with the temple prostitutes, male or female. That was how you worshipped the pagan gods. So the Nicolaitans were teaching Christians that it was okay to continue to do this. It was okay to fit in with the contemporary culture. It was okay to be like everybody else, to be culturally relevant and "politically correct." Nothing has changed. People are still teaching that kind of error today. But God says, "Obey me, not the culture." That is what we need to understand. These people hated the deeds of the Nicolaitans, which Jesus also hates.

> He who has an ear, let him hear what the
> Spirit says to the churches."

Again, this is information for all of the churches.

> To him who overcomes, I will grant to eat of
> the tree of life, which is in the Paradise of God.

The overcomers are the true Christians. They overcome with the Word by obeying Christ. They overcome in His power. We cannot do it on our own; Christ did and does it for us. Philippians 2:13 says, "for it is God who is at work in you, both to will and to work for His good pleasure." He is the victor, He is the ruling king, and in Him is the only way into heaven. By traveling that path of faith and obedience, we are granted access to the tree of life that is in the paradise of God.

CHAPTER 11

The Church in Smyrna

And to the angel of the church in Smyrna write: The first and the last, who was dead, and has come to life, says this: 'I know your tribulation and your poverty (but you are rich), and the blasphemy by those who say they are Jews and are not, but are a synagogue of Satan. "Do not fear what you are about to suffer. Behold, the devil is about to cast some of you into prison, so that you will be tested, and you will have tribulation for ten days. Be faithful until death, and I will give you the crown of life. 'He who has an ear, let him hear what the Spirit says to the churches. He who overcomes will not be hurt by the second death." (Revelation 2:8–11)

Smyrna is located about thirty-five miles north of Ephesus and for-ty-nine miles from Pergamum. It was one of the principal cities of Roman Asia and competed with Ephesus and Pergamum for the title "First City of Asia." During biblical times the population may have been as much as two hundred thousand. Smyrna is the only city mentioned in Revelation that is still in existence. Today it is the mod-ern city of Izmir, Turkey.

The name of the city (Smyrna) is probably from the Hebrew word for *myrrh*.

Robert Mounce, in *The Book of Revelation*, points out that Smyrna

> boasted a famous stadium, library, and public theater [the largest in Asia]. It claimed to be the birthplace of the great epic poet Homer. A famous thoroughfare called the Street of Gold curved around Mt. Pagus [which rose over 500 feet from the harbor] like a necklace on the statue of a goddess. At either end was a temple, one to a local variety of Cybele...and the other to Zeus.

The website biblegateway.com states,

> By the early second century...the congregation at Smyrna had a pastor or bishop named Polycarp. Ignatius of Antioch wrote letters, which still exist, to both Polycarp and his congregation. Polycarp himself wrote a letter to the Philippian Christians in Macedonia and (according to an account in the Martyrdom of Polycarp) was martyred in Smyrna in the year 156. Nowhere were the words be faithful, even to the point of death, and I will give you the crown of life, more aptly fulfilled than in the life and death of Polycarp.

Jesus identifies Himself to the angel (pastor) of the church in Smyrna as the first and the last, who was dead, and has come to life... This statement that He is "the first and the last" would certainly have reminded the pastor and the congregation of the church that Jesus was describing Himself as YHWH God, Who is the Alpha and Omega (the beginning and the end). Jesus is stating that He was in the beginning with God (John 1:1) and He is the eternal One Who lives forever.

One might ask, "How is it that Jesus was dead and has come to life?"

The New American Commentary states,

> MacArthur captures the mystery of the declaration: Here is a profound mystery: How can the ever-living One who transcends time, space, and history die? Peter reveals the answer in 1 Peter 3:18: Christ was "put to death in the flesh, but made alive in the spirit." He died in His incarnate humanness as the perfect sacrifice for sin, but now has come to life [by His resurrection] and lives forever "according to the power of an indestructible life."

Jesus is saying to the church in Smyrna that if they cling fast to Him, even though they may be persecuted for a period, and even martyred for their faith, they will live forever. He commands them to be faithful until death. If they will do so, He will give them the crown of life.

The churches of Revelation were all tempted to make compromises because of the persecution they experienced. Smyrna, in particular, is told by Jesus they would undergo tribulation by the Jews who were not truly Jews, but were, instead, a synagogue of Satan. They would be tested because the devil would cast some of them into prison. We know from many sources that the Christians of the time were persecuted not only by the Romans but also by the Jews who considered the Christians to be blasphemers.

Through John's letter, Jesus tells the pastor that some of the people in the congregation will be tested by tribulation for ten days. He commands the pastor to "be faithful until death." It is not known whether John is saying there will be a specific ten-day period of persecution or whether the ten days is symbolic. But since the Revelation was given by Jesus to communicate (sign) the events to John, the probability is that the ten days are symbolic. Note, however, that being cast into prison was not a long-term affair. The Romans did not normally imprison people for long sentences. A person was normally held only for the period between charges being made and execution. This may be why Jesus tells the people to be faithful until death. He is promising that if they are faithful, even until death, He will give them the crown of life.

Again, the letter to Smyrna, as all are, is written to the churches (plural). Note also that Jesus says it is the Spirit who is speaking to the churches through John. In conclusion, He says the one who overcomes will not be hurt by the second death.

What is the "second death"?

Recall that Christians who believe in Jesus Christ and trust in His finished work on the cross have died to sin. Paul explains in Romans 6:1–11 that Christians who have been baptized into Christ Jesus have been baptized into His death (6:3). That, if they are united with Jesus in His death, they are also united with Him in His resurrection (6:5). Paul writes in Romans 6:11,

> Even so consider yourselves to be dead to sin, but alive to God in Christ Jesus.

Jesus says in John 5:24,

> Truly, truly, I say to you, he who hears My word, and believes Him who sent Me, has eternal life, and does not come into judgment, but has passed out of death into life.

In other words, the person who hears the word of Jesus and believes in Him *has* (present tense) eternal life and will never die. Although the earthly body may cease to function, to be absent from the body is to be with the Lord (2 Corinthians 5:7). The "second death," which is eternal separation from God, has no power over the one who has believed on the Lord Jesus Christ.

CHAPTER 12

The Church in Pergamum

And to the angel of the church in Pergamum write: The One who has the sharp two-edged sword says this: I know where you dwell, where Satan's throne is; and you hold fast My name, and did not deny My faith, even in the days of Antipas, My witness, My faithful one, who was killed among you, where Satan dwells. But I have a few things against you, because you have there some who hold the teaching of Balaam, who kept teaching Balak to put a stumbling block before the sons of Israel, to eat things sacrificed to idols, and to commit immorality. Thus you also have some who in the same way hold the teaching of the Nicolaitans. Repent therefore; or else I am coming to you quickly, and I will make war against them with the sword of My mouth. He who has an ear, let him hear what the Spirit says to the churches. To him who overcomes, to him I will give of the hidden manna, and I will give him a white stone, and a new name written on the stone which no one knows but he who receives it. (Revelation 2:12–17)

Again, John uses a very stylized form of communication. Each of the letters to the churches is written "To the angel" (or pastor) of a particular church. In the "From" section, John includes part of the vision of Christ which he describes in the ending of chapter 1. Each of these parts relate in some way to the particular church being addressed. Jesus says to the pastor, "I know what you are doing." This is usually followed by, "but I have something against you," with Jesus condemning him in some way. And finally, in the phrase "to the one who overcomes," lies a promise. Each of these letters have the same basic structure.

Robert Mounce, in *The Book of Revelation* writes,

> The road north from Smyrna follows the coastline some forty miles, then turns inland in a northeasterly direction along the valley of the Caicus River. About ten miles inland from the Aegean Sea stands the impressive capital city of Pergamum. Pliny called it "by far the most distinguished city in Asia" (Hist. Nat. v. 30). Built on a cone-shaped hill a thousand feet in height, it dominated the surrounding valley of the Caicus. Its very name in Greek (Pergamum) means "citadel."

Mounce further writes,

> Although the site appears to have been inhabited from prehistoric times, its rise to prominence came in the third century BC when it became the capital of the Attalids... It boasted a library of more than 200,000 volumes. Legend has it that parchment was invented there...[since it is known that parchment existed long before the period in which the city was built, the last statement is probably not true].

Mounce continues,

> The most spectacular aspect of this remarkable city was the upper terrace of the citadel with its sacred and royal buildings. Of these, the most remarkable was the great altar of Zeus which jutted out near the top of the mountain. A famous frieze around the base of the altar depicts the gods of Greece in victorious combat against the giants of earth [symbolizing the triumph of civilization over barbarism]... Religion flourished in Pergamum. It was the center of worship for four of the most important pagan cults of the day.

These four cults were: Zeus, prevalent throughout most of the world at that time; Athena, the patron goddess; Dionysus; and Asclepius, the patron saint of healers (whose symbol was a serpent), who was also referred to by the Greeks as "savior." Is it any wonder that the Christians would have a problem with this? Many things were occurring during that period that would have caused the persecution of Christians to be much greater than imagined.

The shrine of Asclepius, the god of healing, attracted people from all over the world. One commentator called it "the Lourdes of the province of Asia." It was where people went for a religious experience of healing. Of greatest import to the Christians living in Pergamum was the fact that it was the official center in Asia of the Imperial cult. Remember that in these times, people worshiped the emperor, as he was considered to be a god. This began with Julius Caesar, who was elevated to godhood after his death. It continued with Augustus, who succeeded him and who was proclaimed a god during his lifetime. This set the precedence of proclaiming the following emperors to be gods. The Romans worshiped their emperors. They built temples dedicated to them. Pergamum was the first city in Asia to be allowed to build a temple to a living ruler.

In 29 BC, Augustus granted permission that a temple be erected in Pergamum to the divine Augustus and to the goddess Roma. Of all the seven cities of Revelation, Pergamum was the one in which the church was most likely to clash with the imperial cult.

> And to the angel of the church in Pergamum write: The One who has the sharp two-edged sword says this... (Revelation 2:12)

Why did Jesus choose this symbology as befitting Pergamum? Since the leader of the city of Pergamum represented the Roman Emperor, he had absolute power. He had the power of the sword to take life or to save it. On the contrary! Jesus is saying, "No, this person is not the one who has absolute power." The One who has the sharp two-edged (literally in Greek, *two-mouthed*) sword says this! Jesus, as the true Ruler of the world, is declaring His power over the secular ruler. The ruler of Pergamum had a temporal power of the sword, but Jesus has the ultimate, eternal power of the sword.

> I know where you dwell, where Satan's throne is...

Why would Jesus make this statement? It was probably because Pergamum, being the center of the Imperial cult, was also the center of four of the major pagan religions of the world at that time. These cults were all immoral and ungodly. Thus, very clearly, this was a place where Satan dwelled. It was a wicked, evil place. It was a place where people worshipped the emperor as a god.

> And you hold fast My name, and did not deny My faith, even in the days of Antipas, My witness, My faithful one, who was killed among you, where Satan dwells.

Jesus is describing this pastor, this "angelos," as a faithful servant. This pastor was teaching correctly that Jesus is the only name by which people can be saved. Is this the kind of clear, uncompromising teaching we see in the church today? Unfortunately, that is not always the case.

We do not know who Antipas was. But no doubt he was someone very well-known at the time. Notice what is said about Antipas:

> My witness, My faithful one, who was killed
> among you, where Satan dwells.

Looking back to chapter 1, verse 5, this is also what is said about Jesus: "from Jesus Christ, the faithful witness, the first-born of the dead." Who would not desire to be commended in the same way as Jesus? This Antipas must have truly been a loyal and steadfast man. He was clearly a martyr, a leader in the church who stood up for Christ. It is a fact that he was killed in Pergamum as a result of his faithful witness. Jesus calls him "My witness, My faithful one."

> But I have a few things against you, because
> you have there some who hold the teaching of
> Balaam.

The name Balaam is derived from the Hebrew word *bala*, meaning "to swallow down," and the word *am*, meaning "people." Therefore, the name means "one who swallows the people," or one who is victorious over the people. In the Old Testament, Balaam was a priest. He was called by the ungodly leaders of Moab to come and curse the Israelites, which he agreed to do for money (Numbers 22). As he was on his donkey, riding toward the encampment of Israel, the donkey came to a certain place and refused to go further. Balaam beat it until finally the donkey spoke to him and told him he had saved his life because the Angel of Wrath was there. Although very little is written about the teaching of Balaam in this incident recorded in the book of Numbers, it is known that he was terribly unsuccessful in his ability to curse the Israelites, who ended up defeating the Moabites. However, much later, due to the teaching of Balaam, the Israelites were eventually overcome by their enemies,

More is revealed about the teaching of Balaam here in Revelation. In verse 14, Jesus states that he "kept teaching Balak to put a stumbling block before the sons of Israel, to eat things sacrificed to idols, and to commit immorality." This was important for Jesus to point out because it was part of the pagan worship system in Pergamum. In many of the temples, the people made a sacrifice and then prepared a meal using the sacrifice (just as in the Old Testament worship). Part of the animal was sacrificed to the god and burned; the rest of it was eaten. The meal was usually followed by acts of sexual immorality with the temple prostitutes, both male and female. This was the way the people communed with their god, and this is clearly what Jesus is condemning in this verse. But He is not only condemning the eating of meat sacrificed to idols but the fact that Christians were actually worshipping in the pagan temples of Satan. Christians in the church of Pergamum were apparently participating in such ungodly worship.

Are these practices prevalent in the churches of today? Is this any different from the Israelites who, for forty years in the desert, had the visible presence of God with them in the column of cloud by day and the column of fire by night? And yet at the same time they were worshipping the star gods and the moon gods and the gods of the planets that they had brought along with them, all in the very presence of God! Many shake their heads and wonder, "How could they do that?" But is this really any different than attending an ungodly worship service today and participating, just to get along, to compromise one's devotion to the living God? This is what Balaam taught Balak. He said to teach the people to compromise, just a little bit. Christians must understand there can be no compromise. We must stand on the Word of God alone (*sola Scriptura*).

Balaam means "swallower," or "conqueror" of the people, and Nicholas (the leader of the Nicolaitans) also means "conqueror of the people." They were both teaching the same kind of false doctrine. Jesus says,

> Thus you also have some who in the same
> way hold the teaching of the Nicolaitans.

Jesus very clearly links them together as they were doing the same thing. He then gives a command:

> Repent therefore; or else I am coming to
> you quickly, and I will make war against them
> with the sword of My mouth.

While reading through the letters to the churches of Revelation, a pattern stands out. To the church at Ephesus Jesus says, "repent," yet to the church in Smyrna He does not. To the church at Pergamum He says, "Repent," and to the church at Thyatira He does not. To every other church He says, "Repent."

When Jesus commands the pastor of the church in Pergamum to "repent," one can see a comparison. Jesus said to the pastor of the church at Ephesus:

> But I have against you, that you have left
> your first love. Remember therefore from where
> you have fallen, and repent and do the deeds you
> did at first. (Revelation 2:4)

The pastor of the church at Ephesus became very legalistic. He tested everybody and made sure they conformed to the Word of God, but he had left his first love. He was too legalistic. The pastor of the church at Pergamum had the opposite problem; he was too lenient. He wanted to get along with everyone. What is desperately needed in the church is a balance between legalism and love. Although doctrine needs to be tested against the Word of God, the examination cannot be done legalistically. It must be done with a good heart, with humility, recognizing that it is God who changes the heart.

> He who has an ear, let him hear what the
> Spirit says to the churches...

These letters are written to the pastor (singular), but at the end, Jesus says, "to the churches" (plural). All the churches were situated along a trade route. A traveler could start at Ephesus then travel to Smyrna, to Pergamum, and on to the other cities. Very likely what happened is that these letters went to the designated church and then were circulated on this trade route so that all the churches would read them and perhaps make a copy. We see this same pattern throughout the New Testament where Paul writes about "my letter to the Laodiceans (which is not part of the New Testament)." The letters from the apostles were apparently read in all the churches as part of their worship services.

It is very important for pastors today not to allow the Nicolaitans and the Balaams into the church unchecked where their teachings will undermine God's Word. This needs to be done in a loving way, with the additional purpose of restoration of bringing that person back into the kingdom.

CHAPTER 13

The Church in Thyatira

And to the angel of the church in Thyatira write: The Son of God, who has eyes like a flame of fire, and His feet are like burnished bronze, says this: I know your deeds, and your love and faith and service and perseverance, and that your deeds of late are greater than at first. But I have against you, that you tolerate the woman Jezebel, who calls herself a prophetess, and she teaches and leads My bond-servants astray, so that they commit immorality and eat things sacrificed to idols. And I gave her time to repent, and she does not want to repent of her immorality. Behold, I will cast her upon a bed *of sickness*, and those who commit adultery with her into great tribulation, unless they repent of her deeds. And I will kill her children with pestilence; and all the churches will know that I am He who searches the minds and hearts; and I will give to each one of you according to your deeds. But I say to you, the rest who are in Thyatira, who do not hold this teaching, who have not known the deep things of Satan, as they call them—I place no other burden on you. Nevertheless what you have, hold fast until I come. And he who overcomes, and he who keeps My deeds until the end, TO HIM I WILL GIVE AUTHORITY OVER THE NATIONS; AND HE SHALL RULE THEM WITH A ROD OF IRON, AS THE VESSELS OF THE POTTER ARE BROKEN TO PIECES, as I also have received *authority* from My Father; and I will give him the morning star. He who has an ear, let him hear what the Spirit says to the churches. (Revelation 2:18–26)

This letter illustrates the very stylized form of writing seen in the other letters. All of them begin with the greeting, "To the angel of the church in (the city is named)," as well as the term *from*, which uses a different part of the imagery in John's vision of Jesus in chapter 1.

Jesus commands John, "To the angel of the church in Thyatira write: The Son of God." This is the only time in the book of Revelation that the title "the Son of God" is used, and it is written very clearly Who "He" is:

The Son of God who has eyes like a flame
of fire, and His feet are like burnished bronze,
says this...

This imagery comes directly out of the vision in Daniel 10:5–6 and Daniel's vison of Jesus Christ.

I know your deeds, and your love and faith
and service and perseverance, and that your deeds
of late are greater than at first.

This statement greatly commended the pastor of the church in Thyatira. Jesus described the pastor of the church at Ephesus as having lost his first love. This description of the pastor of the church in Thyatira is just the opposite. Recall that the Ephesians were caught up in legalism. In their attempt to ensure the church members were doing things according to Scripture, they were doing it harshly and judgmentally, rather than doing it with love.

At first, the church at Thyatira is complimented, but then the hammer falls.

> But I have against you, that you tolerate the
> woman Jezebel.

Who was Jezebel? In the Old Testament, Jezebel was the wife of King Ahab, a wicked ruler of the Northern kingdom of Israel. Jezebel is described at the end of 1 Kings as the archenemy of the prophet Elijah. She promoted Baal worship and practiced idolatry and was herself a conniving, wicked woman. King Ahab wanted the vineyard of Naboth who refused to let the king have it. Jezebel counseled her husband to simply kill Naboth, which was what he did, thus taking over the vineyard.

Evidently, there was an individual in the church in Thyatira who was very similar to the Jezebel in the Old Testament.

> Jezebel, who calls herself a prophetess.

This woman was guilty of being a "false prophet." Like Jezebel, people today may call themselves prophets, but it is God alone who calls and appoints prophets. A prophet in the Old Testament sense was one who was called specifically by God. He received a vision of God (as Isaiah did in Isaiah, chapter 6); he received a specific word from God to speak to a particular people, and he was ordained or given a specific task by God Himself. A prophet in the New Testament sense is one who explains the Scriptures and in so doing "speaks forth" God's Word. There are prophets today in the New Testament sense. Each time a pastor stands before his church and teaches or explains the scriptures, he is prophesying or speaking prophetically. No one today has been given the Old Testament type of prophetic authority by God.

Jezebel obviously was presenting herself as an authoritative Old Testament prophetess. In addition, she was teaching falsely:

> She teaches and leads My bond-servants astray, so that they commit immorality and eat things sacrificed to idols.

Some of the other churches also had problems with temple worship and fornication. They were compromising with the culture: worshipping their idols and adopting their customs.

These seven cities, situated along a trade route, had very strong trade unions. During the time of Revelation, unions were more powerfully influential than the unions of today, especially when it came to forcing a closed union shop. One did not become a silversmith, woodworker, tanner, tentmaker, or any other kind of tradesman unless they belonged the union of his trade. Part of the duties of belonging to that union was to worship the god of that union. Members were required to go to the temple and to participate in the sacrificing and the sacrificial meal. Part of the ceremony likely included fornication with the temple prostitutes, male and female. This was required worship.

A Christian who chose to be a silversmith but confessed to worshipping the one true God, and Him only, would not be allowed to be a silversmith. Neither could he sell, trade, or do anything related in that particular town. This would have a definite effect on one's ability to buy food, housing, and clothing. This was a form of real persecution. For someone to stand up and confess they were a Christian had powerful repercussions. Thus, many did not stand up for Christianity. The person described in the verse as a "Jezebel" was telling others, "It is okay to go to the temples, even if you're a Christian." She was also implying that idols are nothing (*idol* meaning "vanity or nothing"). If one believes there is no other god than the Christian God, what harm is there in going to the temple and participating in the ceremonies? It is all rather meaningless anyway. Such statements are also heard in churches today.

"It's okay to go to a Mormon worship service. Let's build bridges, right?"

Jezebel was saying the same thing. She was teaching that "it is okay to eat meat sacrificed to idols. It is okay to fornicate with the temple prostitutes. A Christian can be a witness to God in other ways. After all, there really is no other choice. Doesn't the Bible say to take care of your family? Do you want them to starve, to do without? 'He who does not take care of his family is worse than an infidel.'" Her message had to have been very powerful and very tempting.

> And I gave her time to repent, and she does
> not want to repent of her immorality.

Jezebel was not an official of the church. Some commentators believe she was like a pagan prophetess. This is unlikely because a pagan prophetess would not have been in the church at Thyatira, and Scripture states very clearly that she was in the church. Jesus said to the pastor (angelos) of the church, "You tolerate the woman Jezebel." She was proclaiming to be a Christian, but from within the church, she was promoting compromise.

> Behold, I will cast her upon a bed of sickness
> [the Greek term refers to a particular kind of bed,
> one for a sick person and not one to sleep in],...
> and those who commit adultery with her...

By this, Jesus is referring to those who follow her and believe her actions and teachings are okay. Often in the Bible, *adultery* does not imply an immoral relation between a man and woman as perceived in modern thinking. It refers primarily to the spiritual condition of the heart. God condemns Israel for having an adulterous affair when they worshipped other gods. This is spiritual adultery. The church is the bride of Christ, and Christ is her husband. He is the One to whom the bride (the church) is committed. He is the One the church is to fear or reverence. He is the One His people serve. When the church compromises, follows after and serves other gods, and does not fear God or obey Him, they are committing adultery. People continuously play mind games. They know God wants them to refrain from sin, but they do it anyway thinking they will repent later. At this point, according to Scripture, they commit adultery.

> [I will cast them] into great tribulation, unless they repent of her deeds. And I will kill her children with pestilence [in the Greek, the word *pestilence* simply means "death"; this is a Hebraism—a Hebrew expression or idiom; to "kill with death" meant to kill ultimately. Thus, her children will not go to heaven] and all the churches will know that I am He who searches the minds and hearts.

God is going to kill these stubborn, disobedient people so that His glory will be paramount. Then people will know that He is the One that searches the minds and hearts. He knows whether they are really Christians, His followers, or not.

> But I say to you, the rest who are in Thyatira, who do not hold this teaching [there were some who did not compromise] who have not known the deep things of Satan, as they call them [one can recognize evil if they know the truth].

Some people say, "How can you condemn adultery unless you have been involved in it?" We can condemn what God says is wrong because when God says it is wrong, it is wrong. What was happening in John's day continues to happen today. People often say, "You cannot condemn something unless you have personal knowledge or awareness of it." This concept comes from the Greek word *gnosis*, "to know." During the time of John, those who believed that one could not know what is evil unless one had direct knowledge of the evil were called Gnostics.

An excellent illustration that actually contradicts this is how bank tellers are trained to recognize counterfeit bills. They are consistently exposed to the real thing. They become so familiar with the feel of the authentic bill that when they see and handle the counterfeit bill, they immediately recognize it as counterfeit. This is the way that God's Word should be to His children. Believers should be able to quickly recognize when something is not in accord with Scripture. Through study and meditation of God's Word, false teaching will be immediately apparent to a believer. Knowing God's Word and truly hiding it in one's heart is the only way to recognize false teaching and be able to combat Gnosticism or any other false religion. True knowledge is not learning everything about Mormonism, Jehovah's Witnesses, or Judaism. True knowledge is regularly and purposefully studying God's Word, in order to prevent being duped by false teachers.

Jesus says,

> And he who overcomes, and he who keeps My deeds until the end, TO HIM I WILL GIVE AUTHORITY OVER THE NATIONS AND HE SHALL RULE THEM WITH A ROD OF IRON, AS THE VESSELS OF THE POTTER ARE BROKEN TO PIECES, as I have also received *authority* from My Father; and I will give him the morning star. He who has an ear, let him hear what the Spirit says to the churches.

In every letter, there is the phrase "he who overcomes." The ones who overcome are the ones who worship God in truth. They are called by Him and are thus willing to firmly take a stand and say, "No, I am not going to do that. I am a Christian, and I am going to follow God's standard, no matter the consequences." It is overcoming without compromising. Do you see the pattern?

> He who overcomes, and he who keeps My deeds until the end...

As Jesus said so clearly,

> If you love me, you will obey my command-
> ments. (John 14:15)

Obedience is the true fruit of loving God, because obeying God is a reflection of genuine love for God.

CHAPTER 14

The Church in Sardis

And to the angel of the church in Sardis write: He who has the seven Spirits of God, and the seven stars, says this: I know your deeds, that you have a name that you are alive, but you are dead. Wake up, and strengthen the things that remain, which were about to die; for I have not found your deeds completed in the sight of My God. Remember therefore what you have received and heard; and keep *it* and repent. If therefore you will not wake up, I will come like a thief, and you will not know at what hour I will come upon you. But you have a few people in Sardis who have not soiled their garments; and they will walk with me in white; for they are worthy. He who overcomes shall thus be clothed in white garments; and I will not erase his name from the book of life, and I will confess his name before My Father, and before His angels. He who has an ear, let him hear what the Spirit says to the churches. (Revelation 3:1–6)

Again, I believe that when Jesus tells John to write to the angel of the church in Sardis, He is speaking about the pastor of the church. It does not make sense for Jesus to instruct John to write a letter to a spiritual being. John is writing to the pastor of each of these individual churches, because the pastor represents the church and is accountable to Jesus for the church. This is made quite clear in the use of the Greek terminology in each of these letters. When Jesus says "I know your deeds," the word *your* is singular. In the Greek, there are different words for *you* singular or *you* plural. When Jesus commands John to write to the angel (or messenger), in every case, it is singular.

This church at Sardis was known in the community for being "alive." It was an active, growing, worshipping church that was alive, at least in appearance. But in reality, it was dead. What is the difference between a church that is alive and a church that is dead? The difference lies not in the physical condition but in the spiritual condition of the church. The Mormon church is one of the fastest-growing churches in America today. And that church is dead, dead, dead. Many who study Mormonism find its teachings to be incredibly doltish! Anyone carefully looking at what Mormonism teaches should quickly recognize its failings and reject it. But nonetheless, Mormonism is growing and has a reputation. Although that church does amazing things to reach out to people, they are spiritually dead. Do not fall for their wonderful commercials!

Sardis was a very interesting place. It was situated in a valley, along a river that ran through the area. It also was located on a trade road that ran east. All the churches of Revelation were located on a circular trade road, with Sardis being inland about fifty miles east of Ephesus. The city was built on a 1,500-foot-high mountain, with sheer cliffs on three sides. Since they only had to defend one side of the city, the people thought they were in an excellent location defensively. Unfortunately, Sardis had been conquered twice in its history. Writers in antiquity reveal that the city had been conquered the same way both times. The first time the invaders sent a climber up the cliff at night. He climbed the cliff and opened the gates on the protected side, allowing the opposing army to storm in and wipe out the city. After Sardis was rebuilt, it fell once again under the same attack strategy. This historical background more fully explains what Jesus says to the pastor of the church in Revelation.

The letter begins, "He who has the seven Spirits of God, and the seven stars, says this." Remember, the seven stars are the seven angels of the churches. In Revelation 1:20, Jesus states to John,

> As for the mystery of the seven stars which you saw in My right hand, and the seven golden lampstands: the seven stars are the angels [or pastors] of the seven churches, and the seven lampstands are the seven churches.

What about the seven Spirits of God? What are they? The Hebrews did not necessarily use numbers in the same manner they are used today. To the Hebrews, numbers had additional meanings. Thus, when Jesus says "seven," He does not necessarily mean the numeral 7 as in seven units of something. Instead, the number 7 conveys the concept of perfection. Thus, seven in the Bible, depending on the context, usually conveys this idea of perfection.
Note Revelation 1:4.

> John to the seven churches that are in Asia: Grace to you and peace, from Him who is and who was and who is to come; and from the seven Spirits who are before His throne.

This verse clearly states there are seven Spirits before the throne of God. Note also Revelation 4:5.

> And from the throne proceed flashes of lightning and sound and peals of thunder. And seven lamps of fire burning before the throne, which are the seven Spirits of God...

In this verse, the seven Spirits are seven lamps burning before the throne. Now look at Revelation 5:6.

> And I saw between the throne (with the four living creatures) and the elders a Lamb standing, as if slain, having seven horns and seven eyes, which are the seven Spirits of God.

The seven Spirits in this verse are seven eyes.
Look at Revelation 8:2.

> And I saw the seven angels who stand before God…

There were seven Spirits who stood before God in chapter 1 verse 4. Here, there are seven angels, or messengers, who stand before God. Isaiah chapter 11 prophesies of the Messiah Who is to come.

> Then a shoot will spring from the stem of Jesse, and a branch from his roots will bear fruit. And the Spirit of the Lord will rest on Him, the spirit of wisdom and understanding, the spirit of counsel and strength, the spirit of knowledge and the fear of the Lord. And He will delight in the fear of the Lord, and He will not judge by what His eyes see.

This is a sevenfold reference to Jesus, the Messiah Who is to come. He will have this sevenfold Spirit of God resting upon Him.

In Zechariah 4, God is describing to Zechariah a vision of the temple. In verses 1–6, we read,

> Then the angel who was speaking with me returned, and roused me as a man who is awakened from his sleep. And he said to me, "What do you see?" and I said, "I see, and behold, a lampstand all of gold with its bowl on the top of it, and its seven lamps on it with seven spouts belonging to each of the lamps which are on the

top of it; also two olive trees by it, one on the right side of the bowl and the other on its left side." Then I answered and said to the angel who was speaking with me saying, "What are these my Lord?" So the angel who was speaking with me answered and said to me, "Do you not know what these are?" And I said, "No, my lord." Then he answered and said to me, "This is the word of the Lord to Zerubbabel saying, 'Not by might nor by power, but by My Spirit,' says the Lord of hosts."

What is God showing Zechariah here? He sees a sevenfold lampstand. Turning back to Exodus 25, God is telling Moses how to build the tabernacle and what to place inside the tabernacle.

Then you shall make a lampstand of pure gold. The lampstand *and* its base and its shaft are to be made of hammered work; its cups, its bulbs and its flowers shall be of *one piece* with it. And six branches shall go out from its sides; three branches of the lampstand from its one side, and three branches of the lampstand from its other side. (Exodus 25:31–32)

He goes on to describe the lampstand and tells Moses how to build it.

Looking at an overall view of the tabernacle (or later the temple), the Holy of Holies was the innermost room in the sanctuary. It held the Ark of the Covenant. Above the ark were the cherubim made of gold, and between their wings dwelt the physical manifestation of God, the Shekinah Glory Cloud. God also dictated the design of the Holy Place. On the right-hand side, as you entered through the curtain, was the table of the Presence. It was also called the table of the showbread, with its loaves of bread and bowls for the wine of the drink offering. On the left side was the golden lampstand.

Probably right in the center in front of the curtain that separated the two compartments was the golden altar, where incense was kept continually burning. There were three coverings over the tabernacle. Inside the tabernacle, it would have been dark; thus one needed a light. The lampstand represented the light of the world coming into the darkness, the Spirit of truth to be a lamp for the feet and a light for the path.

> The Holy Spirit, whom the Father will send in My name, He will teach you all things and bring to your remembrance all that I said to you… But when He, the Spirit of truth, comes, He will guide you into all truth. (John 16:13)

Clearly, it is the Spirit Who gives us truth, Who places upon believers the belt of truth. The seven Spirits of God are the sevenfold perfection of God, all of which are truth and light.

> He who has the seven Spirits of God [again, Jesus has the sevenfold Spirit of God], and the seven stars, says this: I know your deeds, that you have a name that you are alive, but you are dead.

As mentioned earlier, the church had an incredible name in the community. The church was famous in the area. However, its people were not holding to the Word of God, rendering them spiritually dead. In verse 2, Jesus commands the angel (pastor), "Wake up [the Greek actually says 'demonstrate,' or 'show yourself watchful'] and strengthen the things that remain." Historically, the city of Sardis had been conquered twice in the past. The people thought their city was invincible because it had been built on top of a cliff. Twice before, in their history, armies sent climbers up the face of the rock and into the unprotected side of the city to successfully open the city gates, allowing the opposing army to march in. Jesus reminds the church at Sardis not to think they are invincible. This message is also true for believers today. They need to be aware that Satan does not make a frontal attack. This is too obvious. Instead, Satan will sneak into the churches with lies and subtle deception at the point where believers think they are most protected. He will bring in the "Jezebels" who urge compromise with the culture. Jesus warns the church will fall if it is not watchful and consistently vigilant.

> Strengthen the things that remain, which
> were about to die; for I have not found your
> deeds completed in the sight of My God.

Jesus is saying to the pastor and to the churches, "You are not doing the work that God has laid out for you. You have made a name that you are alive, that you are growing. You have a good reputation in the city, but not in the sight of God."

> Remember therefore what you have received
> and heard; and keep *it* and repent.

Again, the same pattern as with the other six churches is evident. Every other church is told to repent. Why? Because they are not doing what God had instructed them to do. The church at Ephesus was complimented but then was told to repent because they had left their first love. To the church at Pergamum, He says, "Repent!" And to the church at Sardis, likewise, He says, "Repent!"

> If therefore you will not wake up, I will
> come like a thief, and you will not know at what
> hour I will come upon you.

Why does Jesus use the analogy of a thief in the night? Many home burglaries occur at night, even while the residents are at home. Thieves break in, silently rifle through closets and drawers, all while the owners are asleep. Similarly, Jesus is saying, "You will not know when I will come." Is He referring to the end of the world? Although this is a popular opinion, the question remains, "To whom is Jesus speaking? He is addressing the pastor (*angelos*), "I will come like a thief in the night; you [singular] will not know when I come." And that He did. The church at Sardis was once a big, thriving, popular church, but it no longer exists. It is apparent the church did not heed God's instructions. Only one of the churches of Revelation remains. All the others are gone. The churches of today needs to heed the warning of Jesus to be faithful to Him.

> But you have a few people in Sardis who have not soiled their garments; and they will walk with me in white; for they are worthy.

Here Jesus is speaking of the people who did not compromise. He may also be speaking of people who were persecuted and not allowed to work in their trade. They did not "soil their garments." Although the Bible speaks in other places about "soiling your garments" by being adulterous, there may be something else being indicated here. When going to worship, particularly as a Hebrew in the synagogue or temple, one went only when they were clean. On Friday night, after finishing work, the Hebrew believer would take a bath and put on clean clothes. Everyone gathered together as the wife initiated the Sabbath by lighting the candle. Similarly, when one went to worship in a pagan temple, they did not go in their work clothes. Instead, they put on their best clothes. This writer used to tell people it was not necessary to put on "Sunday-go-to-meeting" clothes. They could just come as they were. But maybe I was wrong. In the Old Testament there is an emphasis on wearing clean clothes, or one's good clothes, to come into worship. After all, who were they going to see? They were coming before the God of the universe! Today how would one dress to see a president? (When I was in Hawaii, I would go to church in T-shirt, shorts, and shower shoes because that was standard dress. But as I began to learn more, I thought, "Maybe I should put on good shorts and a nice shirt.") There is definitely some significance in this passage.

Jesus says,

> And they will walk with Me in white.

He is saying, "They are pure." He is speaking of the purity of righteousness. In heaven, the people of God will be wearing the pure robes of the righteousness of Jesus Christ. It is not our individual righteousness that is in view but His. In 2 Corinthians 5:21, Paul says,

> God made him who had no sin to be sin for us, so that in Him we might become the righteousness of God.

So once in heaven, will we, as His children, appear in the filthy rags of our own works? No! Everyone will be in their "Sunday-go-to-meeting" finest, which is nothing short of the glorious robes of the righteousness of Jesus Christ Himself.

> For they are worthy.

Why are they worthy? They had not compromised but were faithful, which was only possible because they had the righteousness of Jesus Christ. In the last analysis, it is not what they did but what Jesus did which in turn enabled them to do what they did.

> He who overcomes shall thus be clothed in white garments.

This also appears in Revelation 7:13–14.

> And one of the elders answered, saying to me, "These who are clothed in the white robes, who are they, and from where have they come?" And I said to him, "My lord, you know." And he said to me, "These are the ones who come out of the great tribulation, and they have washed their robes and made them white in the blood of the Lamb."

How is something made white when it is washed in blood? When it is the righteous blood of Jesus Christ. Not the blood, sweat, and tears of His people, but only the blood of Jesus Christ makes the robes of His people white. It is not our works that get us into heaven. It is only the finished, perfect work of Jesus Christ that allows believers into heaven. Yet it is their works that gets them into heaven. That may sound confusing, but the fact is that even though believers are going to heaven on the basis of grace alone, they each will have works, the works which God has prepared for them to carry out (Ephesians 2:10). One who truly belongs to Christ will be doing what God commands.

The two boys who stopped the fatal shootings in Oregon several years ago said they did it because that is what they were raised to do. It was the right thing to do. Christians know the right thing to do because they have the truth. They have the Holy Spirit Who reveals to them the right thing to do. Christians should not lock themselves up in their fortress churches and sit there quaking in their boots waiting on Satan to try to break through the walls. The armor of God is offensive. The shield of faith is like the type of shield the Romans used when they were assaulting the walls. They formed a "turtle" and were completely encased by these shields, and thus, they were practically invulnerable. They would carry a battering ram inside the turtle and walk up to the city gate and pound it until they knocked it down. This is how Christians ought to behave because they have the shield of faith. Can the arrows of Satan harm believers? Can the oil he pours down from the citadel harm them? No, absolutely not. Satan's attacks fall like water off a duck's back. Jesus tells Peter,

> Upon this rock I will build My church and
> the gates of hell shall not withstand it.

Christians ought to be out there kicking down the gates of hell, because they have the shield of faith. They have the strength. That is exactly what the church at Sardis was *not* doing. They were compromising with the ungodly; they had declared a truce with the citadel of

Satan. And in so doing, although they were described as being alive, in fact they were spiritually dead.

> And I will not erase his name from the book of life, and I will confess his name before My Father, and before His angels.

The thought in this passage had a very important part in my personal Christian maturity. When I first became a Christian, I remember talking to people, but I would not tell them I was a Christian. I was afraid of what they might think. I was not secure enough in my belief. How could I witness to them if I did not know enough about Christianity? Later, as I was reading through the Bible, I came across the passage where Jesus says,

> If you are ashamed of me before men, I will be ashamed of you before my Father and His angels. (Mark 8:38, Luke 9:26)

These words brought conviction, and I began to rethink my behavior. Now as I listen to people in conversation, I find myself thinking, "How can I relate this to Christ? How can I bring God into this conversation? How can I tell people that I'm a Christian and what God has done in my life?" This is what really matters. Do I know enough about Scripture to do this? No. Is it necessary for me to know everything about the Bible in order to be a witness? No. What Peter, the other apostles, and others say in the Scriptures, "We simply tell what we know, what we have seen and heard." What is important is what God has done in our life, how we are able to relate this to Scripture. It is not a matter of whether we can memorize large portions of the Bible or list all the kings of the Old Testament. What is important is what God has done in our life. This is what brings life into a church and awakens His people. They will realize that although they are not invincible, they are in an offensive army that will go into the world looking for ways to evangelize, to give people the message of the Good News.

CHAPTER 15

The Church in Philadelphia

Jesus said to John,

> And to the angel of the church in Philadelphia write: He who is holy, who is true, who has the key of David, who opens and no one will shut, and who shuts and no one opens, says this: I know your deeds. Behold, I have put before you an open door which no one can shut, because you have a little power, and have kept My word, and have not denied My name. Behold, I will cause those of the synagogue of Satan, who say that they are Jews, and are not, but lie—behold, I will make them to come and bow down at your feet, and to know that I have loved you. Because you have kept the word of My perseverance, I also will keep you from the hour of testing, that hour which is about to come upon the whole world, to test those who dwell upon the earth. I am coming quickly; hold fast what you have, in order that no one take your crown. He who overcomes, I will make him a pillar in the temple of My God, and he will not go out from it anymore; and I will write upon him

the name of My God, and the name of the city of
My God, the new Jerusalem, which comes down
out of heaven from My God, and My new name.
He who has an ear, let him hear what the Spirit
says to the churches. (Revelation 3:7–13)

It is important to realize that all the cities of Revelation had
common trade unions, and in order to practice a trade, whether tentmaker, bread maker, cobbler, etc., union membership was required.
Why was being a union member such a problem for Christians? Each
union had their own god, and membership in the union involved
worshipping that particular god. Participation in the worship ceremony, which was held at a particular temple, was required of all
members of the union. To refuse participation in the worship ceremony could result in the loss of one's job or prevent employment.

Philadelphia was no different than all the other churches. Jesus
had especially condemned compromise. In virtually every church,
there were situations where an individual or a faction within the
church promoted compromise. Jezebel in the church at Thyatira
taught compromise. She was teaching, "We know that these trade
union gods are nothing but worthless idols. Since we worship the
one true God, it does not really matter if we must participate in some
meaningless ceremony to a god who is nothing. It does not matter if
we partake of the sacrifices, because we know it is not really a sacrifice
to the true God." Quite the contrary! It really *does* matter because our
actions are a testimony. If Christianity is just another religion, why
not pick Hinduism or Mormonism? Why be a Christian if there is
no difference in religions? Very clearly Jesus says there is a difference.
The church in Philadelphia was the only church of the seven that
actually followed God's commands. This was the only church that
Jesus unequivocally complimented.

Philadelphia in Greek means "brotherly love." The name of
the city commemorated the loyalty and devotion of Adolous II to
his brother. He loved his brother and demonstrated his love in such
a way that the city was named for that brotherly love. The city of
Philadelphia was built on a flat plain. Unfortunately, running right

through the center of the city was an earthquake fault. The city had actually been leveled on two different occasions. During the great earthquake of AD 17, the city was destroyed, and its name was changed to Neocessaria (New Caesar) in appreciation of the imperial help it received in rebuilding. At a later date, under the Emperor Vespasian, the name "Flavia" began to appear on their coins. So the city had at least two other names in its history.

As was previously noted, there was something written about each of the seven churches to which the people of the time could relate.

> And I will write upon him the name of My God, and the name of the city of My God, the new Jerusalem, which comes down out of heaven from My God, and My new name."

Jesus states that He is going to give them a permanent name, a statement to which they could relate because of their history.

Since the city was located in a vine-growing district, the worship of Dionysus, the god of wine and revelry, was the chief pagan cult. After Tiberius the Emperor gave them aid, they founded the cult of Germanicus, who was the adopted son and heir of the emperor. This indicated that there was an ongoing struggle between worship of the pagan gods, the Roman emperor, and the true God, Jesus Christ. Again, each of the seven churches had in common this constant temptation to compromise between the worship of the true God and worship of other "gods."

One might ask, "Why did God allow this to continue?" God could have spoken from heaven and with the one breath destroyed all these idolaters. He could have spoken and by the power of His Word instantly transformed everyone into a Christian. But this is not the way He chooses to bring His children to Himself. Instead, as Paul says, God has chosen to use us as "vessels of clay," and He has given us the incredible treasure of the Gospel of Jesus Christ. This is the divine method—God has chosen to work through His people, the church. He puts us in situations to demonstrate our faithfulness, and He will ultimately transform not only individuals but also entire cultures and civilizations in His timing. This is precisely what was occurring in the church in Philadelphia.

> He who is holy, who is true, who has the key
> of David, says this: I know your deeds…because
> you have a little power, and have kept My word,
> and have not denied My name. (3:8)

Most of the other churches had denied Christ. They had large factions that were compromising and denying the Gospel of Jesus Christ. They were saying it was okay to "go along" with the cultural beliefs, to act and look like a pagan. But the church at Philadelphia stood firm.

Jesus says, "You have not denied My name." He also says of the church at Philadelphia, "You have a little power."

In other words, by secular standards, this was probably a small church. Even today, churches that are really being true to the Word of God tend to be smaller churches.

> And to the angel of the church in
> Philadelphia write: He who is holy, who is true,
> who has the key of David, who opens and no one
> will shut, and who shuts and no one opens, says
> this…(3:7)

That sounds quite strange to us. What is this "key of David"? We find the answer by looking in the Old Testament, in Isaiah 22:15–22:

> Thus says the Lord God of hosts, "Come,
> go to this steward, to Shebna [Shebna was a stew-
> ard in the house of David. He was the one who
> controlled a lot of the activity at the temple] who
> is in charge of the royal household, 'What right
> do you have here, and whom do you have here,
> that you have hewn a tomb for yourself here, You

who hew a tomb on the height, you who carve a resting place for yourself in the rock?" [Shebna was apparently someone who thought highly of himself, so much so that he carved a tomb for himself in a place where the kings were buried. God is accusing him of putting himself on the same level as a king.]

Behold the Lord is about to hurl you head-long, O man. And He is about to grasp you firmly, And roll you tightly like a ball, into a vast country; There you will die, and there your splendid chariots will be, you shame of your master's house. And I will depose you from your office, and I will pull you down from your sta-tion. Then it will come about in that day, that I will summon My servant Eliakim the son of Hilkiah And I will clothe him with your tunic, and tie your sash securely about him, I will entrust him with your authority, and he will become a father to the inhabitants of Jerusalem and to the house of Judah. Then I will set the key of the house of David on his shoulder, when he opens no one will shut, when he shuts no one will open.

God is saying that He is going to take this person who thinks very highly of himself, who exalts himself, who elevates himself above his position, and put him where he belongs. As it is written:

God opposes the proud, but gives grace to the humble. (1 Peter 5:5, quoting Proverbs 3:34)

Then He will replace him with one who will have the key of David on his shoulder. The key represented authority. In those days, the key was a large piece of wood that was designed to go into a slot in the door in order to lift a bar on the inside that held the door shut. It was large by design and was carried on one's shoulders.

> He who is holy, who is true, who has the
> key of David, who opens and no one will shut,
> and who shuts and no one opens.

Who has the key to heaven (the key of David)? Jesus Christ, who has been given "all authority in heaven and on earth" (Matthew 28:18). Other religions teach the way of salvation is to earn it, that each person must have their own key. Apparently, what was going on in the city of Philadelphia, and the other cities as well, was that some people were proclaiming, "We Jews are God's chosen people. Therefore, you must be a Jew and follow the law in order to be saved." Is it any different today? No! Virtually all religions in the world today teach a similar "works" salvation. It is the same in every religion—an exclusive claim that one must live out their religion by closely following the rules of that religion in order to enter heaven. But Jesus says, "No, it is not your key, it is MY key, I am the key."

> I am the way and the truth and the light.
> No one comes to the Father except through Me.
> (John 14:6)

Jesus is the key, the One who has earned the right to hold the one and *only* key to heaven.

That is what Jesus means when He says He has the key of David. He opens, and no one will shut. What does that teach us about salvation? Because He alone opens and shut, Jesus is the only way into heaven. If He opens the door for someone, no one is going to shut it for that person. If Jesus opens the door for your salvation, can anyone, including yourself, take away that salvation? No, absolutely not. That is why Jesus teaches that anyone who is saved is in His Father's hand, and no one can remove him, not even God, Himself, because God does not change His mind (John 10:28–29). Thus, salvation is God's choice, not man's choice.

Notice, Jesus says,

> Behold, I will cause those of the synagogue
> of Satan, who say that they are Jews, and are not,
> but lie—behold, I will make them to come and
> bow down at your feet, and to know that I have
> loved you.

As a Christian in those early churches, one was usually from a Jewish background. Yet the church was being opened to believers from a non-Jewish background. Many non-Christian Jews were teaching that one had to be Jewish to receive salvation. A Jew preaching that Jesus was the Messiah would be removed from the synagogue, being excommunicated for believing the truth. Here Jesus gives words of comfort.

> I will cause those of the synagogue of Satan,
> who say that they are Jews, and are not, but lie
> [what an incredible slam!]—behold, I will make
> them to come and bow down at your feet, and
> to know that I have loved you. (Revelation 3:9).

The bottom line is, we cannot just listen to what a church or religion is saying; we have to listen to what God is telling us in His Word.

> Because you have kept the word of My per-
> severance, I also will keep you from the hour of
> testing, that hour which is about to come upon
> the whole world, to test those who dwell upon
> the earth.

Here Jesus speaks of "that hour which is about to come upon the whole world, to test those who dwell upon the earth." Is He talking about something far in the distant future? Absolutely not! The Greek here is very clear—He is speaking of something immediate. We saw it in chapter 1 where John speaks of *the things that are shortly to take place* and *the time is near*. Jesus is teaching the church at Philadelphia—and the other churches that they would be tested. We know from history that the Christians were persecuted terribly between AD 64–68. They were burned at the stake. Nero dipped Christians in pitch and tied them to poles to light up his garden parties.

They went through a three and one half year period of incredible testing, which I believe Jesus is referring to here. He says that those who are faithful, He will protect from that hour of testing. Does that mean they were not going to be burned at the stake? If we are faithful to Christ, does that mean we are not going to have any trials and tribulations? No. Jesus is saying that the temptation, the trial, is not going to change your heart. What is important is your salvation. If you belong to Christ, if God has opened the door with the key of David, there is nothing you or anyone else can do, no matter what trial you go through, that is going to change your heart. I have known people who appeared to be staunch Christians, heavily into the church, evangelism, giving, doing all kinds of things, and when they went through some sort of trial, they thought God hated them and they left the church. So did those people lose their salvation? No, they never had it. They were wolves in sheep's clothing. That is what we need to understand. Jesus says, "It is those who persevere to the end who are saved." That is why it is important for us to understand the words of Jesus to the church in Philadelphia.

> I am coming quickly; hold fast what you
> have, in order that no one take your crown.

If Jesus provides the key that opens the door, why do I have to hold fast so nobody can take my crown? Again, it is a question of our responsibility *and* God's sovereignty. In other words, do your works get you into heaven? No, absolutely not. It is only the perfect work of Jesus Christ that gets you into heaven. Does that absolve you of any good work? No. Scripture teaches that we must work out (our) own salvation in fear and trembling (Philippians 2:13). You see, if you are truly saved, you are saved *unto* good works which God prepared beforehand (Ephesians 2:10). If you really are a Christian, you will be doing good works out of faithful obedience to Jesus Christ. And there is nothing that could possibly happen to you which could change your trust in Jesus Christ.

> He who overcomes, I will make him a pillar
> in the temple of My God, and he will not go out
> from it anymore…

If someone truly is a Christian, he is one who overcomes, and he will be made part of the temple of God. I do not know about you, but to me it is mind-boggling to think I am a living stone in the temple of God!

> And I will write upon him the name of My
> God, and the name of the city of My God, the
> new Jerusalem, which comes down out of heaven
> from My God, and My new name.

What is the name of the city of "My God, the new Jerusalem"? It is the church. It is the "bride of Christ." If you are truly a member of the church, then you are a pillar in the temple of God, which is the church. We will get more into that when we reach Revelation, chapter 22.

Remember, each of these letters was written to the angel of the church, presumably the pastor, as the representative of the church. When Jesus says, "I know your deeds," He is speaking about a particular person, not the church as a whole, yet that person is accountable for the church as a whole. In all these letters, even though they were written to specific churches for specific contemporary reasons, they were most likely read in all the churches. They were circulated between each of the seven churches, so each could benefit from the teaching about the others.

CHAPTER 16

The Church in Laodicea

We have finally come to the last church in John's letter to the churches in the Revelation. It is the church at Laodicea. It was the last city on the big circular trade route on which the other six churches were located.

Jesus said to John,

> And to the angel of the church in Laodicea write: The Amen, the faithful and true Witness, the Beginning of the creation of God, says this: I know your deeds, that you are neither cold nor hot; I would that you were cold or hot. So because you are lukewarm, and neither hot nor cold, I will spit you out of My mouth. Because you say, "I am rich and have become wealthy, and have need of nothing," and you do not know that you are wretched and miserable and poor and blind and naked, I advise you to buy from Me gold refined by fire, that you may become rich, and white garments, that you may clothe yourself, and the shame of your nakedness may not be revealed; and eyesalve to anoint your eyes, that you may see. Those whom I love, I reprove and discipline; be zealous therefore, and repent.

> Behold, I stand at the door and knock; if anyone hears My voice and opens the door, I will come in to him, and will dine with him, and he with Me. He who overcomes, I will grant to him to sit down with me on My throne, as I also overcame and sat down with My Father on His throne. He who has an ear, let him hear what the Spirit says to the churches. (Revelation 3:14–22)

In both this letter and in the letter to Philadelphia, John, under the guidance of the Holy Spirit, deviates slightly from the basic structure of the earlier letters. Jesus refers to Himself through the symbolism in the vision that John had in chapter 1. Here, Jesus says, "I am the Amen." The Greek word *amen* means "so be it," or "truthfully." In the King James Version of the Bible, the phrase "Verily, verily I say unto you" is a translation from the Greek, and the underlying Hebrew/Aramaic words, "Amen, amen." The use of *amen* at the end of a prayer often means "the end." However, in many churches in the South, or even out West, it is common to hear the preacher and members of the congregation repeatedly shouting "Amen." In this context, it means "I feel good," or "I agree with what is being said." Biblically, the word means "truly" or "truthful" or "verily." Thus the use of *amen* actually is affirming that what is being said is true. That is what Jesus means when He calls Himself the "Amen." He is saying "Truly, I am the Truth and the Way and the Light. I am the Amen." Jesus immediately follows that up with *the faithful and true Witness*. Here He is reinforcing this thought with its meaning. He is the "Amen," the One Who is perfect faithfulness and truth.

Jesus is also "the Beginning of the creation of God." This statement conjures up many arguments! What it really means is that the Son of God was present at the beginning of time when God created the world. Jehovah's Witnesses view this differently. They believe it means He (Jesus) was the first *thing* created. They and other Unitarians misinterpret this verse in order to deny the deity of Jesus Christ. If He is *created*, then He certainly cannot be the *Creator*. What they fail to understand is that through carefully examination of this passage and the testimony of the rest of Scripture, it becomes evident that Jesus is not simply the first created thing but He is the Almighty Creator, God Himself. In Colossians 1:15–17 we read,

> For by Him all things were created...all things have been created by Him and for Him. And He is before all things, and in Him all things hold together.

All things have been created *by* Him—the Greek word is *dia*—which means "through the agency of." It was by His agency that all things were created. Thus, the viewpoint of the Jehovah's Witnesses is in error. The issue is not that Jesus was the first thing created but that He was there in the beginning. He is the *Creator*. John says the same thing in his Gospel:

> All things came into being through Him, and apart from Him nothing came into being that has come into being. (John 1:3)

In Revelation 3:15, Jesus tells the angelos (pastor) of the church at Laodicea

> "I know your deeds, that you are neither cold nor hot; I would that you were cold or hot."

This verse does not hold a significant meaning for believers today, and therefore it is interpreted in different ways. Once again, it is important to note both the actual historical and geographical situation of Laodicea. The city was located in a flat valley. About six miles away was the town of Hierapolis, which had been built on top of a high cliff. On the very top of this cliff was a spring of steaming hot, mineral-laden water. This water flowed from the spring, cascading over the cliff. When mineral-laden water is cooled, the minerals in it crystalize. From six miles away, in Laodicea, one could see the huge, white-encrusted cliff with this putrid water coming over its side. On the other side of Laodicea were mountains in which nestled the city of Colossae. Paul wrote a letter to the Colossians and mentioned that he had written a letter to Laodicea (Colossians 4:16). These two cities were very closely intertwined. There was a very clear, sweet, cold spring in Colossae, and there was an aqueduct of stone pipe that brought this refreshing water down to Laodicea.

There are two ways of looking at what is going on here. Jesus says,

> You are neither cold nor hot; I would that
> you were cold or hot.

Many people interpret this verse to mean that Jesus is speaking of spiritual passion. Should we be spiritually hot, or spiritually cold? Why would Jesus ever want His people to be spiritually cold? Yet a lot of theologians think Jesus means that to be spiritual at all means being passionately spiritual. The New American Standard says,

> So because you are lukewarm, and neither
> hot nor cold, I will vomit you out of My mouth.

Some commentators look at the fact that this water from Hierapolis was very putrid and very lukewarm and to drink it was not tolerable. Imagine someone coming in from a long, dusty journey, seeing this water running down from the cliff, making their way to the water to be refreshed, but once they get it into their mouth, they immediately spit it out! Jesus uses a word which means "forcefully ejecting, spewing, or vomiting it out!"

What are the implications here? What Jesus is really saying here is not that the spiritual passion of the people was hot or cold or lukewarm. But instead He had in mind the things they were doing and not doing. It was not so much their heart and their desires that were in view. Rather it was the fact that even though they *were* a church of God, they were not *doing* the things that a church of God would normally do.

Jesus goes on to say,

Because you say, "I am rich."

Historically, Laodicea was one of the richest of the seven cities named in the Revelation. They were known for three things. In regard to the church of Laodicea, Robert Mounce states in his commentary, *The Book of Revelation,*

> In Roman times Laodicea became the wealthiest city in Phrygia. The fertile ground of the Lycus valley provided good grazing for sheep. By careful breeding, a soft, glossy black wool had been produced which was much in demand and brought fame to the region (Strabo xii. 578). Among the various garments woven in Laodicea was a tunic called a trimita. So widely known was this tunic that at the Council of Chalcedon in AD 451 Laodicea was called Trimitaria (Ramsey, L7CA, p. 416). Agricultural and commercial prosperity brought banking industry to Laodicea. Cicero, the Roman statesman and philosopher of the last days of the Republic, wrote of cashing his treasury bills of exchange there... The most striking indication of the city's wealth is that following the devastating earthquake of AD 60 the city was rebuilt without financial aid from Rome. Tacitus wrote, "Laodicea rose from the ruins by the strength of her own resources, with no help from us" (Ann. xiv. 27).

They did not need government help because they were so wealthy.

In addition, Mounce explains that the city was also widely known for their medical school, which had been established in connection with the temple of a god. The temple was thirteen miles to the north and west of Laodicea. A couple of renowned teachers in the medical school theorized that since diseases were compound, compound medicines were necessary for curing patients. As a result, they developed several different compounds that became quite famous. Two of the most outstanding compounds were an ointment of spice nard for the ears and an eye salve made from Phrygian powder mixed with oil.

Therefore, Laodiceans were known for their wealth, their clothing, and their medications. Notice what Jesus says,

> Because you say, "I am rich and have become wealthy, and have need of nothing [they did not need outside help to rebuild the city], and you do not know that you are wretched and miserable and poor and blind and naked."

Jesus is reminding the Laodiceans that they view themselves as having everything they needed through their own wealth. But Jesus says to them,

> I advise you to buy from Me gold refined by fire, that you may become rich, and white garments, that you may clothe yourself, and the shame of your nakedness may not be revealed; and eyesalve to anoint your eyes, that you may see.

It is not the material things that are important. What is important are the things that come from God. Jesus says,

> I advise you to buy from *Me* gold refined by fire, that you may become rich, and white garments, and eyesalve to anoint your eyes...

Jesus is saying, "Buy what you need from *Me*." Indeed! All that is needed or is truly good comes from Jesus.

This confirms the point that this letter to the church at Laodicea would have been especially meaningful to them. They were famous for their wealth. They were famous for their clothing. They were famous for their medication, particularly their eye salve. But Jesus says, "No, none of that is any good, unless it comes from Me."

Jesus says,

> Those whom I love [the Greek is literally "as
> many as I love"] I reprove and discipline...

Wait a minute! Jesus loves me! And yet He is going to discipline me? What is discipline? The biblical word means "to teach" ("to be a disciple"). But we usually think of discipline as a "swat on the rear," or some other form of punishment. God does not wrathfully punish Christians; He lovingly disciplines them. Why does He not punish Christians? He does not do so because all of their sins have already been punished.

> There is therefore now no condemnation
> for those who are in Christ Jesus. (Romans 8:1)

The wrath of God was turned away from Christians at the cross, and they have been adopted into His family as His children. Therefore, He disciplines them, He trains and reproves them, but He does not punish them.

Jesus says,

> As many as I love...

Does this imply that Jesus does not love those who are not experiencing trials and tribulations? No. However, if a person never faces trials and tribulations because of their Christianity, they may need to rethink their relationship with Jesus Christ. An obedient Christian will experience trials and tribulations. God uses these circumstances to teach, to train, to better prepare the believer for His service. He says,

> As many as I love, I reprove and discipline;
> be zealous therefore, and repent.

He is speaking to the church in Laodicea, and He is speaking to believers today.

These seven churches were faced with the specific problem of compromise. Jesus is saying, "No, repent, turn away from compromise and stand out as a Christian."

There are many sermons on verse 20 which have included an evangelistic plea. Jesus says,

> Behold, I stand at the door and knock; if anyone hears My voice and opens the door, I will come in to him, and will dine with him, and he with Me.

The plea often heard is, "Right now Jesus is standing at the door of your heart, knocking. All you have to do is open the door and let Him come in." The problem here is that Jesus is not addressing unbelievers in this passage. Jesus is speaking to the Christians in the church at Laodicea.

If this passage were meant for unbelievers, it would be teaching a "works righteousness way of salvation." It would be teaching that it is up to the unbeliever to open the door and let Jesus in. This would mean that the unbeliever must do something in order to achieve salvation.

A famous painting depicts Jesus standing at a door, knocking. But on His side of the door, something is missing—the doorknob. What does this say? Here is Jesus, powerless, standing out in the cold, forlornly knocking at the door, hoping desperately that the one inside will hear His knock and open the door. Who is in power in this scenario? The person on whom Jesus is waiting. This is not biblical! If God selects an individual, He would boldly open the door, walk in, and command, "Come here!" The way this verse is frequently used rips it out of its context. It must be understood here that Jesus is not talking to unbelievers but to Christians, to the church of Laodicea. He says,

> Behold, I stand at the door and knock; if anyone hears My voice and opens the door, I will come in to him, and will [do what?] dine with him, and he with Me.

What we see is that Jesus is making reference to Communion.

Jesus is simply telling the church that they were lacking something: Him! They needed His fellowship, and they needed to acknowledge their dependence upon Him. In the midst of the wealth they enjoyed, and the priceless resources they were famous for, they had forgotten that in reality they were poor, naked, and blind. The church at Laodicea needed to understand that everything they had came from and would continue to come from Jesus. This attitude is very prevalent in America today as Americans enjoy the abundance and wealth that God has provided. This was the message of Jesus for the church at Laodicea, and this is His message for believers today.

This is what real joy is all about. How joyful would life be if God left believers to run their own lives? Have you ever tried to run your life? Were you very successful? Were you aware of what might happen when you walked around the corner? No.

The world feeds believers the lie of Satan that "you can do it yourself." I used to believe this. I grew up believing that there was nothing that I could not do, given the right circumstances. I had the ability. I had the wherewithal. I had everything I needed to make myself successful, whether I wanted to be president of the United States or something else. Boy, did I get a real shock! People are taught through movies, television, books, and by example that they can succeed in anything through hard work. But when they meet with reality, there is no joy. Instead, there is a great deal of anxiety, frustration, and anger. This is what Christians need to understand about the Christian life. They need to understand that God is in control of all the events in which they are involved. Because He truly loves His children, He is reproving them, He is training them, and He is providing circumstances that will make them better servants in His kingdom. Isn't that a great reason to be joyful? Yes! "Amen!" Amen in the true sense of the word—verily, verily! This was the message of

Jesus to the church at Laodicea, and this is His message to the church today.

Again, Jesus says,

> He who overcomes, I will grant to him to sit
> down with Me on My throne, as I also overcame
> and sat down with My Father on His throne.

Where are we going to be in eternity? We are in Christ! I confess I cannot really comprehend that. It is absolutely mind-boggling to think in terms of sitting on the throne of creation with God, being part of the Godhead in some sense, and sitting on the throne with Jesus. But Jesus says so,

> I will grant to him to sit down with Me on
> My throne.

How then can any Christian be dejected? How then can any Christian in any eternal sense, have sorrow? Yes, in this life there will always be sorrow and anxiety. We are all so self-focused and present-focused. But we need to be God-focused. We need to be future-focused. We need to see the world in terms of God's reality, not whatever the temporary, present situation is. If we had that kind of focus, we could be like Paul or David. We could be like all the saints throughout history who were God-focused. Yes, they struggled with day-to-day events. David went into the depths of depression over his sin and some of the events going on around him. All the biblical characters did. But they were buoyant. Like a cork they bounced right back up to the surface. They all returned to the incredible realization that God was working in and through it all—past tense—and that all they had to do was remember His reality and the future eternity.

What happens when a person is put through a trial that is absolutely devastating? To make it personal, if I were to drive home to the boat on which I used to live in Alameda, California, and as I turn the corner and look where my mast normally sticks up, all I see is the top of it just above the water, I would understand my home and all my belonging are underwater. Everything I own is lost. Then, as I slow down to turn into the parking lot, my engine blows! Smoke and flames pour out. Then my wife steps out of the car to see what is happening, and a semitruck comes flying by and flattens her. Why would God be allowing all this tragedy to happen? It is to teach me to trust in Him. No matter how difficult the circumstances are, believers must understand that God is there, and He is in control. He is limiting what Satan can do, placing a hedge around me. He has me cradled in the palm of His hand. Jesus is the One Who overcame the worst possible circumstances at the cross. This enables believers to become overcomers by trusting in His completed work for them.

When I was growing up, one of my favorite books was *God Is My Co-Pilot*. I must have read it ten times. Although I was not a Christian at the time, as I think back on it now, the title just is not realistic. Is God ever a *co*pilot? Absolutely not! I am the one who is sitting in the back of the bus with my eyes blindfolded, my ears stopped, and my hands tied behind my back! God is the Pilot; He is *not* my copilot. As believers, we desperately need to get away from that kind of thinking.

CHAPTER 17

Suzerain Treaties

Having completed an in-depth look into the seven churches of Revelation, attention will now be directed to the remaining chapters in Revelation. Before continuing, I would like to step aside for a moment and discuss Suzerain Treaties. These treaties were very common in Old Testament times. Suzerain actually means "Great King." The following example illustrates how a Suzerain Treaty would come about. When two armies would come together in battle, the victorious king was seen as the Suzerain or great king. The defeated king became the subject or vassal king. To formalize their new relationship, the two kings would enter into a treaty or covenant. Reading through the Old Testament, we see that God frequently makes or "cuts" a covenant.

This same idea and terminology were used in Suzerain Treaties. Two written copies of the treaty were drawn up in a very stylized format with specific sections. There was a "Preamble," where the Suzerain king stated who he was. There was a "Historical Prologue," which stated his historical accomplishments. The third section documented the "Ethical Stipulations," which were the laws the Suzerain would impose on the land. These would include the organization of the vassal king's government and taxes and the tribute owed the great king. Next there was a section on "Sanctions," including the benefits of obedience (protection and peace) and the consequences of disobedience (punishment and death). The final section concerned

"Succession Arrangements," which laid out how the treaty would continue after either of the parties died.

The treaty was ratified by both kings, with vows and witnesses, at an elaborate ceremony. A number of animals would be sacrificed during the ceremony. Each animal was cut in half, and the pieces would be laid out in two rows between which both of the kings would walk. What was the significance of this? Both parties to the treaty were, in effect, saying, "If either of us break the stipulations of this covenant, if either of us become covenant breakers, may it be to us as these animals are. Let us be torn asunder, let us be killed."

Such details are important because throughout the Bible sections are structured as a Suzerain Treaty. For example, the book of Deuteronomy is structured in that format. All the sections of the treaty are present in it. Each of these sections can be seen very clearly in the book of Exodus, where God gives Israel the Ten Commandments.

Exodus 20:1–5 reads,

> And God spoke all these words I am the LORD you God [this is the "Preamble," where God is stating Who He is, the Suzerain King], who brought you out of Egypt, out of the house of slavery [this is the "Historical Prologue," which recounts what God did, followed by the Stipulations, or laws, what we call the Ten Commandments. It is like saying, "Therefore"]. You shall have no other gods before me. You shall not make for yourself an idol in the form of anything in heaven above or on the earth...

In the Bible, God also includes Sanctions—what He says He will do when His commandments are broken. Throughout the Bible, God consistently lays out cause and effect: "If you break My commandments, this is the consequence." For example, notice in verse 5:

> I the Lord your God, am a jealous God, punishing the children for the iniquity of the

fathers to the third and fourth generations of those who hate me.

God is saying, "If you break My commandments, these are the sanctions." Later on, we also find the "Succession Arrangements."

David Chilton, the author of *The Days of Vengeance*, has validated that the book of Revelation is also written in the form of a Suzerain Treaty. The apostle John, the author of the book of Revelation, would have understood this form of communication. As an elder in the church, he would have been very familiar with the Old Testament and would have noted this specific type of covenantal structure appears in Deuteronomy, in parts of Exodus, in Joshua 24, in Hosea, and other places in Scripture.

In Revelation, the "Preamble" is the first chapter. It describes John's vision of the divine Son of Man, the resurrected and glorified King of Kings, Who is Jesus Christ. In this section, Jesus clearly declares that He is the Suzerain. This is immediately followed by the "Historical Prologue," the letters to the churches: "This is what I have done, how I have taken care of you." It also lays out choices in the present based upon the historical past with future consequences. Next is the "Ethical Stipulations," beginning in chapter 4 with the seven seals. This is followed by the seven trumpets, which are the covenant "Sanctions": "This is what is going to happen if you don't follow My word." Then finally, there are the covenant "Succession Arrangements" and continuity, which are the seven chalices or bowls. Therefore, clearly, the book of Revelation has been structured as a covenant treaty.

One of the most incredible illustrations of the covenant ratification ritual in the Old Testament is when God appears to Abraham and gives him a promise.

> After these things the word of the LORD came to Abram in a vision, saying, "Do not fear, Abram, I am a shield to you; your reward shall be very great." (Genesis 15:1)

The LORD then makes a promise to Abram that he will have many descendants and will possess the land. In verse 8,

> And he [Abram] said, "O LORD God, how may I know that I shall possess it?" [The land that God has promised him.] So He said to him, "Bring Me a three year old heifer, and a three year old female goat, and a three year old ram, and a turtledove, and a young pigeon." Then he brought all these to God and he [Abram] cut them in two, and laid each half opposite the other; but he did not cut the birds. And the birds of prey came down upon the carcasses, and Abram drove them away. Now when the sun was going down, a deep sleep fell upon Abram; and behold, terror and great darkness fell upon him. And God said to Abram, "Know for certain that your descendants will be strangers in a land that is not theirs, where they will be enslaved and oppressed four hundred years." And it came about when the sun had set, that it was very dark, and behold, a smoking oven and a flaming torch which passed between these pieces. On that day the LORD made a covenant [literally, the Lord cut a covenant], with Abram saying to your seed I have given this land, from the river of Egypt as far as the great river. (Genesis 15:8–18)

God, as the Suzerain King, is saying to Abram, the vassal king, "I am cutting a covenant with you." Abram cut the animals and laid them out. God caused a deep sleep to come upon Abram. It was then that God and God alone passed between the animals. This is a picture of the Suzerain Treaty ratification ceremony. As the two kings walked between the cut pieces of the animals, they were promising, "If either of us breaks this treaty, let us be killed as these animals are killed." As God is walking between the animals which have been sacrificed, He is, in effect, saying, "If either of us breaks this treaty, let Me be torn asunder." I do not know about you, but this is almost beyond my comprehension! God promises Abram thousands of years before the fact, knowing that Abraham and his descendants were going to be covenant breakers, and yet, He is promising that He will take upon Himself the penalty for the breaking of *His* covenant.

CHAPTER 18

Worship in Heaven

John writes in Revelation 4:1–11,

> After these things I looked, and behold, a door *standing* open in heaven, and the first voice which I had heard, like the *sound* of a trumpet speaking with me, said, "Come up here, and I will show you what must take place after these things." Immediately I was in the Spirit; and behold, a throne was standing in heaven, and One sitting on the throne. And He who was sitting *was* like a jasper stone and a sardius in appearance; and *there was* a rainbow around the throne, like an emerald in appearance. And around the throne were twenty-four thrones; and upon the thrones *I saw* twenty-four elders sitting, clothed in white garments, and golden crowns on their heads. And from the throne proceed flashes of lightning and sounds and peals of thunder. And *there were* seven lamps of fire burning before the throne, which are the seven Spirits of God; and before the throne *there was*, as it were, a sea of glass like crystal; and in the center and around the throne, four living creatures full of eyes in

front and behind. And the first creature *was* like a lion, and the second creature like a calf, and the third creature had a face like that of a man, and the fourth creature like a flying eagle. and the four living creatures, each one of them having six wings, are full of eyes around and within; and day and night they do not cease to say, "HOLY, HOLY, HOLY *is* THE LORD GOD, THE ALMIGHTY, who was and who is and who is to come." And when the living creatures give glory and honor and thanks to Him who sits on the throne, to Him who lives forever and ever, the twenty-four elders will fall down before Him who sits on the throne, and will worship Him who lives forever and ever, and will cast their crowns before the throne, saying "worthy art Thou, our Lord and our God, to receive glory and honor and power; for Thou didst create all things, and because of Thy will they existed, and were created."

John sees a vision while he is "in the Spirit." He says,

Immediately I was in the Spirit…

It is not certain whether this is a continuation of his original vision, whether it is a more intense vision, or whether there is some period of time between the two. In chapter 1, verse 10, John writes,

I was in the Spirit on the Lord's Day.

Throughout the Old Testament, God calls His prophets into His presence. As believers, in a sense, we are all prophets. *To prophesy* means "to explain Scripture." A pastor is prophesying as he is preaching or teaching. However, there is a difference between the pastor's teaching; a person talking with friends about the Bible; and the proclamations of John, Ezekiel, Isaiah,

Micah, and all the other Old Testament prophets. With virtually no exception, what is clearly seen in the Old Testament is that the prophet was caught up either bodily or in a vision into the very heavenly counsel of God. Isaiah 6 is one of the best examples of this in the Old Testament.

> In the year of King Uzziah's death, I saw the Lord sitting on a throne, lofty and exalted, with the train of His robe filling the temple. Seraphim stood above Him, each having six wings... And one called out to another and said "Holy, Holy, Holy, is the LORD of hosts, the whole earth is full of His glory." And the foundations of the thresholds trembled at the voice of him who called out, while the temple was filling with smoke. Then I said, "Woe is me, for I am ruined. (Isaiah 6:1–5)

The actual word Isaiah uses for *ruined* means *"uncreated"* because he understands that he is so unrighteous and God is perfectly righteous. Even though Isaiah is unrighteous in the sight of God, in his vision he is brought into the very counsel chamber of God where God Himself gives Isaiah his commission. Repeatedly in the Old Testament the prophets are brought into the very presence of God, where God gives them a very specific mission with a very specific message to deliver. These Old Testament prophets were called to the authoritative *office* of prophet.

Today there are no longer prophets in this official interpretation of the Word. Why? Because Scripture is complete. In Hebrews 1:1–2, we are told,

> God, after He spoke long ago to the fathers in the prophets in many portions and in many ways, in these last days has spoken to us in *His* Son, whom He appointed heir of all things, through whom also He made the world.

Jesus Christ was the "Prophet par excellence." He was the final Prophet. He came, and He gave the people God's final Word. There are churches today that claim to have official prophets. This is not biblical. Although the prophet in the Mormon church is proclaimed to be called of God and speaking for Him, clearly Scripture says this is not true. Yes, all believers are prophets in the sense that they proclaim and explain Scripture, but this does not compare to the revelations of God through the Old Testament prophets and thorough the apostles, such as John in the Revelation. In his vision, John is called into the very heavenly counsel of God and given a very specific message by Jesus Christ.

Readers of today may not understand the meaning of the words of John when he describes his vision in chapter 4. What is actually taking place in his vision? Worship! Many believers today do not realize they are, in a sense, "in heaven" every week. Many do not think of the Lord's Day services in this way. But earthly worship is just a glimpse of John's "vision" of heaven. Many churches celebrate Communion the first Sunday of every month. Communion is a miniscule "vision" of what it will be like in heaven when God's children join together at the Table of the Lord with all the saints in history. His people will finish the Last Supper that Jesus Christ arrested when He said,

> This is My blood of the covenant which is poured out for many for forgiveness of sins, But I say to you I will not drink of this fruit of the vine from now on until that day when I drink it new with you in My Father's kingdom. (Matthew 26:28–29)

God has provided these little "glimpses" of what heaven is like. When the church comes together to worship God each week, they are joining in heavenly worship. They come into the very presence of God, joining together with all the saints throughout all of history, lifting their voices in praise to God. This is what John sees in his vision.

Now if this is true, if what John is seeing is a worship ceremony, and if the weekly church worship ceremony is a little foretaste of this, the concern of the congregation should be that they are actually worshiping God in the way He desires. The congregation should be worshipping not only from the heart but according to the pattern which God has given them. This is what the Reformed tradition believes. Scripture teaches that worship of God should not be in any way other than what He has commanded.

In the Old Testament, the high priest officiated in the worship service. He pointed forward to the Mediator, Jesus Christ, Who was to come. He acted as a mediator between the people and God. The high priest dressed in robes decorated with gold and jewels. Over this, he wore a breastplate, a folded pouch on his chest, with twelve jewels each one representing one of the twelve tribes of Israel. Inscribed on each of the jewels was the name of one of the tribes of Israel. There was also a jewel on each of his shoulders with a golden chain from each shoulder which held the breastplate. There were six names of the tribes of Israel on one jewel and six names of the other tribes of Israel on the other. The high priest wore a crown, probably resembling a miter. On the front of the crown was a plate with the inscription "Holy to YHWH." He was set apart, not only from the elders and the other priests, but from the people as well. In and of himself he was not above the other people, but he was called and set apart by God. He was given a particular function. This applies to pastors today who are called out from the people of God. Pastors are not better than any of God's other people, but they are called by God to a particular authoritative function as mediators between God and His people.

What John describes in this part of the Revelation is a worship service in heaven. God is showing John in this vision what true worship should look like. Gathered around the throne of God were the elders and the four living creatures, and they are worshipping before the throne of God, crying out, "Holy, holy, holy." In the same way, this is what is seen in the vision of Isaiah's call in Isaiah chapter 6.

A throne was standing in heaven, and One
sitting on the throne. And He who was sitting

like a jasper stone and a sardius in appearance…
(Revelation 4:2–3)

David Chilton points out in *The Days of Vengeance* that the jasper of today is different than the jasper stone mentioned in the Bible. The jasper in Scripture was probably more like a diamond, a crystalline, clear, kind of stone. A sardius was a red stone much like a ruby. It was named for the town of Sardius and is also called a carnelian. Interestingly, in the Old Testament, the first stone described on the breastplate of the high priest is the jasper. The last stone mentioned is the sardius.

> *There was* a rainbow around the throne, like
> an emerald in appearance.

Upon each of the jewels on the breastplate of the high priest was engraved the name of a particular tribe. An emerald represented the tribe of Judah. Why is that important to the understanding of Revelation? Jesus came from the tribe of Judah; He is the Lion of Judah. Later in chapter 5, Jesus is named not only the Lion of Judah, but also the Lamb of Judah, the Lamb of God. All this would have been easily understood by the people to whom John was writing. They understood the Old Testament symbolism that is foreign to the believers of today.

John sees God sitting on a throne with a rainbow around it that looked much like an emerald in appearance. This is also seen in the calling of the prophet Ezekiel in Ezekiel 1:1–5.

> Now it came about in the thirtieth year, on
> the fifth day of the fourth month, while I was by
> the river Chebar among the exiles [Ezekiel was
> in exile in Babylon] the heavens were opened
> [sounds like John—"a door opened"] and I saw
> visions of God. And as I looked, behold, a storm
> wind was coming from the north, a great cloud
> with fire flashing forth, continually and a bright

light around it, and in its midst something like
glowing metal in the midst of the fire.

This is very similar to John's vision in Revelation 4. The prophet was called into the very presence of God when he was commissioned by God.

And within it there were figures resembling
four living beings. And this was their appearance.

There are some differences between what Ezekiel describes and what John describes. Often, descriptions of a scene are different, depending on the person's viewpoint. Almost everyone describes things a bit differently. Different perspectives are not contradictory but complementary. Each perspective in the Bible is inspired by God, and together the different perspectives form a whole picture. Each prophet is telling people, then and now, what God wants them to hear through the words of the prophet. A close study of the differences will reveal what God is saying and His purpose. Ezekiel goes on after he describes the four living beings and speaks about the throne and the wheels under it.

Now over the heads of the living beings
there was something like an expanse, like the awesome gleam of crystal, extended over their heads.
And under the expanse their wings *were stretched
out*... Now above the expanse that was over their
heads there was something resembling a throne,
like lapis lazuli in appearance; and on that which
resembled a throne, high up, *was* a figure with
the appearance of a man. (Ezekiel 1:22–26)

Ezekiel describes this "expanse" like a sea. John also writes about this same expanse, this "sea of crystal." He says,

And before the throne, as it were, a sea of
glass like crystal...

The only entrance into the tabernacle in the wilderness was from the east, through the tribe of Judah which camped directly in front of the entrance. After passing through the tribe of Judah and entering the curtain which surrounded the tabernacle, one encountered the Altar of Sacrifice. A sacrifice for sin was required before approaching God. Next to the altar was "a sea," a basin of water which was for cleansing or baptizing. In Solomon's temple, this sea was an enormous, bronze laver sitting on the backs of twelve bronze bulls. The volume of water was incredible, and it was used to wash and sprinkle, or baptize. There had to be sacrifice, and there had to be baptism or cleansing, before the priests could further approach to worship God as representatives of the people. Only once a year, on the Day of Atonement, could the high priest enter into the Holy of Holies, the inner chamber of the tabernacle, into the actual presence of God.

In John's vision in Revelation, God reveals what true worship is like in the heavenly tabernacle. God gave Moses a vision of the true tabernacle at Mt. Sinai. Moses built the tabernacle in the desert following precisely the pattern that God had shown him. God also revealed details of the heavenly temple, with its intricate details, to King David, who passed it on to his son Solomon, whom God chose to build His temple. Solomon built the temple following the instructions God had given to David.

The explicit instructions and details that God established for His temple sets the precedent for worship in the church today. Carrying out animal sacrifices or slavishly following manmade rituals is no longer needed because Jesus is the final, once-and-for-all sacrifice. Our Great High Priest sacrificed Himself, which is the only sacrifice of worth. All other sacrifices pointed to God's own promise: "One day I will sacrifice the Lamb of God, the Messiah." This is why the Jews sacrificed a lamb daily, pointing forward in time to its fulfillment in the sacrifice of the Lamb of God, the Son of God.

This will be discussed more thoroughly in the next chapter. Where John writes of seeing the lamb standing "midst" the throne and the elders, the word translated as "standing" is a Hebrew word *tamid*. The lamb that was sacrificed everyday was called the *tamid*, the standing sacrifice.

When worship services are held today, they must be God-focused. Because people are sinful, in order to worship God properly, they must have a sacrifice. It must be understood that Jesus Christ sacrificed Himself for His people and their sins, and they must personally appropriate that salvation by the gift of faith given to them by God (Romans 12:3). Then there must be baptism—symbolizing your cleansing by the blood of the Lamb, the One Who washes away the sins of the world. Then and only then can one enter into the very presence of God in true worship. Yes, anyone can walk through the church door, sit in a seat, sing the songs, and listen to the Word. But this would not be truly worshipping God as He has commanded in His Word.

Just as there are people in the church today who do not understand this, there were people in the days of Moses who did not understand true worship. The children of Israel were in the very *visible* presence of God. As Israel wandered for forty years in the desert, God Himself dwelt between the wings of the cherubim above the Ark of the Covenant in the Holy of Holies in the tabernacle. And above the camp there was a pillar of fire and a pillar of cloud. The people could not miss these visible signs of God's presence! By day, the cloud gave Israel shadow from the heat of the sun and provided shade in the Judean desert. At night, the pillar of fire gave them light and warmth. God was "in their face" every day. Yet what were they doing for forty years in the desert? Complaining! In addition to this, Stephen tells his audience in Acts 7:42–43 that God condemned Israel, saying,

> IT WAS NOT TO ME THAT YOU OFFERED VICTIMS AND SACRIFICES FORTY YEARS IN THE WILDERNESS, WAS IT, O HOUSE OF ISRAEL? "YOU ALSO TOOK ALONG THE TABERNACLE OF MOLOCH AND THE STAR OF THE GOD ROMPHA, THE IMAGES WHICH YOU MADE TO WORSHIP."

They were worshipping these false gods right in the very visible presence of the one and only true God. What did God do about this? All the unbelieving Israelites died in the desert. Sadly, this same scenario is happening in worship services today. People come to worship services and worship other gods in the very presence of God Himself. They worship gods of their own making, fashioned in their own minds in the manner they want or hope or think God is, instead of submitting themselves to the true God and learning what He is truly like from His Word, the Bible, and worshipping Him in the way He tells us in Scripture.

> And from the throne proceed flashes of
> lightning and sounds and peals of thunder...

These are words that resounded at Mt. Sinai! When all of Israel were gathered at the foot of the mountain and God Himself came down in a pillar of cloud and pillar of fire upon the mountain, the very mountain shook. God spoke and gave Israel the Ten Commandments, creating fear among the people as they thought they were going to die! They begged Moses to go talk to Him. "We do not want to hear His voice anymore." They understood this was God sitting in judgment. Back in Revelation 1, John says he heard this voice like that of a trumpet,

> I was in the spirit on the Lord's day and I
> heard behind me a loud voice like of a trumpet.

This incredible, shrieking, windlike trumpet sound was what they were hearing—the voice of God speaking in judgment.

At Mt. Sinai, God's people were quaking in fear. What did the elders do in Revelation chapter 4? They fell down. Moses said, "I tremble with fear." What did Abraham do when God appeared to him in Genesis 17:1–3? He fell facedown in the dirt. What would you do if Jesus Christ were to walk in the door in His full glory as John saw Him? You would fall facedown in the dirt, which is exactly what John did. Many today think of God as a little old, white-bearded Santa Claus in the sky. Or Jesus as the One Who says, "I love you, come to Me no matter what." While the latter is true in a sense, we must remember "the rest of the story." What we continually fail to understand or remember is the awesome majesty of God, His absolute holiness. Reflect upon the words of the four living creatures, who "do not cease to say, 'Holy, holy, holy is the Lord God, the almighty.'" Furthermore, one that is prostrate before God would not be able to raise their face until God reaches out and picks them up. What does Jesus do to John in chapter 1 after John falls on his face "as if dead"? Jesus touches him and "brings him back to life"; thus he gets up. Similar scenes are repeated over and over in Scripture. One example appears in Isaiah 6. We should never go into the presence of God in worship without respect and honor and reverence. This is why the King James translates reverence as "fear." This is not fear in the sense that one is afraid God is going to strike them or send a lightning bolt. Rather, it is fear in the sense of awe due to the recognition of the majesty and transcendence of Almighty God. We have an "awful" God. The definition of the word *awful* has changed. The original meaning of the word *awful* was that something was full of awe, an emotion inspired by the authority or magnificence of what is in view. For example, being invited to the White House and coming into the presence of the president of the United States should fill one with respect and a certain amount of fear—reverence, if you will. We should exhibit this same kind of reverent attitude toward God, except to a vastly greater degree, especially when we gather together for worship. Believers should come recognizing, as the elders do here, that every crown (every honor) belongs to God and that they should throw their crowns at His feet.

CHAPTER 19

The Scroll with Seven Seals

And I saw in the right hand of Him who sat on the throne a book written inside and on the back, sealed up with seven seals. And I saw a strong angel proclaiming with a loud voice, "Who is worthy to open the book and to break its seals?" And no one in heaven, or in the earth, or under the earth, was able to open the book, or to look into it. And I *began* to weep greatly, because no one was found worthy to open the book, or to look into it. And one of the elders said to me, "Stop weeping; behold the Lion that is from the tribe of Judah, the Root of David, has overcome so as to open the book and its seven seals." And I saw between the throne (with the four living creatures) and the elders a Lamb standing, as if slain, having seven horns and seven eyes, which are the seven Spirits of God, sent out into all the earth. And He came and He took *it* out of the right hand of Him who sat on the throne. And when He had taken the book, the four living creatures and the twenty-four elders fell down before the Lamb, having each one a harp and golden bowls full of incense, which are the prayers of the saints. And they sang a new song saying "Worthy are You to take the book, and to break its seals; for You were slain, and did purchase for God with Your blood *men* from every tribe and tongue and people and nation. And You have made them *to be* a kingdom and priests to our God; and they will reign upon the earth. And I looked, and I heard the voice of many angels around the throne and the living creatures and the elders and the number of them was myriads of myriads, and thousands of thousands, saying with a loud voice, "Worthy is the Lamb that was slain to receive power and riches and wisdom and might and honor and glory and blessing." And every created thing which is in heaven and on the earth and under the earth and on the sea, and all things in them I heard saying "To Him who sits on the throne and to the Lamb, *be* blessing and honor and glory and dominion forever and ever. And the four living creatures kept saying "Amen!" And the elders fell down and worshiped. (Revelation 5:1–14)

Beginning with this chapter in the book of Revelation, the most popular understanding of John's letter is that it is a prophecy of the far-distant future. John sees a scroll sealed up with seven seals, and in the following chapters, these seals are broken, leading to a series of events. John continues:

> And I saw in the right hand of Him who sat
> on the throne a book [scroll] written inside and
> on the back. (5:1)

Many people immediately conclude that this is a book of prophecy, that God is revealing to John what is going to happen sometime in the far distant future.

However, there is another interpretation of which many are unaware. The reason is that very few people today are familiar with the Old Testament. John says, "I saw a scroll written inside and on the back," or "on the front and back." That brings to *our* minds writing on both sides of a piece of paper. The problem is that this was not normally done with scrolls. Upon viewing any scroll (even contemporary scrolls), one will see writing on only one side. Nothing appears on the outer or reverse side. The seals (there were normally seven on a testament or covenant document) were placed along the edge of the scroll. Thus, if a scroll was sealed, one would not be able to read its contents. This concept has bothered many commentators, especially those who think this is a book of prophecy. This is the case because John clearly states in verse 1 that the book (scroll) was "written inside and on the back." However, by simply going back to the Old Testament, it is immediately evident there is something with writing on the front and the back.

In a previous chapter, we discovered that the book of Revelation was written in the form of a Suzerain Treaty. This treaty form stated that the Suzerain, or Great King, had conquered a vassal king. Upon his victory, the Suzerain would write a treaty, then hold a covenant ratification ceremony where both kings would "cut the covenant." A clear example of this treaty form appears in Exodus, chapter 20, where God declares, "I am the LORD your God," and then gives Israel His Ten Commandments. These treaties always started with a declaration of sovereignty: "I am the Great King." This was followed by a "Historical Prologue": "This is what I have done to establish this relationship." God tells Israel, "I brought you out of Egypt. I purchased you for My own." Then the Suzerain would state his "Ethical Stipulations," the things required of the vassal king. In Exodus, the stipulations are the Ten Commandments. These were followed by "Sanctions"—blessings if you follow my commands, curses if you do not obey my requirements. Finally, there were "Succession Arrangements," which discussed continuity of the treaty at the death of either of the kings. The entire book of Deuteronomy is also written as a Suzerain Treaty. This treaty form is seen throughout the Old Testament and is also noted in the book of Revelation.

What is fascinating about a Suzerain Treaty is that two copies were made of the treaty, one for the Suzerain and one for the vassal king. Each king would then deposit his copy of the treaty at the feet of his god. When God wrote the Ten Commandments on the tablets of stone, the text states that God wrote on both the front and back (Exodus 32:15). Instead of two tablets with some commandments on one tablet and the rest of the commandments on the other tablet, it is very likely that God wrote out two copies of the treaty. One was deposited at the foot of God (in the Ark of the Covenant above which God Himself dwelt in all His glory over the Mercy Seat between the wings of the cherubim). As the vassal kingdom, the Israelites placed their copy in the same place! Both tablets were placed inside the Ark of the Covenant because their gods were the same. Israel's God was Yahweh God, and Yahweh God had the Israelites put His own copy at His feet as well.

One of my seminary professors, Meredith Kline, did some marvelous work on Suzerain Treaties. He wrote about this in His book, *The Treaty of the Great King*, and I believe he proves the point that the Ten Commandments were two copies of a Suzerain Treaty.

John describes in Revelation a book (scroll) with writing both inside and on the back. This is likely a classic reference to a covenant document. However, this document is sealed. Why does this scroll appear as sealed? Because it is like a time capsule which remains sealed until the time designated for it to be opened. We also find in the Old Testament a reference made to the sealing of a book. At the end of the book of Daniel, in chapter 12:4, the angel Michael commands,

> But as for you, Daniel, conceal these words
> and seal up the book until the time of the end.

What "end"? The end of the Old Covenant era—the period about which Daniel was prophesying.

Similarly, in Ezekiel 2:9–10, it is written,

> Then I looked, behold, a hand was extended
> to me: and lo, a scroll *was* in it. When He spread

it out before me, it was written on the front and
the back: [sounds just like Revelation, doesn't it?]
and written on it were words of lamentations,
mourning, and woe.

What did this covenant document contain? Sanctions! Words
of judgment against Israel! God was simply carrying out the law
agreed to by both parties in the covenant. Because of Israel's disobedience, He is saying, "I am going to do exactly what I said I would
do." These kinds of sanctions are beautifully laid out and contrasted
in Deuteronomy 28: stipulations of blessing for covenant obedience
in the first half of the chapter, sanctions or curses for covenant disobedience in the second half of the chapter.

This is also seen in Revelation 5—a scroll written on the front
and the back. And written on it, as we shall see in later chapters,
are lamentations, mourning, and woe—God's righteous judgment against Israel for covenant disobedience. Now look at Isaiah
29:11–14.

And the entire vision shall be to you like the
words of a sealed book [scroll], which when they
give it to the one who is literate saying, "Please
read this," he will say "I cannot, for it is sealed."
Then the book will be given to one who is illit-
erate, saying, "Please read this." And he will say,
"I cannot read." Then the LORD said, "Because
this people draw near with their words and honor
Me with their lip service, but they remove their
hearts far from Me, and their reverence for Me
consists of tradition learned *by rote*, Therefore
behold, I will once again deal marvelously with
this people."

God then speaks about judgment against the Israelites.
Particularly, He speaks of judgment against the leadership of Israel.
As previously mentioned, the leaders were responsible for what the

people were doing, and the people were responsible for the actions of the leaders since they did not correct the leaders. What we see here in Revelation 5 is God's judgment document against Israel. Revelation is not simply a book of prophecy in the sense that God is revealing what is going to happen. Yes, that is true in a sense, but as Chilton points out in his book, *The Days of Vengeance*, all prophecy is ethical. When most people think of prophecy, they think of events to come in a future time.

But prophecy is not just the foretelling of future events. It is also the forthtelling or explaining of God's Word. All pastors function as prophets. Believers hear a prophecy every Lord's Day morning during the sermon, a forthtelling of the Word of God. All Christians function as prophets when they tell others about the good news of salvation through Jesus Christ. That is what we see over and over again in prophecies in the Bible. God is not simply telling about the events that are about to happen merely to reveal the future. In fact, you never see that in the Bible. God only reveals the events of the future in order to warn people: "If you do not obey My commands, this is what I am going to do." All prophecy in the Bible is ethical. And that is exactly what is happening here in Revelation 5.

Why is the scroll sealed with seven seals? Several commentators have noted the similarity to a Roman testament or will. G. K. Beale, in *The New International Greek Testament Commentary: The Book of Revelation*, writes that the book should be understood

> against the legal background of Roman wills, since the two bear striking similarity: (1) the contents of such a will was sometimes summarized on the back; (2) a will had to be witnessed and sealed by seven witnesses; (3) only on the death of the testator could a will be unsealed and the legal promise of the inheritance executed; (4) a trustworthy executor would then put the will into effect. These similarities appear to be too striking for such wills not to have been in John's mind to some degree.

Herman Hoeksema, in his commentary *Behold He Cometh* states,

> There can be little doubt about the fact that this book is symbolic of the living and powerful decree of God with regard to the things which must shortly come to pass... The breaking of the seals does not simply open the hidden things of God's counsel. Its idea is not simply that of revelation. But the opening of the book signifies the very realization of that powerful, all-comprehensive decree of God. It signifies, therefore, the very realization of the kingdom. He who receives the book and may open the seals receives the living decree of God itself and the power to realize it. He who is honored with the distinction of breaking the seals receives therefore the power to establish and complete the kingdom, actually to bring to pass all that is written in the book... When all of these seals shall have been loosed, the counsel of God shall have been realized and the kingdom shall have been established in glory.

> And I began to weep greatly, because no one was found worthy to open the book [scroll], or to look into it. (Revelation 5:4)

Why would John be so upset and weeping? If people knew that God's judgment was coming, and they also knew that there was a way to prevent His judgment from coming upon them, would they not want to find out how to prevent this from happening? What is obvious here is John's concern for his people, the nation of Israel. He immediately understands that this is a covenant document, that it is a Suzerain Treaty. He knows it contains the sanctions of God against Israel, and so he breaks into tears because no one is worthy of opening it to find out what can be done.

> And one of the elders said to me, "Stop weeping: behold, the Lion that is from the tribe of Judah, the Root of David, has overcome to open the book and its seven seals." (Revelation 5:5)

The Lion of Judah is the son, or root, of David. He is the Messiah, the coming Son of David that was foretold over and over again in the Old Testament. He is the sprig that sprang up from Jesse. He is the root of David. He is the coming Messiah promised by God in the Old Testament. This is why the Jews were so disappointed in Jesus. He was not the kind of Messiah they were expecting. They were expecting a lion, a great warrior, to come riding in on his white charger with sword flashing and wipe out the Romans and everybody except the Jews. And most importantly, they expected Him to restore them to their former glory. But Jesus was not like that. As a matter of fact, John writes,

> And I saw between the throne (with the four living creatures) and the elders a Lamb standing, as if slain.

When most people hear the word *lamb*, they think of a weak, little, helpless, harmless creature that is cuddled in one's arms. Is that the way you think of Jesus? Most people do. They think of him as "gentle Jesus, meek and mild."

But this is not what John is describing here. He writes, "a Lamb standing, as if slain." Now this does sound rather confusing. How can a lamb stand if it is slain? Once again, the problem is unfamiliarity with the Old Testament. When most people read the words "a lamb *standing*," they do not automatically make the same connection that an Israelite of John's day would probably have made. The required daily sacrifice of the lamb in the temple was called a *tamid*, or the "standing sacrifice." Chilton points out in *The Days of Vengeance* that in the book of Revelation, Jesus is called the lamb twenty-nine times. The Greek word used is *arnion*, a word that is only used one time elsewhere in the New Testament. Everywhere else in the New Testament, the word for *lamb* is *amnos*. Why the difference? As Chilton points out, very likely what is going on here is that the Greek translation of the "standing sacrifice" is the word *arnion* plus the Greek word for *standing*.

So what John is describing here is not some mild, meek little lamb that has been slain and yet he is standing up. This would be quite miraculous. Rather, John is writing about the standing sacrifice in the temple. And Who is the standing sacrifice in the temple pointing to? Of course, it is Jesus the Messiah, "the Lamb of God, who takes away the sin of the world" (John 2:29)! That is what is being taught here: The Lion of Judah is the Messiah, the Lamb of God Who is represented by the "standing sacrifice" of a lamb each day in the temple. This is what John's people would have understood. They would not visualize a lamb with its throat cut standing there. Rather, they would have immediately connected John's words to the sacrifice. As a matter of fact, John goes on to say,

> A lamb standing, as if slain, having seven
> horns and seven eyes, which are the seven Spirits
> of God, sent out into all the earth.

It is very difficult to visualize what John is describing. It would be quite a challenge for anyone to paint a picture of a lamb slain, yet standing, with seven horns and seven eyes! And how would one draw the seven Spirits of God? What John is describing in his vision represents biblical symbolism. Virtually everywhere in the Bible the word *horn* represents power. And the number 7 in Scripture represents completeness. Thus, the symbolism here refers to complete power. In modern language, the word used could be *omnipotence* or *all-powerful*.

In reference to the seven eyes, this would create a really distorted lamb. However, the seven eyes represent *omniscience*: complete, perfect vision! This means that the Lamb is omnipotent and omniscient, all-powerful and all-knowing. As for the seven spirits, they represent *omnipresence*! They go out into all the world. In short, what is seen here is God Himself: the Lamb of God Who is God; the Lion of Judah; the omnipotent, omniscient, omnipresent God of the universe.

> And He came and He took (the scroll) out
> of the right hand of Him who sat on the throne.

What is represented here? How can God sit on the throne and yet God stand, giving Himself something from His right hand? How is this possible? How can one be two and yet remain one? Yes, it is difficult to comprehend, but the same kind of vision appears in Daniel 7, where the Divine Messiah comes before the Ancient of Days and receives from Him all power and authority and a kingdom.

It really is not so hard to understand when remembering that God is triune, one God in three persons. God the Father, God the Son, and God the Holy Spirit are the same yet distinct Persons. They do different things and have different responsibilities in the work of salvation. In verse 6, the focus is upon the work of the Lion of Judah, the standing sacrifice, the Lamb of God.

It is only the omniscient, omnipotent, omnipresent Son of God who is able to open the seven seals and complete the decree of God. He is the executor of God's will. He is the One Who completes the realization of the counsel of God and establishes the kingdom in glory. Only Jesus, the Lamb of God, can open the book and establish the plan of God. That is why the four living creatures and the elders fall down before Him in worship.

> And when He had taken the book, the four
> living creatures and the twenty-four elders fell
> down before the Lamb, having each one a harp
> and golden bowls full of incense, which are the
> prayers of the saints.

This scene appears repeatedly in Scripture. This smoke that comes up before God, this incense, this aroma in the nostrils of God, is the prayers of God's people. How much do you pray each day? If the prayers of the saints are the smoke of the incense, the aroma that is pleasing to God, how much do you think you are pleasing God with your prayers? There have been studies done where pastors have been asked, "How much time do you spend each day praying?" The average is five minutes a day! Is this very pleasing to God? No, it is not.

> And they sang a new song, saying "Worthy
> are You to take the book, and to break its seals;
> for You were slain."

John goes on to write about the Lamb Who was slain and Who purchased for God men from every tribe and tongue and people and nations. He relates that the elders sing a new song, saying, "Worthy are you!" There are churches in some denominations that are called "New Song Church." There are many places in the Old Testament where they "sang a new song." When God parts the Red Sea for the Israelites and brings them across on dry land, what do they do? In Exodus 15, they sing a new song! What is seen in the Old Testament record of God's redemptive history, in virtually every juncture where there was a major event, is that the people sang a new song, praising God. "Worthy are you! For…" (and then the reason is cited). And this is exactly what is happening here as well. The saints, elders, and all living creatures are bursting forth in a new song, praising Jesus for His marvelous work of redemption.

> For You were slain and did purchase for
> God with Your blood men from every tribe and
> tongue and people and nation. And You made
> them to be a kingdom…

This verse is a problem for people who believe that Revelation is futuristic. It states, "You were slain [past tense] and purchased [past tense] and You made them to be a kingdom." All the verbs are in the *past tense*. Are you still waiting on the kingdom of God? This verse is one of many that teaches that it is already here. It is something that God has already done at the first advent.

> You made them to be a kingdom and priests
> to our God; and they will reign upon the earth.

How many of you are reigning upon the earth? Every Christian should raise their hand! But what is the typical attitude in the church in America today? "Oh, woe is me! Satan is going to get me. We had better close up the doors and pray that Satan does not knock down the doors of the church." That is the way most churches are today. But Scripture teaches differently. It teaches that the church is the army of God! It is the kingdom! Believers are priests! They are reigning right now upon the earth! One of my favorite things is to remind people that God's first commandment to man in Genesis 1 is twofold. First, man is to be fruitful and multiply, and second, he is to take dominion over the whole earth! Is the church taking dominion in the world today?

> And I looked and I heard the voice of many
> angels around the throne and the living creatures
> and the elders; and the number of them was myr-
> iads of myriads, and thousands of thousands, say-
> ing with a loud voice, "Worthy is the Lamb that
> was slain to receive power and riches and wisdom
> and might and honor and glory and blessing."

Again, this is a clear reference to Daniel chapter 7, where the kingdom is given to the Son of Man.

> I kept looking in the night visions, and
> behold, with the clouds of heaven One like a
> Son of Man was coming, and He came up to the
> Ancient of Days and was presented before Him.
> And to Him was given dominion, Glory and a
> kingdom, that all the peoples, nations, and *men*

> *of every* language might serve Him. His domin-
> ion is an everlasting dominion which will not
> pass away; and His kingdom is one that will not
> be destroyed. (Daniel 7:13–14)

According to Daniel, chapter 2, the kingdom of God came into existence during Roman times, during the first advent of Christ, to include the birth, life, crucifixion, resurrection, and ascension of Jesus. His kingdom is not something that is still in the future, more than two thousand years after the fact. The Scripture teaches very clearly that Jesus ascended to the right hand of the Father and formally received the kingdom and is reigning right now until everything is put under His feet. John was reminding the first-century Christians who were about to undergo severe persecution (and us years later), "We are reigning with Him."

> And every created thing which is in heaven
> and on the earth and under the earth and on the
> sea, and all things in them, I heard saying, "To
> Him who sits on the throne, and to the Lamb,
> be blessing and honor and glory and dominion
> forever and ever." And the four living creatures
> kept saying "Amen."

As a reminder, the word *amen* literally means "so be it," "verily," "in truth." In the King James Version, whenever Jesus says, "Verily, verily, I say unto you," the actual words are "Amen, amen." He's saying "Truly, truly." Thus, the four living creatures are testifying to the truthfulness of what every creature is saying about Jesus.

> And the elders fell down and worshiped.

Again, the primary focus in Revelation is on worship.

Revelation is not simply a book about things that might come to pass someday. We do not need to search the newspapers and TV trying to figure out how all these things mesh with today's current events. It is already all here for us in the Bible. Instead of the newspapers, we need to dig into the Old Testament and study and learn so that we will have the same keys to unlock the meaning of God's Word that the first-century Jewish Christians had. Only then will we discover, as they did, that the Revelation is a letter of comfort and exhortation. Its message is, "Yes, you are going to face tribulation, you are going to face trials, you are going to face terrible persecution. But remember, God is in charge. And also remember what Jesus has accomplished. He has already accomplished all that is necessary for our salvation! Have faith in Him and go out and take dominion! Be bold! Be strong! Always be looking for opportunities to share Christ and extend His kingdom here on earth."

CHAPTER 20

First Five Seals Broken

> And I saw when the Lamb broke one of
> the seven seals, and I heard one of the four liv-
> ing creatures saying as with the voice of thunder,
> "Come." (Revelation 6:1)

Note that none of the writing inside the scroll is yet visible, since it is still rolled up with six other unbroken seals on it. Therefore, the events that are discussed in the coming chapters really have nothing to do with the actual scroll itself and its contents. Rather, John's vision is of what happens as Jesus Christ, the Lamb that was slain, breaks each of the seals, one by one.

> And I saw when the Lamb broke one of
> the seven seals, and I heard one of the four liv-
> ing creatures saying as with the voice of thunder,
> "Come." And I looked, and behold, a white horse,
> and he who sat on it had a bow; and a crown was
> given to him; and he went out conquering, and
> to conquer. When He broke the second seal, I
> heard the second living creature, saying "Come."
> And another, a red horse, went out; and to him
> who sat on it, was granted to take peace from
> the earth, and that *men* should slay one another;

and a great sword was given to him. And when He broke the third seal, I heard the third living creating, saying "Come." And I looked, and behold, a black horse; and he who sat on it had a pair of scales in his hand. And I heard *something* like voice in the center of the four living creatures, saying, "A quart of wheat for a denarius, and three quarts of barley for a denarius; and do not harm the oil and the wine." And when the Lamb broke the fourth seal, I heard the voice of the fourth living creature, saying "Come." And I looked, and behold, an ashen horse; and he who sat on it had the name Death; and Hades was following with him. And authority was given to them over a fourth of the earth, to kill with sword and with famine and with pestilence and by the wild beasts of the earth. (Revelation 6:1–8)

For people who view Revelation as futuristic and think that this scroll is going to reveal the events of the future, it is important to emphasize that absolutely nothing has yet been revealed from the scroll itself. The passage above describes the first four seals that have been broken. However, there are still three seals left on the scroll; therefore, it is still tightly sealed—a "closed book." Specific events occur as each of the seals is broken.

This passage is often referred to as "The Four Horsemen of the Apocalypse." The late evangelist, Dr. Billy Graham, wrote an immensely popular book titled *Approaching Hoofbeats: The Four Horsemen of the Apocalypse.*

According to the scenario described in this interpretation of the verses, a white horse appears with a rider who is a conqueror. Next, a red horse appears whose rider is war. Following this, there is a black horse which is ridden by famine, and finally, a mottled gray (the Greek word is actually *green*) horse whose rider is Death, and Hades is sitting behind him. The "four horsemen" gallop out bringing about an "end of the world" situation.

> And I looked, and behold, a white horse, and he who sat on it had a bow; and a crown was given to him; and he went out conquering, and to conquer.

Who should this remind us of? Jesus Christ! After all, is He not the Mighty Conqueror? Is He not the One Who receives the crown? Is He not the One Who is given the eternal kingdom and absolute authority by the Ancient of Days in Daniel 7? As a matter of fact, David Chilton, in *The Days of Vengeance*, has a wonderful exposition of the significance of the rider on the white horse holding a bow. Turn back to Habakkuk, that little book near the end of the Old Testament. In 3:3–11, we read,

> God comes from Teman, and the Holy One from Mount Paran. His splendor covers the heavens, and the earth is full of His praise. *His* radiance is like the sunlight; He has rays *flashing* from His hand, and there is the hiding of His power. Before Him goes pestilence, and plague comes after Him. He stood and surveyed the earth; He looked and startled the nations. Yes, the perpetual mountains were shattered, the ancient hills collapsed. His ways are everlasting. I saw the tents of Cushan under distress, the tent curtains of the land of Midian were trembling. Did the LORD rage against the rivers, or was Your anger against the rivers, or was Your wrath against the sea, that You rode on Your horses, on Your chariots of salvation? Your bow was made bare, the rods of chastisement were sworn. You cleaved the earth with rivers. The mountains saw You and quaked; the downpour of waters swept by. The deep uttered forth its voice, it lifted high its hands. Sun *and* moon stood in their places; They went away at the light of your arrows.

What is Habakkuk describing? He is prophesying the judgment of God against the nation of Israel. This characterization of the mountains being cleaved and the sun being dark is the same kind of apocalyptic language of decreation that is found in Matthew 24. It is also found in Revelation 6:12.

> The sun became black as sackcloth *made* of
> hair, and the whole moon became like blood.

What is being described in biblical language is the judgment of God, His judgment upon the nation of Israel.

John is not describing some kind of global cataclysm that will unfold in the future. He is using language that the Christian people of his time would have immediately understood because they had an in-depth knowledge of the Old Testament. They would have immediately recognized this "One coming forth to conquer," this "One with the bow," this "One that causes all these cataclysmic things to occur," this "One who is accompanied by death and pestilence." They would have immediately come to the conclusion that this is God coming in judgment.

On the other hand, people today who think Revelation is describing future events interpret this person on the white horse in different ways. Hal Lindsey, one of the very popular dispensational writers who has been read by millions of people, even goes so far as to declare that only the Antichrist could possibly accomplish all of these feats. Now, please do not misread what I am saying. Hal Lindsey has accomplished some marvelous things, and many people have come to Christ as a result of his books. But that is in spite of the fact that he has completely misinterpreted what the Scripture is teaching here. If he would only go back and dig into the Old Testament, he would see that it is Christ who has the bow, it is Christ who has the crown, and it is Christ who goes out conquering and to conquer. As a matter of fact, when the seal is broken, where does the command come from for this rider on the white horse to come forth? From one of the four living creatures, the ones who are immediately around God. They are the ones who are orchestrating these events. Thus, it is God Himself

Who is sending forth these riders, not some Antichrist as believed by and taught by so many teachers. It is Christ Himself Who comes forth on the white horse.

Remember that Psalm 45 is known as a "Messianic Psalm." It is one that virtually everyone understands is speaking of Jesus Christ. That Psalm states,

> Gird Your sword on *Your* thigh, O mighty one, *in* Your splendor and Your majesty! And in Your majesty ride on victoriously, for the cause of truth and meekness *and* righteousness; let Your right hand teach You awesome things. Your arrows are sharp; the peoples fall under You. *Your arrows are* in the heart of the King's enemies. (Psalm 45:3–5)

This is speaking about Christ riding forth to conquer. Perhaps this is precisely what is seen in the sixth chapter of Revelation.

> And when He broke the second seal, I heard the second living creature saying "Come." [Again, there is a living creature around the throne of God, who calls forth the second rider.] And another, a red horse, went out; and to him who sat on it, was granted to take peace from the earth, and that men should slay one another; and a great sword was given to him. (Revelation 6:3–4)

The purpose of Jesus Christ and the great sword He was given, in regard to this verse, is to divide. He came to bring truth and righteousness. He did not come to say "Welcome" to everyone. Although He does say that, it is directed only to those whom He will save. He said,

> Do not think that I came to bring peace on the earth; I did not come to bring peace, but

a sword. For I came to SET A MAN AGAINST HIS FATHER, AND A DAUGHTER AGAINST HER MOTHER, AND A DAUGHTER-IN-LAW AGAINST HER MOTHER-IN-LAW; and A MAN'S ENEMIES WILL BE THE MEMBERS OF HIS HOUSEHOLD. He who loves father or mother more than Me is not worthy of Me; and he who loves son or daughter more than Me is not worthy of Me. (Matthew 10:34–37)

I believe that is what we are seeing here. Jesus has come not to bring peace but a sword. The sword of the Word of God divides between the saved and the unsaved. The sword divides even families because of belief or unbelief. The rider on the red horse is granted authority to take peace from the earth. It is only by God's grace that there is any peace at all. Look around you and see what is happening in the world today: road-rage killings, school shootings, etc. It is only by the grace of God that things are not much, much worse than they are.

And when he broke the third seal, I heard the third living creating saying "Come." And I looked, and behold, a black horse; and he who sat on it had a pair of scales in his hand.

Look back at Ezekiel chapter 4:1–3. God says to Ezekiel,

Now you son of man, get yourself a brick, place it before you, and inscribe a city on it, Jerusalem. Then lay siege against it, build a siege wall, raise up a ramp, pitch camps, and place battering rams against it all around. Then get yourself an iron plate and set it up as an iron wall between you and the city, and set your face toward it so that it is under siege, and besiege it. This is a sign to the house of Israel.

This sounds like the events that happened in AD 70, when the Roman army came in and laid siege to the city of Jerusalem for over two years.

> Moreover, He said to me, "Son of man, behold, I am going to break the staff of bread in Jerusalem, and they will eat bread by weight and with anxiety, and drink water by measure and in horror, because bread and water will be scarce; and they will be appalled with one another and waste away in their iniquity." (Ezekiel 4:16–17)

Again, this is a quote that appears to be describing the destruction of Jerusalem by the Romans in AD 70. Such facts are known through the works of Josephus. He was a Jewish historian who was with the Roman army that laid siege to Jerusalem and destroyed the city and the temple. He described the things that were happening, and he was allowed access into the city, even while it was under siege. He writes about the people scraping up the straw from the bricks for food, as well as fighting over rat dung and other detestable things. They were literally eating the leather off their shields and shoes because being under siege for two years led to a great famine.

> And I looked, and behold, a black horse; and he who sat on it had a pair of scales in his hand. And I heard *something* a voice in the center of the four living creatures saying, "A quart of wheat for a denarius, and three quarts of barley for a denarius; and do not harm the oil and the wine."

A denarius was a day's wage, therefore, because of the famine, grain became very expensive. Interestingly enough, extra-biblical evidence reveals that when the army came in, the Roman general instructed that no harm was to be done to the olive trees and the vineyards. Everything else could be completely destroyed, but no harm was to come to the oil and the wine. God is so incredibly sovereign that He controls even the hearts of the ungodly that He sends against His people.

> And when the Lamb broke the fourth seal, I
> heard the voice of the fourth living creatures saying "Come." And I looked, and behold, an ashen
> horse.

The King James Version says a "pale horse." The word is actually an interesting Greek word that is very familiar to us in one form. The Greek word is *chloros*, which means "green," as in *chlorophyll!* The word is one that is taken directly from the Greek word. Thus, this is a "sickly green horse."

> And he who sat on it had the name Death;
> and Hades was following with him.

Pictures of this horse and rider show Hades, with a hideous grin on his face, perched on Death's back.

> And authority was given to them over a
> fourth of the earth, to kill with sword and with
> famine and with pestilence and by the wild beasts
> of the earth.

Wow! Does this mean one fourth of the people of the whole earth are going to be killed? Has this already happened? Yes! It is stated in Ezekiel 14:21:

> For thus says the Lord GOD, "How much
> more when I send My four severe judgments
> against Jerusalem: sword, famine, wild beasts,
> and plague to cut off man and beast from it!

God's judgment against Israel is prophesied in these verses. Ezekiel presents each of the four judgments God will use against Israel: to kill with sword, famine, pestilence, and by the wild beasts of the earth.

What about the question of a fourth of the earth being killed? Unfortunately, the word *earth* here is, I believe, a mistranslation because the translators were thinking in futuristic terms. The Greek term is actually the normal word for *land*. Referring back to the writings of Josephus and noting the number of Jews that were killed in the ensuing wars, siege, and destruction of Jerusalem, I would venture a guess the number would be at least a fourth of the people of the land, if not more!

Notice that as each of the first four seals is broken, John hears the voice of a living creature saying, "Come." But now there is a shift in emphasis:

> And when the Lamb broke the fifth seal, I
> saw underneath the altar the souls of those who had
> been slain because of the word of God, and because
> of the testimony which they had maintained.

John hears something at the breaking each of the first four seals; however, on the fifth seal he actually sees something.

Once again, at this point, none of the writing in the scroll has been revealed. Even when the fifth seal is broken, the scroll is still sealed. There remain two more unopened seals that prevent anything in the scroll being seen. Therefore, people who interpret the action at the breaking of the seals as what the scroll is saying about the distant future simply have not read the Scriptures very carefully. These are events that John heard and saw as each seal was broken, but nothing in the scroll has yet been revealed.

> I saw underneath the altar the souls of those
> who had been slain because of the word of God,
> and because of the testimony which they had
> maintained.

The souls underneath the altar who have been slain, I believe, are the early Christian martyrs. Hal Lindsey writes that they are the souls of the people in the future who will not be raptured. But I believe they are martyrs contemporary to John's audience, people they personally knew who were slain because of the Word of God and because of their testimony. In the previous chapters John reveals the Christians are about to enter a period of time in which they will experience terrible persecution. John is writing a letter of comfort to these Christians, saying, "Even through you are going to be horribly persecuted: even though you are going to be thrown to the wild beasts and torn apart; even though you will dipped in pitch, put on poles, and set ablaze as torches to light up Nero's garden parties; even though you will suffer many other horrific persecutions, God is in control and Jesus Christ is victorious and is coming in judgment."

What is seen here, I believe, are the martyrs of those early days, the souls of those who had been slain because of the Word of God. They had stood up proclaiming, "Thus says the Lord. We testify to the word of Jesus," and they were killed for their testimony.

> And they cried out with a loud voice, saying "How long, O Lord, holy and true, will you refrain from judging and avenging our blood on those who dwell on the earth."

Chilton brings out an interesting point here. According to this verse, the blood of the martyrs is crying out from under the altar. When the sacrifice was accomplished in the temple, the animal was sacrificed, and the blood ran down into a trench around the altar and was then flushed into the Kidron ravine. Recall that it was the priests who sacrificed these animals. This correlates to the persecution of the early Christians that was being done by Jewish priests and religious leaders. It was the leadership of the Jewish nation in league with the Roman government that ruthlessly and relentlessly persecuted the early Christians. Thus, what Chilton points out here is that it may be referring to the blood of those that were slain by the Jewish leadership.

> And they cried out with a loud voice, saying "How long, O Lord, holy and true, will you refrain from judging and avenging our blood on those who dwell on the earth."

Again, I believe the word translated *earth* should actually be translated *land*. It is referring to the land of Israel not the whole earth.

> And there was given to each of them a white robe; and they were told that they should rest for a little while longer, until *the number of* their fellow servants and their brethren who were to be killed even as they had been, should be completed also.

Here, the martyrs are told to rest for "a little while longer" (*not* thousands of years). Therefore, what is seen here are not the souls of all the martyrs all throughout history crying out to God. Instead, John is referring more specifically to the early Christian martyrs who were killed from Stephen on through the period before the temple was destroyed. They are naturally asking God how long He will let this persecution continue and how long before He will destroy the Israelite religious system that persecuted them. And God replies, "Hold on just a little bit longer, for 'the time is at hand,' and then My judgment will come."

CHAPTER 21

The Sixth Seal Broken

And I looked when He broke the sixth seal, and there was a great earthquake; and the sun became black as sackcloth *made* of hair, and the whole moon became like blood; and the stars of the sky fell to the earth, as a fig tree casts its unripe figs when shaken by a great wind. The sky was split apart like a scroll when it is rolled up; and every mountain and island were moved out of their places. Then the kings of the earth and the great men and the commanders and the rich and the strong and every slave and free man, hid themselves in the caves and among the rocks of the mountains; and they said to the mountains and to the rocks, "Fall on us and hide us from the presence of Him who sits on the throne, and from the wrath of the Lamb; for the great day of their wrath has come; and who is able to stand?" (Revelation 6:12–17)

Has it ever been recorded throughout history that the sun became black as sackcloth made of hair? Has the whole moon ever become like blood? After reading this passage, many people conclude, "Obviously, this has not yet happened. Therefore, it must be speaking of future events." Quite the contrary, according to Scripture, these things have already happened! One of the things that convinced me of the orthodox preterist view of Revelation was reading all the Old Testament references in their original context. In this particular passage, we see very similar language to Matthew 24:29,

> But immediately after the tribulation of those days THE SUN WILL BE DARKENED, AND THE MOON WILL NOT GIVE ITS LIGHT, AND THE STARS WILL FALL from the sky, and the powers of the heaven will be shaken.

Although this reads almost exactly like Revelation 6:12, Matthew 24:29 is a quote from Isaiah 13:10.

> For the stars of heaven and their constellations will not flash forth their light; the sun will be dark when it rises, and the moon will not shed its light.

What is Isaiah prophesying about? Again, a passage must always be interpreted by the context. Verse 1 of Isaiah 13 teaches that the passage is an oracle or prophecy which Isaiah, the son of Amos, saw concerning Babylon. This raises the question: "What is Isaiah writing about?" He is actually prophesying the destruction of Babylon. Look at Isaiah 13:17,

> Behold, I am going to stir up the Medes against them [the Babylonians].

We know from history and extra-biblical documents that the Medo-Persian Empire is the one that wiped out the Babylonian Empire and took it over around 500 BC. So what Isaiah is writing about in Isaiah 13 has already happened. Now think about it. Did the sun actually become black? No. Isaiah is not speaking about the sun literally ceasing to give light; he is writing about the awesome terror of God's judgment blotting out the world's greatest power of that day, symbolized by the darkening of the sun. That is what we need to understand.

In the Bible, the symbols of the sun, moon, and stars have to do with governments. That is very easy to prove. Look at Genesis 1:14–16.

> [Then God said] let there be lights in the expanse of the heavens to separate the day from the night, and let them be for signs, and for seasons, and for days and years; and let them be for lights in the expanse of the heavens to give light on the earth"; and it was so. And God made the two great lights, the greater light to govern the day, and the lesser light to *govern* the night; *He made* the stars also.

People who are steeped in the Old Testament and who have memorized great portions of it, who have heard it over and over again, would not think of the literal sun and moon and stars as we do when John mentions them. They would automatically know that what was in view here was the political structure of the world. These heavenly bodies symbolize or represent governing authorities. What Jesus is speaking of in Matthew 24 is not the destruction of the literal sun, literal moon, and literal stars. It is the destruction of the governmental system. We still do this today. What do we have on the flag of the United States? We have fifty stars to represent each of the fifty states, with their respective state governments. It is the same kind of use of symbolism we see here in Revelation.

> The sky was split apart like a scroll when it is rolled up; and every mountain and island were moved out of their places.

There is an interesting thing here that I will go into very quickly. Years ago, when I first looked at Revelation, I thought of

Revelation in the same way Hendrickson does in his book, *More Than Conquerors*. In that book, Hendrickson sees Revelation as a sevenfold recapitulation of history, because there are obviously a lot of "sevens" here. A man by the name of Vern Poythress who was a professor at Westminster Theological Seminary in Philadelphia did a massive study of Revelation in which he showed that Revelation is put together as a whole series of seven sevens. Because the Jews did not have many books, they used a lot of mnemonics (memory tricks) to memorize great portions of Scripture.

The Jews used a "chiasm," or a "chiastic structure," to aid them in memorizing written material. What you would see throughout the Old Testament is an "A thought." Then that would be followed by a "B thought" and then a "C thought," and then there would be a repeat of the "B thought," then there would be a repeat of the "A thought." What that would do is form an arrow pointing to the central thought of the passage. For example, the whole book of Ecclesiastes has this chiastic structure, pointing to one central thought in the book. Within that are chiasms within chiasms within chiasms. The whole book of Revelation is like this. Vern Poythress has a massive outline that shows how all of these "sevens" are put together. Seven upon seven upon seven upon seven. What I want to point out here is that we are speaking about the seven seals and that there are seven judgments listed here at the sixth seal. Chilton goes into them in his book. Number 1 is the earth, then the sun, the moon, the stars, and the firmament, the land, and then man. The passage speaks of God's judgment against those seven things.

> And I looked when He broke the sixth seal, and there was a great earthquake [earth]; and the sun [sun] became black as sackcloth *made* of hair, and the whole moon [moon] became like blood; and the stars [stars] of the sky fell to the earth, The sky was split apart like a scroll [firmament] when it is rolled up; and every mountain [land] and island were moved out of their places. (Revelation 6:12)

Then comes the judgment against man, which is also set out in sevens.

> And the kings of the earth and the great
> men and the commanders and the rich and the
> strong and every slave and free man…

Did you notice how many items there were in John's list? Yes, there are seven! Now, if you were Hebrew and living two thousand years ago, you would immediately understand this kind of structure. Its meaning would jump right out at you. But it does not appear obvious to us because we are not trained that way. We have not grown up saturated in the Old Testament. And we do not generally see these kinds of things unless someone points them out to us. But once we do, suddenly we have an "aha" experience. We understand and wonder why we did not see it before.

There are seven items in John's list, because this is God's sevenfold judgment against the sevenfold creation. The other thing that is interesting (Chilton points this out in *The Days of Vengeance*) is that you see this same sevenfold judgment not only in Revelation 6, but also in Matthew 24 and Mark 13 and Luke 21. Remember Matthew 24, Mark 13, and Luke 21 are parallel passages talking about the destruction of the temple in AD 70. You have war, international strife, famine, pestilence, persecution, and earthquakes. These six things are mentioned in almost the same sequence, and you begin to understand that they are all talking about the same thing.

What I want you to understand is that Revelation is based on the other parts of the Bible. It is not something new and different and boldly futuristic. It is something that someone who was steeped in the Old Testament and Hebrew tradition would have seen and understood.

> And the kings of the earth and the great men
> and the commanders and the rich and the strong
> and every slave and free man, hid themselves in
> the caves and among the rocks of the mountains.

Who are these men? What kind of people are they? They are the great, the rich, the powerful, and they are also slaves and free men. Are they saved or unsaved? They *must be unsaved* because they are hiding from the One Who sits on the throne. When Christians read this and think "I must hide because God is coming!" that is the wrong attitude because it is not true. Revelation is telling us about judgment against the ungodly, the sinful, those who are hiding from God. When Adam and Eve sinned, and God came walking through the garden in the wind of the Spirit, with this incredible shrieking trumpet blast, rushing water, hurricane-wind type of sound of God coming in judgment, what did they do? They hid because they knew they had sinned and were in trouble. That is exactly what you see happening here.

> And they said to the mountains and to the rocks, "Fall on us and hide us from the presence of Him who sits on the throne, and from the wrath of the Lamb; for the great day of their wrath has come, and who is able to stand?"

Praise God that no Christian ever has to fear the wrath of God. Why? Because He has already poured out His just wrath for our sins upon His Son, Jesus Christ. There is no future judgment for our sin because in Christ God sees us as sinless, as perfectly righteous. Paul says in Romans 8:1,

> Therefore there is now no condemnation for those who are in Christ Jesus.

You and I who believe in Jesus Christ do not have to fear the wrath of God. Rather, when we hear that trumpet sound, it is going to be a sound of pure joy.

> After this I saw four angels standing at the four corners of the earth, holding back the four winds of the earth, so that no wind would blow

on the earth or on the sea or on any tree. And I saw another angel ascending from the rising of the sun, having the seal of the living God; and he cried out with a loud voice to the four angels to whom it was granted to harm the earth and the sea, saying, "Do not harm the earth or the sea or the trees, until we have sealed the bondservants of our God on their foreheads." (Revelation 7:1–3)

This would have referred John's original readers to Ezekiel 9:1–4,

> Then He cried out in my hearing with a loud voice saying, "Draw near, O executioners of the city [the city of Jerusalem], each with his destroying weapon in his hand." And behold, six men came from the direction of the upper gate which faces north, each with his shattering weapon in his hand; and among them was a certain man clothed in linen with a writing case at his loins. And they went in and stood beside the bronze altar. Then the glory of the God of Israel went up from the cherub on which it had been, to the threshold of the temple. And He called to the man clothed in linen at whose loins was the writing case. And the LORD said to him, "Go through the midst of the city, *even* through the midst of Jerusalem, and put a mark on the foreheads of the men who sigh and groan over all the abominations which are being committed in its midst."

God is saying in Ezekiel that He is going to destroy Jerusalem because of their unbelief. But before He does, He commands that a mark be placed on the foreheads of those who believe in Him, those who are crying out because of the abominations being done.

There is a very interesting thing about this mark. First, the Israelites were marked on their head and their hand. Remember, in the Old Testament, God said to bind the law on your head and on your hand:

> You shall bind them (the Laws) as a sign on
> your hand and they shall be as frontals on your
> forehead. (Deuteronomy 6:8)

The Jews of Jesus's day took that literally. They made what were called phylacteries, which were cases containing little pieces of Scripture. They wore these phylacteries prominently on their foreheads and bound them on their hand. Jesus condemns them for their hypocrisy for doing so in Matthew 23:5.

> But they do all their deeds to be noticed
> by men; for they broaden their phylacteries and
> lengthen the tassels of their garments.

But even this is not what John is referring to. We need to go to Ezekiel to understand the peculiarity of this mark. God is preparing to bring judgment upon the people of Jerusalem in that day, and we read God saying in verse 4.

> Go throughout the midst city, *even* through
> the midst of Jerusalem, and put a mark on the
> foreheads of the men who sigh and groan over all
> the abominations which are being committed in
> its midst.

What God literally commands is to put a Hebrew letter *tav* (pronounced "tove") on every man's forehead. The Hebrew letter *tav* was the last letter of the Hebrew alphabet. The form in which it was written in that day would look very familiar to our eyes. The original form looked like a cross. In Ezekiel, hundreds of years before Christ, before the cross, before the Romans ever even thought about crucifixion, God commands the man in Ezekiel's vision to go through the city and put a cross on the foreheads of those "who are truly My people."

I think we need to ask ourselves at this point, "What does it mean to have the mark of God upon you?" And conversely, "What does it mean to have the mark of the beast upon you?" (More on that later!) The mark is a symbol of authority or ownership. An example is the tomb of Christ. The Jewish leaders requested that the tomb be sealed by the Romans, which probably meant they put some sort of a ribbon around the stone with a wax impression of the seal of Caesar upon it. What did this seal of Caesar mean? It meant ownership. It meant "this belongs to Caesar and you had better not break this seal, because you are dealing with Caesar's property." We used to do the same things with letters; by putting wax seals on them, that meant it was authoritatively your letter.

It is the same thing here. To have the seal of God upon your forehead means that you belong to Jesus Christ. Is there really going to be a big "666" branded on somebody's forehead? No, the mark of the beast is simply talking about loyalty, recognizing to whom a person belongs. That is why it is laughable when people talk about 666 being included in the UPC (Universal Product Code) and say the government is going to put a chip in your hand and forehead, and everyone will have the mark of the beast. Notice in the context that it is only those who *worship* "the beast and his image, and receives a mark on his forehead or upon his hand" (Revelation 14:9). Christians do not have to worry because they have already received a mark, the mark of the cross, the mark of Jesus Christ. That is what is important. In both Ezekiel and Revelation, before God's wrath is poured out, He says, "Go through and mark those who belong to Me." As Christians, we are already branded as those who are in service to God.

CHAPTER 22

The Mark of God and the 144,000

In the last chapter the discussion was centered on the fact that the sealing of God's people on their foreheads goes back to the book of Ezekiel, chapter 9. There, God is speaking about bringing judgment upon Jerusalem.

> And He called to the man clothed in linen at whose loins was the writing case. And the LORD said to him, "Go through the midst of the city, *even* through the midst of Jerusalem, and put a mark on the foreheads of the men who sigh and groan over all the abominations which are being committed in its midst." (Ezekiel 9:3–4)

What God is speaking about here is marking the people who believe in Him. He literally says to "set a *tav*" [pronounced 'tove'] on the foreheads of the men." The current form of the Hebrew letter *tav* looks like this ת. It is the last letter of the Hebrew alphabet. If you go back in history and study the history of the language, what you find is that the original form of the Hebrew letter *tav* was a cross. In Ezekiel 9, when God says "put a tav on the heads of the men," He means to put a cross on the foreheads of the men who sigh and groan over the abominations.

This is also what we see in Revelation. It is not the mark of the beast that we need to be concerned about as Christians. There is a lot of anxiety in the Christian world today that we are going to have a computer chip in our forehead and in our hand. This should not be our concern. As Christians, we are already marked by God. That is what you see in Ezekiel and in the Revelation.

Notice the four angels are told not to do anything to "harm the earth or the sea or the trees, until we have sealed the bondservants of our God on their foreheads." You see that theme throughout Revelation. Even if all the terrible things we see in Revelation were to literally come upon our world, which I do not believe they will, Christians are not there to endure them. If you read Revelation carefully, you will see the Christians are never there during the tribulations described. We need to understand that all of these terrible curses are upon the ungodly. They are God's wrath upon the ungodliness of Rome and of Jerusalem.

The next few verses are difficult to understand. There has been a lot of conjecture about them. John says,

> And I heard the number of those who were sealed, one hundred and forty-four thousand sealed from every tribe of the sons of Israel: From the tribe of Judah, twelve thousand *were* sealed, from the tribe of Reuben twelve thousand, from the tribe of Gad twelve thousand, from the tribe of Asher twelve thousand, from the tribe of Naphtali twelve thousand, from the tribe of Manasseh twelve thousand, from the tribe of Simeon twelve thousand, from the tribe of Levi twelve thousand, from the tribe of Issachar twelve thousand, from the tribe of Zebulun twelve thousand, from the tribe of Joseph twelve thousand, from the tribe of Benjamin, twelve thousand *were* sealed. After these things I looked,

and behold, a great multitude, which no one could count, from every nation and *all* tribes and peoples and tongues, standing before the throne and before the Lamb, clothed in white robes, and palm branches *were* in their hands; and they cry out with a loud voice saying "Salvation to our God who sits on the throne, and to the Lamb." And all the angels were standing around the throne and *around* the elders and the four living creatures; and they fell on their faces before the throne and worshiped God, saying, "Amen, blessing and glory and wisdom and thanksgiving and honor and power and might, to our God forever and ever. Amen." Then one of the elders answered, saying to me, "These who are clothed in the white robes, who are they, and where have they come from?" I said to him, "My lord, you know." And he said to me, "These are the ones who come out of the great tribulation, and they have washed their robes and made them white in the blood of the Lamb. For this reason, they are before the throne of God; and they serve Him day and night in His temple; and He who sits on the throne shall spread His tabernacle over them. They shall hunger no more, neither thirst anymore; nor will the sun beat down on them, nor any heat; for the Lamb in the center of the throne will be their shepherd, and shall guide them to springs of the water of life, and God shall wipe every tear from their eyes." (Revelation 7:4–17)

The question is, "Who are the 144,000?" If you are a Jehovah's Witness, you are taught they are a literal 144,000 people who are saved. Initially, the Jehovah's Witnesses taught that only 144,000 would go to heaven. But obviously, as people were designated one of the 144,000, they very quickly ran out of spaces in the group. So the

Jehovah's Witnesses actually proposed another class of people who are not the 144,000. The Jehovah's Witnesses say the 144,000 go to be with God around the throne. The other saved people actually live on the earth. One of the books they hand out teaches that *You Can Live Forever in Paradise on Earth.*

David Chilton, in his book *The Days of Vengeance,* goes into a separate section regarding this subject. Interestingly, remember that we are saying that Revelation is picturing a worship service. Chilton and others have seen that what is being discussed here in Revelation is a picture of the tabernacle in the wilderness. Remember that the tabernacle was a tent, around which was the white linen curtain. As a person entered the complex, the altar of sacrifice was the first thing encountered. Next came the baptismal laver, and then the tabernacle itself. The tent was divided into two sections. The outer section, the Holy Place, contained the Table of the Presence on the right side (the north). On that table was the showbread, the twelve loaves representing the twelve tribes and bowls for the drink offering of wine. On the other side (to the south) was the Golden Lampstand. The golden altar of incense was right in the front of the veil (to the west) that divided the two compartments. In the inner compartment, the Holy of Holies, was the Ark of the Covenant, where God Himself dwelt between the outstretched wings of the cherubim. The twelve tribes of Israel were camped in a specific order around the tabernacle, but that order does not match what is here in Revelation. Chilton and others have done a lot of work trying to figure out why the order in Revelation is different from the one in the Old Testament. Personally, I do not think anyone has yet come up with a good answer.

But why 144,000? Twelve times twelve thousand equals 144,000. There were twelve tribes. Remember, the Israelites did not have numbers like we do; they actually used letters of their alphabet. Each letter had a numerical equivalent. In our numbering system, each number is simply a label specifying a very definite quantity.

To the Hebrews, however, numbers had meaning. When you look, for instance, at the number 5 in Scripture, it has to do with grace. God initially called Abram called out of Ur of the Chaldees. When God made the covenant with Abram, He changed his name to Abraham. God added the Hebrew letter *hay*, which is the fifth letter of the Hebrew alphabet. He gave grace to Abram. We see that over and over in Scripture. To the Hebrews, the number 3 represented perfect unity. We have a triune God. Our God is Father, Son, and Holy Spirit—a perfect unity. The number 7 meant completeness. God made the world in six days, and on the seventh He rested—completeness. To the Jews, 10 was a perfect number because it represented the union of perfect unity and completeness (7 + 3). They saw that as a perfect number. So 10 × 10 × 10 was a complete perfection.

I think (Chilton and others agree, I did not come to this by myself) that what is being written about in regard to the 144,000 is that those people whom God will save are perfectly numbered. There is a specific number of people who will be saved. There is another reason I think that. If you go through the book of Revelation, you will see a pattern developing. In chapter 6:1, John says, "And I *heard* one of the four living creatures," and then in verse 2 he says, "And I *looked*, and behold, a white horse." In verse 3, "I *heard* the second living creature saying come," "and I *saw* something." You see this pattern of John hearing something and then seeing something. Notice in chapter 7, verse 4,

I *heard* the number of those being sealed…

Verse 9,

After these things I *looked*, and behold, a great multitude.

If you were reading along, would you think the 144,000 were part of the great multitude? I would not. If I were reading this as a while male in the twentieth century, that would mean to me a definite number of 144,000 people and a different group that was a great multitude. But when I look at Revelation, I see this pattern structure. When John says that he heard one of the four living creatures and then he looked and saw something that related to what he heard, and then we read,

> I *heard* the number of those being sealed…

Verse 9,

> After these things I *looked*, and behold, a great multitude…

I think John is telling us who the 144,000 really are. What he is saying is that the people of God are definitely numbered. What does it mean to be elect? It means to be picked out, chosen, numbered. The elect of God are numbered. God knows exactly how many are going to be saved. After all, He chose those who would be saved before the foundation of the world (Ephesians 1:4). There is no question in the mind of God when someone is going to be saved or if someone is going to be saved. If there was a question in God's mind, He would not be God. He would not be omniscient. He would not *know* all things. God knows the number of those who are going to be saved, and they are a great multitude.

Over and over in Scripture we read there is going to be a remnant that is going to be saved. What is a remnant? It is a tiny portion. But in God's economy, over the course of history, that remnant is going to be huge. It is going to be as if the whole world had been saved. In fact, it is going to be the whole world of the elect, of those who are chosen by God. It is going to be a great multitude that no one can number.

CHAPTER 23

The Seventh Seal

And when the Lamb broke the seventh seal, there was silence in heaven for about half an hour. And I saw the seven angels who stand before God; and seven trumpets were given to them. Another angel came and stood at the altar, holding a golden censer; and much incense was given to him, that he might add it to the prayers of all the saints upon the golden altar which was before the throne. And the smoke of the incense, with the prayers of the saints, went up before God out of the angel's hand. Then the angel took the censer; and filled it with the fire of the altar and threw it to the earth; and there followed peals of thunder and sounds and flashes of lightning and an earthquake. And the seven angels who had the seven trumpets prepared themselves to sound them. (Revelation 8:1–6)

This is a part of Revelation that people really have a problem understanding. If you are looking at Revelation as futuristic, then this has not yet happened. No one has heard the angels' trumpets blowing; people have not seen all these horrible things happening. But I want to remind you that, along with the author David Chilton and others,

I see Revelation as a Suzerain Treaty document. Remember that the Suzerain Treaty was a document that was drawn up by the conquering king (the Suzerain king) and the vassal king, the king who had been conquered. They made two copies of this treaty. The treaty had a very specific format. In the first part, the "Preamble," the Suzerain king stated, "This is who I am." The second part was the "Historical Prologue," in which the Suzerain stated, "This is what I have done." The third part listed the "Ethical Stipulations": "These are my commands that you must follow." The next section was the "Sanctions": "If you do not follow my commands, this is what I am going to do." The last part of the treaty was a "Succession Arrangement": "This is what must happen if either of us dies." Beginning with chapter 8, what we see in the Revelation are the "Sanctions." God is saying, "This is what I am going to do because you have not done what I told you to do." My position is, these are sanctions that we see against the Roman state and against apostate Israel.

> And when He broke the seventh seal.
> (Revelation 8:1)

Remember, we are reading about the scroll that was sealed with seven seals. So far, the scroll has not yet been opened. It still has one final seal on it, and now that seal is being opened, and what happens—"there was silence in heaven for about half an hour." Why? What in the world is going on here? Alfred Edersheim wrote *The Life and Times of Jesus the Messiah*, in which he tells us what the culture was like in Israel during the time of Jesus Christ. David Chilton quoted an excerpt of Edersheim's book *The Temple,* describing this temple ceremony.

> Slowly the incensing priest (the one who is
> to burn the incense) and his assistants ascended
> the steps to the Holy Place.

Remember, the tabernacle and then the temple was divided into two compartments. There was the outer compartment called the Holy Place into which the priests could go. On the right hand, or north side, was the Table of the Presence, or showbread, which had the twelves loaves of bread which represented the twelve tribes of Israel and bowls for the drink offering of wine. On the left, or south side, was the Golden Lampstand. In front of the veil that separated the two compartments stood the golden altar of incense. Behind the veil, God Himself dwelt in glory between the wings of the cherubim on the Ark of the Covenant above the Mercy Seat.

Now when they would burn incense, which was a daily function, Edersheim writes,

> Slowly the incensing priest and his assistants ascended the steps to the Holy place, preceded by the two priests who had formally dressed the altar and the candlestick, and who now removed the vessels they had left behind, and, worshipping, withdrew. Next, one of the assistants reverently spread the coals on the golden altar [the coals came from the bronze Altar of Sacrifice; God Himself had started that fire and the priests did not let that fire go out. They kept it burning and the coals that were used for burning the incense actually came from this sacrificial altar] the other arranged the incense [he did not put it on yet, just arranged it]; and then the chief officiating priest was left alone within the Holy Place to await the signal of the president [the High Priest] before burning the incense.

In other words, they would all go in and set it up, and everyone would leave except for the priest who had been chosen by lot to burn the incense. Edersheim writes,

> It was probably while thus expectant that the angel Gabriel appeared to Zacharias [Luke 1:8–11]. Remember while Zacharias was in the

Holy Place in the temple, the angel Gabriel appeared to him and told him that he would have a son who would be named John (Luke 1:8–13).

Edersheim continues,

> As the president gave the word of command which marked that "the time of incense had come," "the whole multitude of the people without" [outside] withdrew from the inner court [directly around the holy place] and fell down before the Lord, spreading their hands in silent prayer.

In other words, everyone would back away from the inner court around the Holy Place into the outer court of the temple. They would all fall down with their hands spread out in prayer.

> It is this most solemn period, when throughout the vast Temple buildings deep silence rested on the worshipping multitude, while within the sanctuary itself, the priest laid the incense on the golden altar, and the cloud of "odours" [5:8] rose up before the Lord, which serves as an image of the heavenly things in this description.

If you understand what is going on in the temple, you can see how much sense this part of Revelation makes. In his vision, John is seeing a worship service in heaven. Remember, the temple service had been patterned after what Moses had seen at Mt. Sinai. Here John sees the prayers of the saints, the incense, going up before God. That was the symbolism. When the priest would go in and burn incense on the golden altar, it represented the prayers of the saints going up before God. In the temple service that Edersheim is describing, all the people are backing away, bowing down to God, and spreading out their hands in prayer. The whole temple area is silent in worshipful prayer before God. I believe that is what we see here in Revelation chapter 8.

Edersheim points out that the practice of folding the hands together in prayer dates from the fifth century of our era and is of purely Saxon origin. The bowing of the heads and the folding of the hands is not traditional Jewish worship. The Jews actually stood up to pray with their hands held up in the air.

We bow our heads or bow down in a sign of reverence. But what is important is that your heart is reverent. The position of your body is not essential. As Christians, we bow our heads as a sign of reverence to God, as a sign of submission, and there are scriptures that support that.

> Another angel came and stood at the altar, holding a golden censer; and much incense was given to him, that he might add it to the prayers of all the saints upon the golden altar which was before the throne.

Notice that the incense here represents the prayers of the saints. In fact, Revelation 5:8 states,

> When He had taken the book, the four living creatures and the twenty-four elders fell down before the Lamb, each one holding a harp, and golden bowls full of incense, which are the prayers of the saints.

What we should understand in the symbolism here is that the golden altar of incense continuously had incense burning before God. This tells us that there ought to be continuous prayer from the people of God. Not that we have to be on our knees in prayer twenty-four hours a day; obviously we could not do that, but our lives should be lived in an attitude of prayer. When you are driving down the freeway, you can pray. Please do not bow your head in the Saxon form. Keep your head up and your eyes open in the Israelite form and pray. We need to have every thought captive to Christ; that is the attitude we need to have as Christians. We ought to be in constant communication with God. That is what is represented here.

In our culture, we are too often compartmentalized. We pray at a particular time, we eat at a particular time, we go to work at a particular time, and we worship God on a particular day. But our lives ought to be in a continual relationship with God and in continuous communication with Him. That is what we see in the continuous smoke of the incense.

> Then the angel took the censer; and he filled it with the fire of the altar and threw it to the earth; and there followed peals of thunder and sounds and flashes of lightning and an earthquake.

A censer is a pan or container which held the coals which were placed on the golden altar to burn the incense. Why in the world would the angel take the censer, fill it with the fire of the altar, and throw it to the earth, and then all these terrible things begin to happen? That too comes from Old Testament symbology. In the Old Testament, God speaks of putting a city under the ban. The word is *corban*, which means dedicated to God. It is dedicated as a sacrifice to God. Nothing in the city belongs to men; it all belongs to God. The fire that was used to bring the judgment of God upon the city came from the altar of sacrifice. When fire was brought into the city, it was brought from the altar of sacrifice, and the city was burned to the ground.

The city of Jericho was put under the ban (Joshua 6:17), and everything was supposed to be burned as a sacrifice to God, as a judgmental sacrifice to God. Achan, of course, took the gold and silver and the beautiful mantle which belonged to God. As a result, the Israelites were defeated at Ai. Achan was stealing from God. That is why God condemned he and his whole family.

> And there followed peals of thunder and sounds and flashes of lightning and an earthquake.

What John sees here is a vision of the judgment of God. As Chilton and others have pointed out, the same words were used when God came down on Mt. Sinai to give the Law. There were peals of thunder, this incredible cloud, flashes of lightning, a horrendous noise which the Israelites could not stand. They sent Moses to talk to God because they feared they would die if they heard the voice of God in judgment. The Israelites told Moses, "We will listen to you, we do not want to listen to God." The words being used here—the "peals of thunder and sounds and flashes of lightning and an earthquake"—are speaking about God's judgment upon Israel. That is further verified as we proceed.

> And the seven angels who had the seven trumpets prepared themselves to sound them. The first sounded, and there came hail and fire, mixed with blood, and they were thrown to the earth; and a third of the earth was burned up, and a third of the trees were burned up, and all the green grass was burned up. The second angel sounded, and *something* like a great mountain burning with fire was thrown into the sea; and a third of the sea became blood, and a third of the creatures, which were in the sea and had life, died; and a third of the ships were destroyed. The third angel sounded, and a great star fell from heaven, burning like a torch, and it fell on a third of the rivers and on the springs of waters. The name of the star is called Wormwood; and a third of the water's became wormwood, and many men died from the waters, because they were made bitter. (Revelation 8:6–11)

If we interpret Revelation in a strictly literal sense, this has obviously not yet happened. But if it is symbolic—as I believe it is—if it is using Old Testament symbols to tell the Christians of the first century about God's grace, God's mercy, and that God was going to be with them and if it is pointing out that God was going to pour out judgment against Israel and the Roman system, that He was going to protect the Christians, then it is much easier to explain these things.

> The first sounded, and there came hail and
> fire, mixed with blood.

That should remind everyone of the plagues of the judgment of God upon the gods of Egypt. Remember, when God promised to bring the Israelites out of Egypt, He told Moses,

> I will harden [Pharaoh's] heart so that he
> will not let the people go. (Exodus 4:21)

God brought ten plagues upon the Egyptian gods; one of which was fire and hail. Very large hail came down and broke down the plants and killed people who refused to understand. Fire came down out of heaven and ran along the ground (Exodus 9:22–25). Just as Exodus shows us the judgment of God upon the disobedient nation of Egypt, the Revelation shows us the judgment of God upon the disobedient nation of Israel.

Remember that in Exodus, Moses dipped his staff into the Nile, and all the water became blood. We see the same kind of imagery in verse 8. The Israelites, most of whom were familiar with the Old Testament and understood the plagues against Egypt were a sign of the judgment of God, would have known this part of John's vision was referring to the judgment of God. Remember, these plagues are being done to the ungodly, the enemies of God's people. This is judgmental language. What is in view here is the terribleness of the judgment of God, the hail, and the fire and the blood.

> The second angel sounded, and *something*
> like a great mountain burning with fire was
> thrown into the sea; and a third of the sea became
> blood...

A great mountain burning with fire—has that happened yet? Maybe he is speaking of volcanoes...but "thrown into the sea"?

Daniel 9:20 says that Israel is the mountain of God. Also, in Jeremiah 51:24, God says,

> "But I will repay Babylon and all the inhabitants of Chaldea for all their evil that they have done in Zion before your eyes declares the LORD. Behold, I am against you, O destroying mountain. Who destroys the whole earth," declares the LORD, "And I will stretch out My hand against you, and roll you down from the crags and I will make you a burnt out mountain. And they will not take from you *even* a stone for a corner nor a stone for foundations, But you will be desolate forever," declares the LORD.

Zion is the mountain of God. Zion represented Israel. In Jeremiah God is condemning Babylon and Chaldea for all the evil they have done in Israel, and He is speaking of Babylon as a destroying mountain.

David Chilton, in *The Days of Vengeance*, points out that here in the Revelation, God is speaking of Israel in terms of Babylon. That apostate Israel, by their disobedience, have demonstrated they are not part of the family of God. By their incredible rebellion, by their ignorance, by their ignoring what God had commanded them to do, they are now being spoken about in terms of Babylon. They are the burning mountain that is going to be thrown into the sea. Judgment is coming upon Israel.

Chilton points out that believing people understood this and that the Christians prayed for God's judgment upon the apostate Jews.

> God reins down his judgments upon the earth in specific response to the liturgical worship of His people. As part of the formal, official

> worship service in heaven, the angel of the altar offers up the prayers of the corporate people of God; and God responds to the petitions, acting into history on behalf of the saints. The intimate connection between liturgy and history is an inescapable fact, one that we cannot afford to ignore... The point here is that the official worship of the covenantal community is cosmically significant. Church history is the key to world history.

That is what we as a church do not understand today.

What I believe we see here in the Revelation is God symbolically pouring out judgment upon Jerusalem. It is a prophecy of His coming judgment in AD 70. There is a pattern here. Notice that when the seventh seal was opened, there were seven trumpets given to the angels. When the seventh trumpet sounds, there are seven bowls of the wrath of God. The pattern of sevens indicates the Scripture is speaking of the complete judgment of God upon Jerusalem.

In Isaiah 14:12–15, we read that God says through the prophet Isaiah,

> How you have fallen from heaven, O star of the morning, son of the dawn! You have been cut down to the earth, you who have weakened the nations! But you said in your heart, "I will ascend to heaven; I will raise my throne above the stars of God, and I will sit on the mount of assembly in the recesses of the north. I will ascend above the heights of the clouds; I will make myself like the Most High." Nevertheless you will be thrust down to Sheol, to the recesses of the pit.

God is prophesying through Isaiah specifically against Babylon. He is predicting judgment (verse 4) "against the king of Babylon." What God is predicting here is the destruction of the king of Babylon who said, "I am going to make myself like God." The passage may also be speaking about Satan because he said, "I am going to put myself above God." That was his sin. By the way, that is our sin too. "I want to be like God." That was the temptation in the garden and that is the ultimate sin. We want to be like God knowing good and evil.

> Therefore thus says the LORD of hosts, the God of Israel, "behold, I will feed them, this people, with wormwood and give them poisoned water to drink. I will scatter them among the nations, whom neither they nor their fathers have known; and I will send the sword after them until I have annihilated them." (Jeremiah 9:15–16)

Who is God prophesying about? Look back up to verse 11–15:

> And I will make Jerusalem a heap of ruins, a haunt of jackals; and I will make the cities of Judah a desolation, without inhabitant. Who is the wise man that may understand this? And *who is* he to whom the mouth of the LORD has spoken, that he may declare it? Why is the land ruined, laid waste like a desert, so that no one passes through? The LORD said, "Because they have forsaken My law which I set before them, and have not obeyed My voice nor walked according to it, but have walked after the stubbornness of their heart and after the Baals, as their fathers taught them," therefore thus says the LORD of hosts, the God of Israel, "behold, I will feed them, this people [Israel, Judah], with wormwood and give them poisoned water to drink."

What is being prophesied in the Revelation is exactly what Jeremiah was prophesying—that God would pour out upon Israel

His judgment because of their disobedience. I do not think this is some futuristic incredible thing that is yet to occur. I think this is something the believing Jewish Christians would have understood, because they understood Isaiah, Jeremiah, and the Psalms. They understood the temple worship, and they understood that what God was speaking about here was His judgment against ungodly Israel.

These Jewish background believers were steeped in the Old Testament. Instantly, when they heard about the seven trumpets, they would be thinking temple liturgy. When they heard wormwood, they would be thinking of Jeremiah's prophecy against Jerusalem. When they heard of the burning mountain, they would be thinking of Isaiah and his prophecy against Jerusalem as Babylon.

CHAPTER 24

The Fifth and Sixth Trumpet

Then the fifth angel sounded, and I saw a star from heaven which had fallen to the earth; and the key of the bottomless pit was given to him. He opened the bottomless pit; and smoke went up out of the pit, like the smoke of a great furnace; and the sun and the air were darkened by the smoke of the pit. And out of the smoke came forth locusts upon the earth; and power was given them, as the scorpions of the earth have power. They were told not to hurt the grass of the earth, nor any green thing, nor any tree, but only the men who do not have the seal of God on their foreheads. And they were not permitted to kill anyone, but to torment for five months; and their torment was like the torment of a scorpion when it stings a man. And in those days men will seek death and will not find it; they will long to die and death flees from them. The appearance of the locusts was like horses prepared for battle; and on their heads appeared to be crowns like gold, and their faces were like the faces of men. They had hair like the hair of women, and their teeth were like *the teeth* of lions. They had breast-

plates of iron; and the sound of their wings was
like the sound of chariots, of many horses rushing to battle. They have tails like scorpions, and
stings, and in their tails is their power to hurt
men for five months. They have as king over
them, the angel of the abyss; his name in Hebrew
is Abaddon, and in the Greek he has the name
Apollyon. (Revelation 9:1–11)

What or who is the star from heaven? I believe it is Lucifer or Satan.
What leads to that conclusion? Remember when we looked at chapter 8:10–11,

> The third angel sounded, and a great star fell
> from heaven, burning like a torch, and it fell on
> a third of the rivers and on the springs of waters;
> The name of the star is called Wormwood.

We noted the fact that this is a reference to Isaiah 14:12–15
where Isaiah is prophesying about Babylon. He was predicting that
because Babylon, particularly Nebuchadnezzar, had said, "I, myself,
have built this great kingdom." God was going to bring judgment
upon him. Babylon was one of the greatest cities that the world had
ever seen. God took this great star and brought it down. But most
commentators believe (and I also believe) the passage is also speaking
about Lucifer (his name means "Lightbearer")—that he was a star,
he was an angel. He refused to obey God, and he fell from heaven
and became the prince of this world. In Luke 10:17–19, when the
seventy whom Jesus sent out "returned with joy, saying, 'Lord, even
the demons are subject to us in Your name.' He said to them, 'I was
watching Satan fall from heaven like lightning. Behold, I have given
you authority to tread on serpents and scorpions, and over all the
power of the enemy, and nothing will injure you.'"

Notice also that Jesus tells His disciples He has given them
"authority to tread on serpents and scorpions and over all the power
of the enemy, and nothing will injure you." More about that later.

In Jeremiah 9:15, we read that Jeremiah speaks of feeding wormwood to Israel. God says of Israel, because they have not believed, because they have been disobedient, "I will feed them, this people, with wormwood." Then in Jeremiah 23:15, God repeats that promise of judgment. In Amos 5:7, God condemns Israel for having turned justice into wormwood. He is saying that He is going to make things bitter for them. He is going to bring about judgment upon Israel because they were acting like Babylon. They were saying, "We ourselves have done all of this," and they were not giving credit to God. Isaiah is writing about the prophecy against Babylon; then Jeremiah refers that to Israel. God is saying, in effect, Israel has become like Babylon—a pagan nation.

With that background, remember that the people of the seven churches to whom John was writing would have understood. They knew the Old Testament backward and forward. They would have understood that God was saying, "I am going to bring judgment against Jerusalem."

This key of the bottomless pit is given to Satan himself. This bottomless pit, the word here means *abyss*, is referred to seven times in Revelation. Where did Satan get the key? It was given to him. It came from God. What we need to understand is that even in this, God is in control. He gives the key of the abyss to this fallen angel, to Satan, and allows him to open it. What comes out? Smoke.

> He opened the bottomless pit; and smoke
> went up out of the pit, like the smoke of a great
> furnace; and the sun and the air were darkened
> by the smoke of the pit. Then out of the smoke
> came forth locusts upon the earth.

These were not ordinary locusts.

Does the five-month period during which the locusts were allowed upon the land have any significance? Yes, everything in Scripture has significance. David Chilton, in *The Days of Vengeance* asks,

> Why does the locust plague last for five
> months? This figure is first of all a reference to

> the period of five months from May through
> September when locusts normally appeared.

Locusts actually appear during a five-month period of the year. He points out that though they appear all through that period, they do not actually live for the whole five months.

> The unusual feature here is that *these* locusts
> *remain* for the entire period.

Locusts normally live about one week, but they actually appeared during this whole period.

While we may not be able to say with certainty what the locusts refer to, what we can know is that whatever the locusts were symbols of, God limited their power. They were not allowed to hurt anything except those who did not have the seal of God on their forehead. Remember, that refers to Ezekiel 9:4 where God tells the man clothed in linen, the one with a writing case to, "put a mark [Hebrew letter *tav*; pronounced 'tove'] on the foreheads of" those who are believers. Remember also the original form of the Hebrew letter was a cross. The locusts were only able to torment for five months those who did not have the mark of Christ. This was all in God's plan.

What we as Christians need to remember is that we do not have to worry about this torment. Even if it is futuristic, it is only going to happen to those who are not Christian, who do not have the seal of God on their forehead. Those who believe in Jesus Christ as their Lord and Savior have the mark of the ownership of God on them. Remember that a seal in those days was a mark of ownership. If you are truly a part of the body of Christ, the church, you are under the protection of God. Romans 8:1 states,

> Therefore there is now no condemnation
> for those who are in Christ Jesus.

You see, even if you believe in a future tribulation, when you read through the book of Revelation, there is never a case where the Christians suffer any of the judgment of God. Read carefully, and you will see the Christians are never under the judgment of God. He has already poured out His wrath for our sin upon His own Son, Jesus Christ.

> They have as king over them, the angel of the abyss; his name in Hebrew is Abaddon [that word in Hebrew means "destruction"] and in the Greek he has the name Apollyon.

In Greek, the word means "destroyer"; it has the same connotation. One is destruction, one is the destroyer; it is the same root. What does that tell us that Satan is trying to do? He is trying to destroy the work of God, the kingdom of Jesus Christ.

Genesis 1:1–2 tells us,

> In the beginning, God created the heavens and the earth. And the earth was formless and void.

It was chaos. It was abyss. What did God do? He brought order out of chaos. Satan is trying to bring chaos out of order. He is trying to create a false creation. Remember he is the father of lies. He is trying to undo what God does. He is trying to say, "God did not really say this." We need to understand that the chaos we see in our society today is a result of Satan. It is the work of sinfulness. We live in a world polluted by sin. We have the results of our old sinful nature hanging on. Even though God is bringing order into the universe through Jesus Christ, Satan is doing his best trying to bring disorder, trying to bring destruction. So those who have the mark of the beast, who serve Satan, are headed for destruction.

> The first woe is past; behold, two woes are still coming after these things. (Revelation 9:12)

Wait a minute! Demons from the pit, and this is only the first of three woes! Wow! We must be in big trouble! No, we are not, but the people under the judgment of God certainly were.

> The first woe is past; behold, two woes are still coming after these things. And the sixth angel sounded, and I heard a voice from the four horns of the golden altar which is before God, one saying to the sixth angel who had the trumpet, "Release the four angels who are bound at the great river Euphrates." And the four angels, who had been prepared for the hour and day and month and year, were released, so that they might kill a third of mankind. And the number of the armies of the horsemen was two hundred million; I heard the number of them. (9:12–16)

The sixth angel sounds his trumpet, and John hears a voice coming from the altar. What is significant about the golden altar? Remember, Revelation tells us that the smoke of the incense going up from the golden altar is the prayers of the saints.

Chilton points out that the Christians were praying for the destruction of the ungodly. It appears they were praying imprecatory prayers for the destruction of the Jewish system, the ungodly Jews who refused to obey God. Revelation very clearly teaches that in response to the prayers of the saints, God is sending out all these judgments upon Israel. So when this voice comes from the four horns from the golden altar of incense, what would these Christians understand? God is hearing my prayers! God is answering my prayers! I believe they would have clearly understood, and that would have been a great comfort to them.

John hears the voice of "one saying to the sixth angel who had the trumpet, 'Release the four angels who are bound at the great river Euphrates.'"

What is the significance of the great river Euphrates? That is where the Garden of Eden was. In Genesis 2:10, we are told,

> Now a river flowed out of Eden to water the garden; and from there it divided and became four rivers... And the fourth river is the Euphrates.

When you look at the Mediterranean, with Israel to the south and the Euphrates to the north, where did all the invaders of Israel come from? They came from the north, from the Euphrates. They crossed the Euphrates. The judgment of God was to come from the north.

In verse 15, it is important to notice three things. First, the four angels "had been prepared for the hour and day and month and year." The form of the original language is such that a particular hour in a particular day in a particular month and a particular year is meant. In other words, God had already decreed the exact time when these events would occur. Secondly, the verb form of "had been prepared" means that it was determined in the past with continuing results into the present and the future. Again, God had already determined when these angels would be released. The final thing to note is that the four angels were released "so that they might kill a third of mankind." The angels did this through the three plagues that came from the mouth of the horses. The text is very clear that it is the four angels who do the killing through the three plagues of fire, smoke, and brimstone (verse 18).

> And the number of the armies of the horsemen was two hundred million; I heard the number of them.

Normally, the New American Standard Bible (NASB) is a more literal translation, but the translators of the NASB, along with most every translation, do a terrible work here. Most translations say, "The number of the armies of the horsemen was two hundred million," but that is not what the text literally says. What the Greek actually says is that John states he "heard the number of the horsemen was double myriads myriads." In the Greek it is the same word and its double; the word for *myriad* doubled has *dis* in front of it, and then *myriads*, which is many. What John really writes in Greek is "double many, many"—in other words, "a lot, a huge number." It does not state a particular number. It is just a huge number. The translators state "two hundred million" to note it is a large number.

The final point to realize in this part of the passage is that even though a third of mankind was killed by the plagues of the four angels, the rest of mankind "did not repent of the works of their hands, so as not to worship demons, and the idols…and they did not repent of their murders nor of their sorceries nor of their immorality nor of their thefts."

All the people in view in this passage are unbelievers. It is the judgment of God upon their unbelief. Even though they see the futility of their rebellion and even though they see the judgment of God upon those around them, they do not repent and turn to God.

CHAPTER 25

The Seventh Angel

And I saw another strong angel coming down out of heaven, clothed with a cloud; and the rainbow was upon his head, and his face was like the sun, and his feet like pillars of fire; and he had in his hand a little book which was open. And he placed his right foot on the sea and his left on the land; and he cried out with a loud voice, as when a lion roars; and when he cried out, the seven peals of thunder uttered their voices. And when the seven peals of thunder had spoken, I was about to write; and I heard a voice from heaven saying, "Seal up the things which the seven peals of thunder have spoken, and do not write them." And the angel whom I saw standing on the sea and on the land lifted up his right hand to heaven, and swore by Him who lives forever and ever, who created heaven and the things in it, and the earth and the things in it, and the sea and the things in it, that there shall be delay no longer, but in the days of the voice of the seventh angel, when he is about to sound, then the mystery of God is finished, as He preached to His servants the prophets. (Revelation 10:1–7)

There should be no doubt in anyone's mind that this angel is Jesus Christ. He is clothed with a cloud. A rainbow is upon His head. His face is like the sun and His feet like pillars of fire. Remember John's description of Jesus in Revelation 1:15.

> His feet *were* like burnished bronze, when it
> has been caused to glow in a furnace.

David Chilton, in *The Days of Vengeance*, points out that this description is very much like what we see of God in Exodus at Mt. Sinai. The presence of God was represented by a pillar of fire and a pillar of cloud. M. G. Kline in *Images of the Spirit* proves—I think conclusively— that there were two pillars coming out of the Shekinah Glory Cloud that represented the presence of God. These pillars represented the legs, the feet of God standing upon the earth in the midst of His people. The fact that John sees the angel with His right foot on the sea and His left foot on the land represents His absolute dominion over all the earth. Ephesians 1:22 tells us that God "put all things in subjection under His [Christ's] feet and gave Him as head over all things to the church."

The rainbow upon the head of the angel would have reminded John's readers of Ezekiel's vison of God. In Ezekiel 1:27–28, the prophet writes,

> Then I noticed from the appearance of
> His loins...and downward I saw something like
> fire; and there was a radiance around Him. As
> the appearance of the rainbow in the clouds on a
> rainy day, so was the appearance of the surround-
> ing radiance. Such was the appearance of the like-
> ness of the glory of the LORD. And when I saw it,
> I fell on my face and heard a voice speaking.

In *Images of the Spirit*, M. G. Kline says of the voice of God,

> [It] is characteristically loud, arrestingly
> loud. It is likened to the crescendo of ocean and

storm, the rumbling of earthquake. It is the noise of war, the trumpeting of signal horns and the din of battle. It is the thunder of the storm-chariot of the warrior-Lord, coming in judgments.

Scripture consistently represents the voice of God coming in judgment as this incredibly loud, roaring sound. In Jeremiah 25:30, the prophet is told by God,

> Prophesy against [Jerusalem] all these words, and you shall say to them, "The LORD will roar from on high And utter His voice from His holy habitation; He will roar mightily against His fold. He will shout like those who tread the grapes, Against all the inhabitants of the earth."

David Chilton states in *The Days of Vengeance*,

> *In worshipful response to His Voice*, the seven peals of thunder uttered their voices.

Virtually everyone wonders what the seven peals of thunder uttered, but John is told by a voice from heaven to "seal up the things which the seven peals of thunder have spoken and do not write them." There are some things that God reveals to some men which others are not to know. Remember that the Apostle Paul states in 2 Corinthians 12:4 that he "was caught up into Paradise and heard inexpressible words, which a man is not permitted to speak."

> And the angel whom I saw standing on the sea and on the land lifted up his right hand to heaven, and swore by Him who lives forever and ever, who created heaven and the things in it, and the earth and the things in it, and the sea and the things in it, that there shall be delay no longer. (Revelation 10:5–6)

Some commentators believe that since the angel swears by God, "Him who lives forever and ever, WHO CREATED HEAVEN AND THE THINGS IN IT, AND THE EARTH AND THE THINGS IN IT, AND THE SEA AND THE THINGS IN IT" the angel cannot be Jesus Christ. They reason that would mean that God is swearing by Himself. But God repeatedly swears by Himself because there is nothing higher by which to swear. In *The Days of Vengeance*, David Chilton reminds us,

> The Lord God swears oaths throughout Holy Scripture (cf. Gen. 22:16; Isa. 45:23; Jer. 49:13; Amos 6:8), and in fact our salvation is based on God's faithfulness to His covenant oath, the ground of the Christian's assurance and hope (Heb. 6:13–20).

> But in the days of the voice of the seventh angel, when he is about to sound, then the mystery of God is finished, as He preached to His servants the prophets. (Revelation 10:7)

We should remember that mystery in Scripture is not something that needs to be solved but something that has been hidden and is now revealed. The Apostle Paul ends his letter to the church at Rome with these words:

> Now to Him who is able to establish you according to my gospel and the preaching of Jesus Christ, according to the revelation of the mystery which has been kept secret for long ages past, but now is manifested, and by the Scriptures of the prophets, according to the commandment of the eternal God, has been made known to all the nations, leading to obedience of faith; to the only wise God, through Jesus Christ, be the glory forever. Amen. (Romans 16:25–27)

Notice that although the mystery has been kept secret for long ages past, it is now manifested or made known by the Scriptures of the prophets. By the commandment of the eternal God, the mystery has been made known to all the nations…to obedience of faith.

When is the mystery of God made known? It is finished "in the days of the voice of the seventh angel, when he is about to sound."

When did the seventh angel sound? Revelation 11:15 tells us,

> And the seventh angel sounded; and there arose loud voices in heaven, saying, "The kingdom of the world has become the kingdom of our Lord, and of His Christ; and He will reign forever and ever."

When did the kingdom of the world become the kingdom of our Lord and of His Christ? The prophet Daniel writes in Daniel 7:13–14:

> I kept looking in the night visions, and behold, with the clouds of heaven one like a Son of Man [Jesus] was coming, and He came up to the Ancient of Days and was presented before Him. And to Him [Jesus] was given dominion, Glory and a kingdom, that all the peoples, nations, and men of every language might serve Him. His dominion is an everlasting dominion which will not pass away; and His kingdom is one which will not be destroyed.

I believe the mystery of God was made known by the work of Jesus Christ on the cross in our behalf. One of the last words of Jesus on the cross was, "It is finished!"

CHAPTER 26

Judgment against Jerusalem

Then there was given me a measuring rod like a staff; and someone said, "Get up and measure the temple of God and the altar, and those who worship in it. Leave out the court which is outside the temple and do not measure it, for it has been given to the nations; and they will tread under foot the holy city for forty-two months. And I will grant *authority* to my two witnesses, and they will prophesy for twelve hundred and sixty days, clothed in sackcloth." These are the two olive trees and the two lampstands that stand before the Lord of the earth. And if anyone desires to harm them, fire proceeds out of their mouth and devours their enemies; and if anyone would desire to harm them, in this manner he must be killed. These [the two witnesses] have the power to shut up the sky, in order that rain may not fall during the days of their prophesying; and they have power over the waters to turn them into blood, and to smite the earth with every plague, as often as they desire. And when they have finished their testimony, the beast that comes up out of the abyss will make war with them, and overcome them and kill them. And their dead bodies *will lie* in the street of the great city which mystically is called Sodom and Egypt, where also their Lord was crucified. And those from the peoples and tribes and tongues and nations *will* look at their dead bodies for three days and a half, and will not permit their dead bodies to be laid in a tomb. And those who dwell on the earth *will* rejoice over them and make merry; and they will send gifts to one another, because these two prophets tormented those who dwell on the earth. And after three days and a half the breath of life from God came into them, and they stood on their feet; and great fear fell upon those who were beholding them. And they heard a loud voice from heaven saying to them, "Come up here." And they went up into heaven in the cloud, and their enemies beheld them. And in that hour there was a great earthquake, and a tenth of the city fell; and seven thousand people were killed in the earthquake, and the rest were terrified and gave glory to the God of heaven. The second woe is past; behold, the third woe is coming quickly. (Revelation 11:1–14)

John is given a measuring rod and told to "measure the temple of God, and the altar, and those who worship in it." The thing to realize here is that John is told to measure the true temple of God, the church. In fact, he is specifically told to "leave out the court which is outside the temple, and do not measure it, for it has been given to the nations; and they will tread under foot the holy city for forty-two months." The word that is translated "leave out" is a word which is used in Scripture for excommunication, for "casting out" unbelievers. Those who are not the true temple or church of God are being given over to the nations (Gentiles) for judgment. Apostate Jerusalem is being "cast out" or excommunicated and given to the Gentile army under the Roman general Vespasian and his son, Titus, for destruction. Ralph E. Bass Jr. in his commentary *Back to the Future* includes the quote,

> Vespasian received his commission from Nero, and declared war on Jerusalem February, A. D. 67. The siege ended with the fall of Jerusalem, the burning of the city and temple, in August, A. D. 70. This computation of dates yields the forty-two months for Jerusalem to be "trodden under foot."

Who are the two witnesses who are going to prophesy for 1,260 days? By the way, 42 months is 1,260 days and also 3 1/2 years. One possibility for the two witnesses is Joshua and Zerubbabel, from the book of Zechariah. Another possibility is Moses and Elijah, the lawgiver and the prophet. In Herman Hoeksema's commentary on Revelation, *Behold He Cometh*, he writes there are as many theories as there are people who have written commentaries.

What does Zechariah tell us about the two lampstands? In Zechariah 4:1–3, the prophet writes,

> Then the angel who was speaking with me returned, and roused me as a man who is awakened from his sleep. And he said to me, "What do you see?" And I said, "I see, and behold, a lampstand all of gold with its bowl on the top of it, and its seven lamps on it with seven spouts belonging to each of the lamps which are on the top of it; also two olive trees by it, one on the right side of the bowl and the other on its left side."

What Zechariah sees in this vision is a lampstand that has two olive trees one on either side of the lampstand. We are told in

Scripture there are two golden pipes that are taking oil from these two olive clusters to the lampstand (verse 12).

> Then [Zechariah] answered and said to the angel who was speaking with me saying, "What are these, my lord?" So the angel who was speaking with me answered and said to me, "Do you not know what these are?" And I said, "No, my lord."

What does that tell us? Why in the world would the angel ask Zechariah if he knew what the symbols were, when Zechariah had just asked him, "What are these?" I think he is saying that Zechariah should have known what they were. How would Zechariah have known? He should have known from Scripture. I think clearly the angel is saying Zechariah should have known the answer to his question by studying Scripture.

> Then he answered and said to me, "This is the word of the LORD to Zerubbabel saying, 'Not by might nor by power, but by My Spirit,' says the LORD of hosts."

Who is Zerubbabel? His name means seed or offspring of Babylon. He was the grandson of a king of Judah and he rebuilt the rubble of Jerusalem. He was sent back in the initial wave of those returning from exile when King Cyrus put out his decree to rebuild Jerusalem and the temple. Zerubbabel was the governor of Jerusalem under King Cyrus. He led the people and began to rebuild the city during the time of Ezra and Nehemiah.

The question Zechariah is asking the angel, "What are these, my lord?" is what are the two olive trees. The angel answers,

> This is the word of the LORD to Zerubbabel saying, "Not by might nor by power, but by My Spirit," says the LORD of hosts. "What are you,

> O great mountain? Before Zerubbabel you will become a plain; and he will bring forth the top stone with shouts of "Grace, grace to it!" Also the word of the LORD came to me saying, "The hands of Zerubbabel have laid the foundation of this house, and his hands will finish it. Then you will know that the LORD of hosts has sent me to you. For who has despised the day of small things? But these seven will be glad when they see the plumb line in the hand of Zerubbabel—*these are* the eyes of the LORD which range to and fro throughout the earth."

What are the seven eyes of the LORD which range to and fro through the earth? The seven eyes of the LORD represent His Spirit, which represents His omnipresence—His complete eyesight, if you will, His perfect seeing of all things. The Spirit of God is everywhere. There is no place you can go and be hidden from the vision of God. In Psalm 139, David says, "if I ascend to the heights, you are there. If I descend to the depths, you are there. If I go anywhere, you are there."

The seven eyes that we see in the Old Testament, the seven eyes in Revelation represent the omnipresence of God, the omniscience of God, this all-knowing, all-present Spirit of God.

> Then I answered and said to him, "What are these two olive trees on the right of the lampstand and on its left?" And I answered the second time and said to him, "What are the two olive branches which are beside the two golden pipes, which empty the golden *oil* from themselves?" So he answered me saying, "Do you not know what these are?" And I said, "No, my lord." Then he said, "These are the two anointed ones, who are standing by the Lord of the whole earth." (Zechariah 4:11–14)

What is God's Word telling us here? What is the angel telling us through the prophet Zechariah? He is telling us these two olive branches are the two anointed ones who are standing by the Lord of the whole earth. Who stands by God? The Holy Spirit and Jesus Christ. What is the angel telling Zechariah? I believe he is saying the two witnesses are Jesus and the Holy Spirit. The name by which Jesus is called in the Old Testament is the Messiah; in Hebrew, the *meshiach*. The word literally means "the anointed." What is Jesus called in the New Testament? He is the Christ. *Christos* in Greek means "anointed." In the Old Testament, anointing represented authority. The king was anointed to show his authority was from God. The prophet Samuel anointed both Saul and David as kings over Israel. The priests were also anointed. Aaron, when he was made High Priest, and his sons when they were made priests under him were anointed with the oil that God had commanded Moses to make. Anointing symbolizes the outpouring of the Spirit, the anointing of the Holy Spirit, and the authority given to the person anointed. This person is set apart. This person is a representative, or a witness, of God.

Who are the two witnesses? As stated previously, I believe they are the witness of the Holy Spirit and Jesus Christ through the church. Remember, Scripture requires two witnesses to confirm every fact. First Timothy 5:19 teaches,

> Do receive an accusation against an elder except on the basis of two or more witnesses.

The Old Testament also requires two witnesses. Deuteronomy 19:15 states,

> A single witness shall not rise up against a man on account of any iniquity or any sin which he has committed; on the evidence of two or three witnesses a matter shall be confirmed.

The New American Standard Bible (NASB) reads in Zechariah 4:14, "anointed ones." Literally it is "sons of fresh oil." The term *anointed ones* is an interpretation; the translators realize that what is being written about here is an anointing, so they are using the term *anointed*, but literally it is "sons of fresh oil." The oil represented the Holy Spirit. Therefore, I think what we can see in Zechariah 4 is that the two witnesses that are being written about are the Holy Spirit and Jesus Christ. They are the two witnesses who testify to the faithfulness of God. God the Son and God the Holy Spirit testifying to the faithfulness of God the Father. Some might say, "Wait a minute. Can God testify to himself?" Yes. Why can He do that? Because He is God and He is the faithful one. He can swear by Himself and no other because He is the highest authority there is. There are many other interpretations of this passage; therefore, I am not adamant about this. But personally, I am convinced that the two witnesses are the Holy Spirit and Jesus Christ.

David Chilton in *The Days of Vengeance* has a different understanding. He writes,

> *The two witnesses are identified as the two olive trees and the two lampstands that stand before the Lord of the earth.* At this point the imagery becomes much more complex. St. John returns again to Zechariah's prophecy of the lampstand. The seven lamps on the lampstand are connected to two olive trees…from which flow an unceasing supply of oil, symbolizing the Holy Spirit's filling and empowering work in the leaders of His covenant people. The meaning of the symbol is summarized in Zechariah 4:6: "Not by might nor by power, but by My Spirit says the LORD of hosts." The same passage in Zechariah also speaks of two Witnesses, two *sons of oil* ("anointed ones"), who lead God's people: Joshua the *priest* and Zerubbabel the *king*… In brief, then, Zechariah tells us of an olive tree/lampstand complex repre-

senting the officers of the covenant: two Witness figures who belong to the royal house and the priesthood. The book of Revelation freely connects all of these speaking of two shining lampstands which are two oil-filled olive trees, which are also two Witnesses a king and a priest—representing a Spirit inspired prophetic testimony of the Kingdom of priests.

What Chilton suggests is that this is a combining of the types represented by the king and the priest of the Old Testament. The New Testament brings them together in the officers of the church. Who are the kings and the priests in the church today? All believers function as kings, priests, and prophets, in one sense. But specifically in an official, ordained capacity, we have kings, prophets, and priests in the Reformed church today. The ruling elder is functioning as the king. The teaching elder functions as the prophet. The deacons function as the priests. What Chilton is saying is that the two types, the prophetic function and the kingly function, are being brought together. All "representing a Spirit inspired prophetic testimony of the kingdom of priests." In other words, the New Testament church. A major aspect, he says, of John's message is that the new covenant church comes into the full inheritance of the promises as a true kingdom of priests. The royal priesthood in which all the Lord's people are prophets. As Christians, we all *function* as prophets, priests, and kings. We are a kingdom of priests who prophesy. What does it mean to prophesy? It means to proclaim God's Word to those around us who do not know Him. It means to explain God's Word. That is what the pastor of a church does every Sunday. He prophesies, not in the sense of foretelling the future, but forthtelling or explaining the Word of God.

Chilton goes on to say,

> St. John now speaks of the two witnesses in terms of the two great witnesses of the Old Testament, Moses and Elijah—the Law and the

Prophets. *If anyone desires to harm them, fire proceeds out of their mouth and devours their enemies.* In Numbers 16:35, fire came down from heaven at Moses' word and consumed the false worshippers who had rebelled against him; and similarly, fire fell from heaven and consumed Elijah's enemies when he spoke the word (2 Ki. 1:9–12).

The first passage is dealing with Korah's rebellion. Remember Korah and his followers questioned the authority of Moses and asked, "Who made you king over us? Who made you priest over us?" Korah and his followers wanted to have the same authority to lead as Moses had. Moses, in effect, said, "Okay, we will let God decide who is the leader." The ground opened up and swallowed Korah and his followers into Sheol. In another case fire came down out of heaven and consumed Nadab and Abihu. They were sons of Aaron, who was the high priest. Nadab and Abihu are specifically mentioned as the ones who went up to Mt. Zion when God gave Moses the law, and they ate on the mountain in the very presence of God, in the presence of the Shekinah glory cloud. God had told Israel through Moses, "When you bring fire in to burn the incense before Me, you must take the coals off the altar of sacrifice and you must bring the coals into the Holy Place (of the tabernacle), and you must burn the incense with those coals and those coals only." Remember that initially, the fire on the altar came down from God and consumed the first sacrifice. But Nadab and Abihu, in spite of the fact that they had had communion with God on Mt. Zion, when they came down from the mountain, they brought strange fire into the Holy Place before the Lord. They made their own fire and brought it in their fire pans. They came in to worship God in violation of His commandment, and what happened? Fire from heaven came down and consumed them. What does that tell us? We must follow the rules of God given to us in His Word, the Holy Scriptures. We must worship God only in the way God commands us to worship Him. In Reformed churches, we speak of the Regulative Principle of Worship. We do what God commands in His Word and nothing else.

> And if anyone desires to harm them, fire proceeds out of their mouth and devours their enemies... (Revelation 11:5)

We see the same idea in Jeremiah 5:14, which says,

> Therefore, thus says the LORD, the God of hosts, because you have spoken this word, behold I am making My words in your mouth fire and this people wood, and it will consume them.

How should we be fighting our enemies? With Scripture. That is the judgment fire of God. That is what God uses to testify to people. It is Jesus Christ, the incarnate Word. It is the Holy Spirit speaking through the Word of God that either convicts people of their sin and changes their heart and makes them become a Christian, *or* the Word of God consumes them by the judgment of God if they refuse to believe.

> When they have finished their testimony, the beast that comes up out of the abyss will make war with them, and overcome them and kill them. And their dead bodies *will lie* in the street of the great city which mystically is called Sodom and Egypt, where also their Lord was crucified. Those from the peoples and tribes and tongues and nations will look at their dead bodies for three and a half days, and will not permit their dead bodies to be laid in a tomb. And those who dwell on the earth *will* rejoice over them and celebrate; and they will send gifts to one another, because these two prophets tormented those who dwell on the earth. But after the three and a half days, the breath of life from God came into them, and they stood on their feet; and great fear fell upon those who were watching them. And they

heard a loud voice from heaven saying to them, "Come up here." Then they went up into heaven in the cloud, and their enemies watched them. And in that hour there was a great earthquake, and a tenth of the city fell; seven thousand people were killed in the earthquake, and the rest were terrified and gave glory to the God of heaven. The second woe is past; behold, the third woe is coming quickly. (Revelation 11:7–14)

David Chilton in *The Days of Vengeance* states,

> With the death of the witnesses their voice of condemnation is silenced and now those from the people and tribes and nations regard the church itself as dead. Openly displaying their contempt for God's people whose dead bodies lie unburied in the street under an apparent curse. For they will not permit their dead bodies to be laid in a tomb.

He notes several Old Testament references where that same idea appears. Chilton continues,

> The desire for insertion into the Promised Land in death was a central concern to the faithful Witness of the Old Covenant, as a pledge of their future resurrection... The oppression of the kingdom of priests by the heathen was often expressed in these terms.

He quotes Psalm 79:1–3.

> O God, the nations have invaded Thine inheritance;
> They have defiled Thy holy Temple;

They have laid Jerusalem in ruins.

They have given the dead bodies of Thy servants for food to the birds of the heavens, The
flesh of Thy godly ones to the beasts of the earth.

They have poured out their blood like water
out about Jerusalem;

And there is no one to bury them.

Remember that we are speaking about two things going on.
There is Old Testament symbology, which the people who were
steeped in the Old Testament would have understood. But I also
believe that beginning with chapter 11, this is a prophecy about the
judgment of God upon unbelieving Jerusalem. Therefore, when John
writes about measuring the temple of God, casting out the outer
court, giving it to the nations to tread the Holy City underfoot for
forty-two months, I believe he is writing about the Romans coming
in for three and one half years (forty-two months) and destroying the
city. It appears to everyone the Jewish believers have been destroyed.
The temple has been demolished. Even the Christians are being
killed and being persecuted by the Israelites and by the Romans. It
probably seemed to the Christians that the church was going to be
wiped out. Remember, I believe that Revelation is a letter of comfort
to the churches. God is promising that even though the testimony is
going to be put down for a while, it will be raised back up and the
church will survive.

Over and over again in Scripture there are references to a
short-term victory by the enemy. When Jesus died on the cross, the
unbelieving leadership of the Israelites thought they had won! This
rebellion has been put down! These Christians, this sect that was following this false leader, was destroyed! Yet I believe, as Chilton and
others have pointed out, what appeared to be a victory by the enemy
of God overcoming the Spirit and the Word is, in fact, in accordance
with the plan of God and He is still with His church.

Then the seventh angel sounded; and there
were loud voices in heaven, saying, "The king-

dom of the world has become the kingdom of our Lord and of His Christ; and He will reign forever and ever." And the twenty-four elders, who sit on their thrones before God, fell on their faces and worshiped God, saying, "We give You thanks, O Lord God, the Almighty, who are and who were, because You have taken Your great power and have begun to reign." (Revelation 11:15–17)

What is the significance of the sounding of the seventh angel? I believe the people of John's day would have immediately associated it with the Feast of Trumpets, one of the feasts which God commanded Israel to observe on an annual basis.

In an article titled "The Feast of Trumpets" at Ligonier Ministries, the author writes,

> Since the Feast of Trumpets marked the beginning of the civil calendar in ancient Israel, the Jews eventually came to refer to the holiday as *Rosh Hashanah*, which in the Hebrew literally means "head of the year" or New Year's Day. This day began the seventh month of the religious calendar (Tishri), a month in which the solemn Day of Atonement and the festive Feast of Booths were also celebrated (Lev. 23:23–44). In addition to a day of rest and special food offerings (Num. 29:1–6), all that Scripture prescribes for the Feast of Trumpets is a "blast of trumpets" (Lev. 23:23–25). While trumpets were blown on other occasions, it seems that at the Feast of Trumpets the instruments were sounded continuously from morning until evening.
>
> What was the purpose of the trumpet soundings? One answer is that the trumpet blast was a call for the people to assemble to hear the voice of God just as it was at the foot of Mt. Sinai. (Ex.

19:13). Given that the feast was celebrated even during the times God was not actively providing new revelation, it would seem that at every Feast of Trumpets there was an anticipation that the Lord might reveal Himself in power once more, especially to consummate the salvation of His people (Isa. 27). Seven is the number of completeness in Scripture, and the fact that the Feast of Trumpets was held in the seventh month of the year confirms this idea.

In a September 2000 article in the *Jews for Jesus Newsletter*, titled "The Feast of Trumpets: Background and Fulfillment," we read the following:

> Leviticus 23:23–27 maps out God's commandments concerning this festival: "Then the Lord spoke to Moses, saying, 'Speak to the children of Israel, saying: "In the seventh month, on the first day of the month, you shall have a sabbath-rest, a memorial of blowing of trumpets, a holy convocation. You shall do no customary work on it; and you shall offer an offering made by fire to the Lord.""
>
> The only other reference to this festival in the Torah (Pentateuch) is Numbers 29:1*ff.* Neither passage provides much information regarding the original meaning of this feast. But, by examining the text in Leviticus 23, we note that the day was to be a "*memorial*" with blowing of trumpets. This is our only clue. The word "memorial" indicates that the event to be remembered had taken place prior to this ordinance.
>
> To solve the puzzle, we must ask ourselves what extremely significant event, involving the blowing of trumpets, took place in the national

life of Israel? What spiritual event was of such great importance that God commanded the people to remember it every year? I believe the Bible points to one outstanding event—connected to the blowing of trumpets—that required memorializing.

When the ram's horn sounds a long blast, they shall come up to the mountain. So it came about on the third day, when it was morning, that there were thunder and lightning flashes and a thick cloud upon the mountain and a very loud trumpet sound, so that all the people who were in the camp trembled. And Moses brought the people out of the camp to meet God and they stood at the foot of the mountain. Now Mount Sinai was all in smoke because the Lord descended upon it in fire; and its smoke ascended like the smoke of a furnace, and the whole mountain quaked violently. When the sound of the trumpet grew louder and louder, Moses spoke and God answered him with thunder (Exodus 19:13*b*, 16–19).

In Exodus chapters 19 and 20, we read the account of God's appearance on Mount Sinai and the initial giving of the Ten Commandments. Exodus 19:5 depicts God inviting the children of Israel into a covenant: the Mosaic Covenant. In a spectacular revelation, God manifested His presence in the smoke and fire on Mount Sinai— as He came to covenant with His people amidst the sound of a trumpet that caused the people to tremble. They promised to do everything that the Lord commanded.

This cataclysmic event was to be stamped indelibly upon the memory of the people of Israel. Every year, at the Feast of Trumpets, those same-sounding trumpet blasts reminded Israel that they were a people under covenant; a nation who had accepted the responsibilities of being God's people. By doing so, the nation also prepared herself for the Day of Atonement, eight days later, when they would repent and find atonement for all they had done to break this covenant.

In *The Days of Vengeance*, David Chilton writes,

> In terms of the Biblical calendar the "seventh trumpet" was sounded on Tishri 1, the first day of the seventh month in the liturgical year... Rosh Hashanah, the Day of Trumpets.

Chilton then includes a long quote from Ernest L. Martin, *The Birth of Christ Recalculated*. Martin writes,

> Each of the Jewish months was officially introduced by the blowing of trumpets (Num. 10:10)...the last month (Tishri) was the last month for a trumpet introduction. This is one of the reasons that the day was called "the Day of Trumpets." The "last trump" in the series was always sounded on this day—so, it was the final trumpets' day (Lev. 23:24; Num. 29:1).
>
> This was the exact day that many of the ancient kings and rulers of Judah reckoned as their inauguration day of rule... Indeed, it was customary that the final ceremony in the coronation of kings was the blowing of trumpets...

Chilton continues,

> All this would naturally be in the minds of St. John and his first-century audience at the

mention of the great Seventh Trumpet. Now, he adds a new dimension of symbolism, by showing the Christian significance of Rosh Hashanah, that to which it has always pointed: The Day of Trumpets is the Beginning of the New World, the New Creation, the coronation-day of the King of kings, when He is enthroned as supreme Judge over the whole world.

In regard to the birth of Christ, Chilton writes,

> Sundown on September 11, 3 BC, was the beginning of Tishri 1 in the Jewish calendar—Rosh Hashanah, the Day of Trumpets! Martin summarizes, "The central theme of the Day of Trumpets is clearly that of enthronement of the great King of kings. This was the general understanding of the day in early Judaism—and it certainly is that of the New Testament. In Revelation 11:15 the seventh angel sounds his 'last trump' and the kingdoms of this world become those of Christ.

As both Martin and Chilton point out, John is referring his readers (and us) to the fact that Jesus Christ has been enthroned over all the kingdoms of the world.

> Then the seventh angel sounded; and there were loud voices in heaven, saying, "The kingdom of the world has become the kingdom of our Lord and of His Christ; and He will reign forever and ever." And the twenty-four elders, who sit on their thrones before God, fell on their faces and worshiped God, saying, "We give You thanks, O Lord God, the Almighty, who are and who were, because You have taken Your great power and have begun to reign." (Revelation 11:15–17)

CHAPTER 27

The Great Sign in Heaven

And a great sign appeared in heaven: a woman clothed with the sun, and the moon under her feet, and on her head a crown of twelve stars; and she was with child; and she cried out, being in labor and in pain to give birth. And another sign appeared in heaven: and behold, a great red dragon having seven heads and ten horns, and on his heads were seven diadems. And his tail swept away a third of the stars of heaven, and threw them to the earth. And the dragon stood before the woman who was about to give birth, so that when she gave birth he might devour her child. And she gave birth to a son, a male, who is to rule all the nations with a rod of iron; and her child was caught up to God and to His throne. And the woman fled into the wilderness where she had a place prepared by God, so that there she might be nourished for one thousand two hundred and sixty days. (Revelation 12:1–6)

John writes,

And a great sign appeared in heaven...

Many of those who believe in a futuristic interpretation of the Revelation would agree this part of John's letter is symbolic, since he clearly states that a sign appeared in heaven. But many also believe the rest of Revelation is literal. How might we respond to that?

Remember, in chapter 1, verse 1, John states this letter is,

> The revelation of Jesus Christ which God gave him to "sign" to his bondservants the things which must shortly take place.

Clearly, the Word of God is teaching us that the Revelation is a sign which God has given to teach His people about things which would shortly take place during the time of the Apostle John.

The word *sign* is used seven times in God's letter to His church through John. Remember that in Revelation there are repetitive issues, patterns that are seen. Three of the uses of the word *sign* occur in regard to heaven—the one here in chapter 12, verse 1; in chapter 12, verse 3; and in chapter 15, verse 1. Four of the uses of the word *sign* occur in regard to things happening on earth, and they are signs of what the wicked are doing, what the beast-powered prophets are doing to lead people astray.

Very clearly the sign John writes about here is referring to Jesus. Notice that it says the woman "gave birth to a son, a male *child*, who is to rule all the nations with a rod of iron; and her child was caught up to God and to His throne."

It is obvious that John is telling us about the Messiah. He is the One Who will rule the nations. He is the One Who will shepherd the nations with a rod of iron. King David, prophesying of the coming reign of God's Messiah, writes in Psalm 2:7–9,

> I will surely tell of the decree of YHWH: He said to Me, "You are My Son, Today I have begotten You. Ask of Me, and I will surely give the nations as Your inheritance, And the very ends of the earth as Your possession. You shall

break them with a rod of iron, You shall shatter them like earthenware."

Clearly, the "sign" of the Son Who would rule the nations with a rod of iron is a sign about Jesus. What is it saying about Jesus? Why would John write that "a great sign appeared in heaven: a woman clothed with the sun, and the moon under her feet, and on her head a crown of twelve stars"?

The Apostle Paul writes in Galatians 4:22–26,

> Abraham had two sons, one by the bond-woman and one by the free woman. But the son by the bondwoman was born according to the flesh, and the son by the free woman through the promise. This is allegorically speaking, for these women are two covenants: one proceeding from Mount Sinai bearing children who are to be slaves; she is Hagar. Now this Hagar is Mount Sinai in Arabia and corresponds to the present Jerusalem, for she is in slavery with her children. But the Jerusalem above is free; she is our mother.

Therefore, I believe the woman in Revelation 12:1 represents the heavenly Jerusalem. She is crowned with twelve stars which represent the twelve tribes of Israel.

But there may be much more included in the sign about which John tells us.

How many people today know the constellations of the Zodiac? Many have never even heard of the constellation Virgo, the Virgin. Does anyone today know how Virgo is portrayed in symbols? She actually has twelve stars in her crown. David Chilton writes in *The Days of Vengeance*,

> It is important to realize the relationship of all this to the very obvious astronomical symbolism in the text. The word St. John uses for

sign was the term used in the ancient world to describe the constellations of the Zodiac; St. John's model for this vision of the Church is the constellation of Virgo, which does have a "crown" of *twelve stars*. (There are twelve that are visible to the naked eye.) It seems likely that the twelve stars also represent the twelve signs of the Zodiac, from ancient times regarded as symbols of the twelve tribes of Israel.

Chilton then refers to a book titled *The Birth of Christ Recalculated*, written by Ernest Martin. Chilton writes,

> Prof. Ernest Martin carefully and painstakingly narrows down the probable date of Christ's' birth to sometime in September, 3 B. C. Martin then adds the icing to the cake: "In the period of Christ's' birth, the Sun entered the head position of the Woman (Virgo) about August 13, and exited from her feet about October 2. But the Apostle John saw the scene when the Sun "clothes" or "adorns" the Woman. This surely indicates that the position of the Sun in the vision was located somewhere mid-bodied of the Woman—between the neck and knees.(The Sun could hardly be said to 'clothe' the Woman if it were situated in her face or near her feet.)
>
> The only time in the year that the Sun could be in a position to 'clothe' this celestial Woman (to be mid-bodied) is when it was located between 150 and 170 degrees along the ecliptic (which is a line across the sky where the zodiacal signs are). This "clothing" of the Woman by the Sun occurs for a 20-day period each year. This 20-degree spread could indicate the general time when Christ was born. In 3 B. C., the Sun would

have entered this celestial region about August 27 and exited from it about September 15. If John in the Book of Revelation is associating the birth of Christ with the period when the Sun is mid-bodied to the Woman, then Christ would have had to be born within that 20-day period... Even today, astrologers recognize that the sign of Virgo is the one which has reference to a messianic world ruler to be born of a virgin...

There is another apparent key here. David Chilton points out,

> The key is the Moon. The apostle said it was located "under her feet." What does the word "under" signify in this case? Does it mean that the Woman of the vision was standing on the Moon when John observed it or does it mean that her feet were positioned slightly above the Moon? John does not tell us. This, however, is not of major consequence in using the Moon to answer our question, because it would only involve the difference of a degree or two... In the year 3 B. C., these two factors [the moon under the feet of Virgo and the sun midbodied] came to precise agreement for less than 2 hours, as observed from Palestine...on September 11... This is the only day in the whole year that this could have taken place.

Chilton continues,

> An added bonus: Sundown on September 11, 3 B. C., was the beginning of Tishri 1 in the Jewish calendar—Rosh Hashanah, the Day of Trumpets! Martin summarizes: "The central theme of the Day of Trumpets is clearly that of

enthronement of the great King of kings. This was the general understanding of the day in early Judaism—and it certainly is that of the New Testament. In Revelation 11:15 the seventh angel sounds his 'last trump' and the kingdoms of this world become those of Christ."

If Jesus was born on September 11, 3 BC, why does the church celebrate His birth on December 25? Chilton points out one possible reason in a footnote on page 302–303. He writes,

What about December 25, the traditional date of the Nativity? As Martin demonstrates, there were numerous startling astronomical phenomena taking place during the years 3–2 B. C. Chief among these celestial events was the fact that Jupiter, recognized by Jews and Gentiles alike as the "Planet of the Messiah," was located in Virgo's womb and standing still, directly over Bethlehem, on December 25, 2 B.C., when the Child was a little over a year old. (Matthew states that the holy family was settled in a house, not a stable, by the time the Magi visited [Matt. 2:11]. Moreover, Herod ordered the slaughter of the innocents "from two years old and under, according to the time which he had ascertained from the Magi" [Matt. 2:16] indicating that the Child was no longer a newborn.)

Now there is another interesting thing here. John writes in Revelation 12:3–4,

Then another sign appeared in heaven: and behold, a great red dragon having seven heads and ten horns, and on his heads were seven diadems. And his tail swept away a third of the stars of heaven and threw them to the earth. And the dragon stood before the woman who was about to give birth, so that when she gave birth he might devour her child.

Who is this great red dragon? Verse 9 tells us,

And the great dragon was thrown down, the serpent of old who is called the devil and Satan, who deceives the whole world...

Interestingly, in the zodiac constellations at this particular time, the constellation of Scorpio was stretched across the sky. The sign of Scorpio was also known in ancient times as the dragon. Those who have investigated this (Chilton, Martin, and others) believe that what John is writing about is the time of the birth of Christ. The serpent, the great dragon, who is called the devil and Satan, is waiting to devour the Christ-Child.

Chilton writes,

The Dragon's goal is to abort the work of Christ, to devour and kill Him... This conflict between Christ and Satan was announced in Genesis 3:15, the war between the two seeds, the Seed of the Woman and the seed of the Serpent.

That is the message throughout the entire Bible. Satan, the devil, the serpent is trying to disrupt God's plan and destroy the seed of the woman, but her seed will crush the head of the seed of the serpent. We see that in the struggle between Jacob and Esau, which began in the womb of Rebekah and with God's promise that the older would serve the younger. We see it in the story of Jael in Judges 4:21. She drove a tent peg into the head of Sisera, the enemy of Israel. We see it in the story of the wicked king Abimelech in Judges 9:53, whose head was crushed by a millstone thrown from a tower by a woman.

Chilton continues,

> This pattern comes to a dramatic climax
> at the birth of Christ, when the Dragon pos-
> sesses King Herod, the Edomite ruler of Judea,
> and inspires him to slaughter the children of
> Bethlehem (Matt. 2:13–18).

In spite of the fact that the dragon attempts to destroy the child of the woman, whom many believe is Israel from whom the Messiah will come, God clearly protects her.

> And the woman fled into the wilderness
> where she had a place prepared by God, so that
> there she might be nourished for one thousand
> two hundred and sixty days. (Revelation 12:6)

Why 1,260 days? We need to remember the Jews used a lunar calendar of twelve thirty-day months (360 days). In that case, the 1,260 days works out to be three and one half years, or forty-two months. Clearly, this number is symbolic in Scripture. Remember that God told John the Gentiles would tread the Holy City underfoot for forty-two months.

What we should see here is that God protected the woman (Israel, from whom the Messiah would come) in the wilderness for 1,260 days. We should also remember this is not strictly historical as we might read it, it is symbolic. The numbers were symbols to which the Jewish Christians of John's day would have related. It is interesting that although Israel was protected by God in the wilderness for forty years, there were forty-two camps in the wilderness. Additionally, the genealogy of Jesus in Matthew 1:1–17 includes forty-two generations.

In Revelation 12:14 we are told,

> And the two wings of the great eagle were
> given to the woman, in order that she might fly

into the wilderness to her place, where she was
nourished for a time and times and half a time,
from the presence of the serpent.

Again, we see the symbol of time times and half a time (3 1/2),
or 1, 260, or 42.

While we tend to read the words of John's letter in a linear and
literalistic way, we need to remember his writing is symbolic. It is a
Revelation of or about Jesus Christ. In Revelation chapter 12, John
telescopes the entire history of the earthly ministry of Jesus Christ
from His birth until He is caught up to heaven in His ascension. His
point here is to ensure the people of God that the Lord's Anointed
One completely escapes the power of the dragon.

CHAPTER 28

Persecution by the Beast (Revelation 13:1–10)

> And he stood on the sand of the seashore.
> (Revelation 13:1)

Who is the *he* that is referred to in this verse? If in fact it is a *he*. The New American Standard Bible (NASB) has a marginal note that states some manuscripts read, "I stood on the sand of the seashore." Other translations, such as the New American Standard Update (NASU), state, "The dragon stood on the sand of the seashore." This should not confuse us or make us think that Scripture is wrong. Rather, the translators want to be very fair, and since there are some manuscript copies which read "And *I* stood on the sand of the seashore" and others that read "*He* stood on the sand of the seashore," the translators insert a note so that people are aware there are differences. In the NASU, the translators have decided it is "he" but have inserted "the dragon" because the previous verse is speaking of the dragon. Very likely the word is actually "he" because the majority of the manuscript copies are referring back to the dragon. Therefore, we should accept the NASB,

> And he (the dragon) stood on the sand of
> the seashore. And I saw a beast coming up out of

the sea, having ten horns and seven heads, and on his horns were ten diadems, and on his heads were blasphemous names. And the beast which I saw was like a leopard, and his feet were *like those* of a bear, and his mouth like the mouth of a lion. And the dragon gave him his power and his throne and great authority.

Who is standing on the sand of the seashore? The dragon. What is coming up out of the sea? A beast. If you look back to Revelation 12:3, you will notice it reads, "And another sign appeared in heaven: and behold, a great red dragon having seven heads and ten horns, and on his heads were seven diadems." Who is the great red dragon? John tells us in Revelation 12:9, "[He is] the serpent of old who is called the devil and Satan, who deceives the whole world."

What is going on here is that John is describing the political entity of the Roman Empire that received its power from Satan.

Nearly all commentators agree the beast being described is Rome. Several point out that the beast is coming up out of the sea. Not only did the Jews consider the sea a biblical metaphor for the nations or the Gentiles, the sea was also a metaphor for the chaos of evil. It would also appear to the Christians that Rome was rising out of the sea as it came from the west.

In verse 2, John describes the beast "as like a leopard, and his feet were *like those* of a bear, and his mouth like the mouth of a lion. And the dragon gave him his power and his throne and great authority."

Where else in Scripture have we seen a beast that looks like a leopard, a beast that looks like a bear, and a beast that looks like a lion? These three are listed in reverse order in Daniel 7:3–6. In that vision, Daniel is describing three world kingdoms that will arise and lead to a fourth kingdom, the Roman Empire. He describes that kingdom as a "fourth beast, dreadful and terrifying and extremely strong…and it had ten horns."

Daniel tells us the ten horns are ten kings who will arise in the time of the fourth beast. Therefore, they must be ten rulers of the

Roman Empire. Although Scripture does not detail who the ten rulers are, we can know for certain that their power comes from Satan.

> And *I saw* one of his heads as if it had been slain, and his fatal wound was healed. And the whole earth was amazed *and followed* after the beast; and they worshipped the dragon, because he gave his authority to the beast; and they worshipped the beast, saying, "Who is like the beast, and who is able to wage war with him?" And there was given to him [the beast] a mouth speaking arrogant words and blasphemies; and authority to act for forty-two months was given to him. And he opened his mouth in blasphemies against god, to blaspheme His name and His tabernacle, *that is,* those who dwell in heaven And it was given to him [the beast] to make war with the saints and to overcome them; and authority over every tribe and people and tongue and nation was given to him. And all who dwell on the earth will worship him, *everyone* whose name has not been written from the foundation of the world in the book of life of the Lamb who has been slain. If anyone one has an ear, let him hear. (Revelation 13:3–9)

Note that everyone "whose name has not been written in the book of life of the Lamb who has been slain" are those who worship the dragon. Those who are not saved (their names are not in the book of life of the Lamb) are the ones who worship the dragon and the beast to whom he gave power.

Remember, John was writing to Christians who were shortly to undergo intense persecutions by the Roman government and by the Jews. The Christians were persecuted by the Romans as traitors and idolaters because they would not vow obedience to the Roman Emperor as a god. The only requirement to live in peace in the empire was to burn incense to the emperor and declare, "Caesar is Lord." Since the Christians believed there was only one Lord and God, they refused to do so. Christians were persecuted by the Jews who believed they were a blasphemous sect who did not worship the one true God.

The great fire in Rome started in the coliseum in July AD 64. Although no one really knows who or how it started, the Roman emperor Nero blamed the Christians and began to persecute them. That persecution lasted from November AD 64 until the death of Nero in June AD 68, a period of forty-two months.

An additional period John may have had in mind is noted by Ralph E. Bass, Jr. in his commentary *Back to the Future*. He states,

> Vespasian (a Roman General) received his commission from Nero, and declared war on Jerusalem February, A. D. 67. The siege ended with the fall of Jerusalem, the burning of the city and temple, in August, A. D. 70. This computation of dates yields the forty-two months for Jerusalem to be "trodden under foot."

A very important point to remember is that the beast (the Roman government) was given his power by the dragon. Who is it that gives the dragon his power? It is God. He is sovereign over all of creation, even Satan. It is God who places any governing authority in power.

Romans 13:1 states,

> There is no authority except from God, and those which exist are established by God.

That is why we must not resist the governing authorities unless we are commanded by them to do what is contrary to the Word of God. The early Christians were willing to live as good citizens in the Roman Empire, but they were not willing to acknowledge that Caesar, a mere man, was Lord or God.

Additionally, we need to remember that even when the government is against us as Christians and even if we are being persecuted,

God is still in control. Romans 8:28 teaches us "that God causes all things to work together for good to those who love God, to those who are called according to *His* purpose" (NASB).

Remember what happened to Joseph. He was sold into slavery by his brothers, and they told his father Joseph had been killed. Joseph lived seventeen years as a prisoner and a slave before God raised him up to be the most powerful man in the known world. He was second only to Pharaoh, who was considered to be a god. At the end of the book of Genesis, after the father of Joseph and his brothers had died, they realized Joseph had the power of life or death. His brothers went to him and begged his forgiveness for their sin against him and pledged to be his servants.

Joseph acknowledges that their actions were sinful, but he also points out that God used their sinful acts for good. In Genesis 50:20, Joseph says,

> As for you, you meant evil against me, but
> God meant it for good in order to bring about
> this present result, to preserve many people alive.

The Apostle Peter makes the same point in Acts 2:22–23 when he preaches,

> Men of Israel, listen to these words: Jesus
> the Nazarene, a man attested to you by God with
> miracles and wonders and signs which God per-
> formed through Him in your midst, just as you
> yourselves know—this Man, delivered over by
> the predetermined plan and foreknowledge of
> God, you nailed to a cross by the hands of godless
> men and put Him to death.

Peter states very clearly that although the crucifixion of Jesus Christ was carried out by the hands of godless Jews and Romans, it was also done according to the predetermined plan and foreknowledge of God.

In other words, the most wicked act in all of history, the crucifixion of the sinless Son of God, was caused by the predetermined plan of God to bring about the salvation of His people.

What that means for us as Christians is that even though we may suffer persecution by governments or people given power by Satan, God is in control and will use even wicked events to bring about good for His people.

CHAPTER 29

The Mark of the Beast (Revelation 13:11–18)

Then I saw another beast coming up out of the earth; and he had two horns like a lamb and he spoke as a dragon. He exercises all the authority of the first beast in his presence. And he makes the earth and those who dwell in it to worship the first beast, whose fatal wound was healed. He performs great signs, so that he even makes fire come down out of heaven to the earth in the presence of men. And he deceives those who dwell on the earth because of the signs which it was given him to perform in the presence of the beast, telling those who dwell on the earth to make an image to the beast who had the wound of the sword and has come to life. And it was given to him to give breath to the image of the beast, so that the image of the beast would even speak and cause as many as do not worship the image of the beast to be killed. And he causes all, the small and the great, and the rich and the poor, and the free men and the slaves, to be given

> a mark on their right hand or on their forehead,
> and *he provides* that no one will be able to buy or
> to sell, except the one who has the mark, *either*
> the name of the beast or the number of his name.
> Here is wisdom. Let him who has understanding
> calculate the number of the beast, for the number
> is that of a man; and his number is six hundred
> and sixty-six. (Revelation 13:11–18)

John writes that he saw another beast coming up out of the land. In most translations the word is translated *earth*, but in the Revelation, the Greek word typically refers to "the land of Israel." This beast who comes up out of the land of Israel is the false prophet about which Jesus had warned His disciples. In Matthew 24, Jesus is teaching His disciples (Peter, James, John, and Andrew) what they would experience at the end of the Jewish age. He states in verse 5,

> Many will come in My name, saying, "I am
> the Christ," and will mislead many.

In verse 11, Jesus states,

> Many false prophets will arise and will mis-
> lead many.

In verse 24, Jesus states,

> For false Christs and false prophets will arise
> and will show great signs and wonders, so as to
> mislead, if possible, even the elect.

Moses had prophesied in Deuteronomy 13:1–5,

> If a prophet or a dreamer of dreams arises
> among you and gives you a sign or a wonder, and
> the sign or the wonder comes true, concerning

which he spoke to you, saying, "Let us go after other gods (whom you have not known) and let us serve them," you shall not listen to the words of that prophet or that dreamer of dreams; for YHWH your God is testing you to find out if you love YHWH your God with all your heart and with all your soul. You shall follow YHWH your God and fear Him; and you shall keep His commandments, listen to His voice, serve Him, and cling to Him. But that prophet or that dreamer of dreams shall be put to death, because he has counseled rebellion against YHWH your God who brought you from the land of Egypt and redeemed you from the house of slavery, to seduce you from the way in which YHWH your God commanded you to walk. So you shall purge the evil from among you.

Notice that Moses tells us that the false prophet, in order to deceive the people, will even be able to perform signs and wonders that come true. Moses warns that the people should not listen to the words of the false prophet, even if those signs and wonders come true. They should follow God and keep His commandments. Jesus, in Matthew 24, teaches that the false prophets will mislead (or deceive) many.

This beast from the land of Israel is specifically identified as a false prophet in Revelation 19:20:

And the beast was seized, and with him the false prophet who performed the signs in his presence, by which he deceived those who had received the mark of the beast and those who worshiped his image; these two were thrown alive into the lake of fire which burns with brimstone.

In Revelation 20:10, the dragon (the devil) is thrown into the lake of fire and brimstone where "the beast and the false prophet are also; and they will be tormented day and night forever and ever."

What we should understand in this part of John's vision is that this beast is the false prophet of the Jewish leadership who were trying to destroy the Christian church in the years after the death and resurrection of Jesus Christ. Although this false prophet/beast looks like a lamb (he pretends to speak for God), he speaks as a dragon (verse 1). In Matthew 7:15, Jesus warned His followers to "beware of the false prophets, who come to you in sheep's clothing, but inwardly are ravenous wolves."

While the false prophet may look like a Christian; while false prophets may claim to be prophets of God, if their message is not in accordance with the revealed Word of God, they are speaking falsely. They are seeking someone to devour.

David Chilton, in *The Days of Vengeance* points out,

> The Jewish leaders, symbolized by this Beast from the Land, joined forces with the Beast of Rome in an attempt to destroy the Church... Apostate Judaism became completely subservient to the Roman State.

Chilton continues,

> The Jewish synagogues enforced submission to the Emperor...they organized economic boycotts against those who refused to submit to Caesar as Lord...

He quotes Austin Farrar, in *The Revelation of St. John the Divine*, who states the leaders of the synagogues were *"forbidding all dealings with the excommunicate."*

What does it mean that the beast causes all to receive a mark on their right hand or their forehead?

Many in the modern world, particularly in America, believe that someday soon every person will be required by the government to receive a mark in order to conduct business. Many believe this "mark" will be a computer chip of some kind by which the government can keep track of each person.

What you should understand is that the mark being written about here is a mark of ownership.

Further, you should understand the mark is not simply a computer chip or other physical mark. Remember, the Revelation is a vision given to John to "sign" to the people of Jesus. It is written in symbolic language.

You should also understand that no Christian will ever receive the mark of the beast. Every Christian has already received the name of God. They are under His ownership. They have been chosen by God, in love, before the foundation of the world (Ephesians 1:4).

CHAPTER 30

Babylon the Great
The Mother of Harlots

There is a great deal of confusion among Christians and even among commentators about Babylon the great or the great city and who or what is the Mother of Harlots.

The majority of Christians and commentators believe that Babylon the great is the city of Rome. That opinion is based on the fact that the Revelation, in speaking of the great harlot that sits on a scarlet beast with seven heads (Revelation 17:1–3), states,

> Here is the mind which has wisdom. The
> seven heads are seven mountains on which the
> woman sits...

Since everyone is aware that Rome was built on seven hills, many believe it follows that Babylon must be the city of Rome.

However, David Chilton, in a footnote in his commentary *The Days of Vengeance* states,

> The Harlot is seated on the Beast, and thus
> on the seven hills of Rome, in other words, apos-

tate Judaism, centered in the City of Jerusalem, is supported by the Roman Empire.

His point is that although the seven hills/mountains refer to the city of Rome, the Harlot is *not* Rome. The Harlot is "*apostate Judaism, centered in the City of Jerusalem,*" which is supported by the Roman Empire.

While clearly "the seven heads" of the Beast on which the harlot is seated are "seven mountains," we should not assume therefore that the city of Rome is Babylon the great. In fact, Ralph E. Bass notes in his commentary, *Back to the Future,* the woman (the harlot) is not equated to the seven mountains; she sits on them. The two, the harlot and the city, are "*separate and distinct entities. The* seven mountains (17:9) *equate to Rome and* the woman (17:9) *equates to Jerusalem who rides on, and is supported by Rome.*" Bass points out that although the seven mountains are the city of Rome, the woman (the harlot) is not Rome. The harlot equates to the city of Jerusalem.

Both Chilton and Bass note that Scripture equates the harlot with Jerusalem and not Rome.

Rather than accept what the majority of people believe, we must look at the whole of Scripture to determine what is being taught in any particular verse. To that end, we need to look at other scriptures in Revelation and in the rest of the Bible to determine the identity of the harlot or Babylon the great.

Revelation 11:8 states,

> And their dead bodies [the bodies of the two witnesses] *will lie* in the street of the great city which mystically is called Sodom and Egypt, where also their Lord was crucified.

Clearly the great city in this verse is the city of Jerusalem. That is the city where Jesus, the Lord of the two witnesses and our Lord, was crucified.

In Jeremiah 23:14, the LORD, YHWH, complains of the wickedness of Jerusalem and her prophets by stating,

> Also among the prophets of Jerusalem I have seen a horrible thing; The committing of adultery and walking in falsehood; And they strengthen the hands of evildoers, So that no one has turned back from his wickedness. All of them have become to Me like Sodom, and her inhabitants like Gomorrah.

God, through the prophet Jeremiah, condemns the apostasy or adultery of the prophets of Jerusalem and states the city has become to Him like Sodom and Gomorrah. Although they should have been taking the truth of the Word of God to the nations, they were turning to other gods (adultery) and spreading falsehood rather than truth.

In Isaiah 1:21, speaking of Judah and Jerusalem, the prophet quotes God condemning the "faithful city" for having become a harlot:

> How the faithful city has become a harlot,
> She *who* was full of justice! Righteousness once lodged in her, But now murderers.

According to God, speaking through the prophet—the faithful city (Jerusalem) which once was full of justice, which once had righteousness residing in her, where Jesus was crucified—has now become a harlot.

In Revelation 14:6–10, John sees

> another angel flying in midheaven, having an eternal gospel to preach to those who live on the earth, and to every nation and tribe and tongue and people; and he said with a loud voice, "Fear God, and give Him glory, because the hour of His judgment has come; worship Him

who made the heaven and the earth and sea and springs of waters." And another angel, a second one, followed, saying, "Fallen, fallen is Babylon the great, she who has made all the nations drink of the wine of the passion of her immorality." Then another angel, a third one, followed them, saying with a loud voice, "If anyone worships the beast and his image, and receives a mark on his forehead or on his hand, he also will drink of the wine of the wrath of God, which is mixed in full strength in the cup of His anger; and he will be tormented with fire and brimstone in the presence of the holy angels and in the presence of the Lamb.

The Jamison, Fausset, Brown (J. F. B.) commentary points out,

Babylon—here first mentioned; [is] identical with the harlot, the apostate Church; distinct from the beast, and judged separately.

Verse 8 describes Babylon the great as "she who has made all the nations drink of the wine of the passion of her immorality." Literally, the word translated as *passion* is the same Greek word translated as *wrath* in verse 10 when speaking of the wrath of God. Notice also Babylon the great has made the nations drink of the wine of wrath and that anyone who receives the mark of the beast will drink of the wine of the wrath of God.

In Revelation 16:19, John writes,

The great city was split into three parts, and the cities of the nations fell. Babylon the great was remembered before God, to give her the cup of the wine of His fierce wrath.

In this verse "the great city" and Babylon the great are the same. The city is "split into three parts" and "remembered before God, to give her the cup of the wine of His fierce wrath."

Some commentators have pointed out this division of the city into three parts may be what is referred to by Josephus in *The Jewish War*. As a Jew writing as an eye-witness to the siege of Jerusalem by the Roman army and their defeat of the Jews, Josephus writes,

> [The city was divided] into three factions, which became acute after the return of Titus. While Titus was besieging [the city of Jerusalem] from without, the three rival factions were fighting fiercely within: but for this the city might have staved off defeat for a long time, even perhaps indefinitely, for no great army could support itself for long in those days in the neighborhood of Jerusalem; there was no water and no supplies. This fighting within the city delivered it quickly into the hands of Titus...

Notice also that God has given the great city (which is Jerusalem and is also Babylon the great) the cup of the wine of His fierce wrath. Literally, the last phrase is "the wrath of His anger." The words have to do with the "boiling over" of the wrath of God against the city where His Son was crucified. Because of their apostasy or adultery in chasing after other gods and their spreading of falsehood rather than truth, God is boiling over angry with them.

> Then one of the seven angels who had the seven bowls came and spoke with me, saying, "Come here, I will show you the judgment of the great harlot who sits on many waters, with whom the kings of the earth committed *acts of* immorality, and those who dwell on the earth were made drunk with the wine of her immorality." And he carried me away in the Spirit into a wilderness;

> and I saw a woman sitting on a scarlet beast, full of blasphemous names, having seven heads and ten horns. The woman was clothed in purple and scarlet, and adorned with gold and precious stones and pearls, having in her hand a gold cup full of abominations and of the unclean things of her immorality, and on her forehead a name *was* written, a mystery, "BABYLON THE GREAT, THE MOTHER OF HARLOTS AND OF THE ABOMINATIONS OF THE EARTH." And I saw the woman drunk with the blood of the saints, and with the blood of the witnesses of Jesus. (Revelation 17:1–6)

There are several things to note in this passage. First, remember that God has condemned Jerusalem (the great city) for her adultery (harlotry) and is going "to give her the cup of the wine of His fierce wrath" (Revelation 16:19).

In Revelation 17:3–5, John writes that in his vision, the angel showed him the "judgment of the great harlot." What John sees is "a woman sitting on a scarlet beast" and the "woman was clothed in purple and scarlet, and adorned with gold and precious stones and pearls, having in her hand a gold cup full of abominations and of the unclean things of her immorality, and on her forehead a name *was* written, a mystery, 'BABYLON THE GREAT, THE MOTHER OF HARLOTS AND OF THE ABOMINATIONS OF THE EARTH.'"

It has already been shown that Babylon the Great is the great city, Jerusalem. The mother of harlots, or Babylon the great, is the woman sitting on the scarlet beast. In the symbolism of Revelation, the woman is apostate Judaism represented by the city of Jerusalem, which is supported by the power of the beast or the Roman Empire.

Of special note here is that the woman is dressed in "purple and scarlet, and adorned with gold and precious stones and pearls." That would have reminded John's readers (and should remind us) of the dress of the high priest. When he was ministering in the tabernacle or temple, he wore a robe of purple and scarlet, which was adorned with gold and precious stones. He also wore a turban with a gold plate on the front (on his forehead), on which was written "Holy to YHWH."

Note also, the woman, who is dressed as a high priest, has "in her hand a gold cup full of abominations and of the unclean things of her immorality." She is "drunk with the blood of the saints, and with the blood of the witnesses of Jesus." Rather than drink of the wine of the drink offering that represented the blood of the Lamb of God being poured out for the sacrifice of sin, this harlot is drinking and has become drunk on the blood of the saints and witnesses of Jesus.

This picture of the woman would have reminded John's readers and should remind us of the condemnation of Jesus against the leadership of Israel for their repeated refusal to hear the prophets and wise men and scribes sent by God to warn Jerusalem of their apostasy.

In Matthew, chapter 23, Jesus condemns the scribes and Pharisees (the leaders of Judaism) by calling down eight "woes" upon them. In Matthew 23:33–37, Jesus says to them,

> You serpents, you brood of vipers, how will you escape the sentence of hell? Therefore, behold, I am sending you prophets and wise men and scribes; some of them you will kill and crucify, and some of them you will scourge in your synagogues, and persecute from city to city, so that upon you may fall *the guilt of* all the righteous blood shed on earth, from the blood of righteous Abel to the blood of Zechariah, the son of Berechiah, whom you murdered between the temple and the altar. Truly I say to you, all these things will come upon this generation. Jerusalem, Jerusalem, who kills the prophets and stones those who are sent to her! How often I wanted to gather your children together, the way a hen gathers her chicks under her wings, and you were unwilling.

Jesus condemns the apostate Jewish leadership as those who kill the prophets and wise men and persecute them from city to city. He further states they are guilty of all the righteous blood shed on the earth. Jesus laments that Jerusalem is the city who kills the prophets and stones those sent to her. Immediately after His condemnation of the Jewish leadership, Jesus begins His prophecy of the destruction of Jerusalem in Matthew 24.

After explaining the rest of John's vision in regard to the beast in verses 8 through 17, the angel further identifies the woman in John's vision.

> The woman whom you saw is the great city, which reigns over the kings of the earth. (Revelation 17:18)

Many have used this verse to identify the woman with the great city of Rome because Rome was the city that reigned over the world of the time. It is clear, however, from other verses that the great city is not Rome but is Jerusalem. How is it then that Jerusalem can be said to be a city that "reigns over the kings of the earth"?

David Chilton in *The Days of Vengeance* provides the clue when he writes,

> If the City is Jerusalem, how can she be said to wield this kind of worldwide political power? The answer is that *Revelation is not a book about politics; it is a book about the Covenant*, Jerusalem *did* reign over the nations. She *did* possess a Kingdom which was above all the kingdoms of the world. She had a covenant priority over the kingdoms of the earth. Israel was a Kingdom of priests (Ex. 19:6), exercising a priestly ministry of guardianship, instruction, and intercession on behalf of the nations of the world.

The world of the time understood the centrality of the Jewish worship in Jerusalem. Even the leaders of the Roman Empire valued the sacrifices made in the temple on their behalf. In a footnote on page 443 of *The Days of Vengeance*, David Chilton writes,

> Josephus points out repeatedly that the nations had historically recognized the sanctity and centrality of the temple: "This celebrated place...was esteemed holy by all mankind" (*The Jewish War*, v.i. 3; cf. v.ix. 4; v.xiii. 6). In fact, the action of Jewish rebels, in the summer of A.D. 66, of halting the daily sacrifices for the Emperor (in violation, Josephus points out, of long-standing practice) was the single event which finally precipitated the Roman war against the Jews... Even at the very end, as Titus prepared to raze the city to the ground, he was still pleading with the Jewish priests to offer up the sacrifices, which by now had been entirely discontinued...

Because of the disobedience of the Jewish leadership to the commandments of God, His anger "boils over" against them, the city and the temple. Because the Jews refused to acknowledge the final sacrifice of Jesus Christ, the Lamb of God, God sent the Roman army to destroy the city and the temple. Jesus prophesies in Matthew 24 about that destruction of Jerusalem. His prophecy is more fully revealed to John in Revelation 18, God's prophecy of the covenantal destruction of Babylon the great, the city of Jerusalem.

> After these things I saw another angel coming down from heaven, having great authority, and the earth was illumined with his glory. And he cried out with a mighty voice, saying, "Fallen, fallen is Babylon the great! She has become a dwelling place of demons and a prison of every unclean spirit, and a prison of every unclean and

hateful bird. For all the nations have drunk of the wine of the passion of her immorality, and the kings of the earth have committed *acts of* immorality with her, and the merchants of the earth have become rich by the wealth of her sensuality." I heard another voice from heaven, saying, "Come out of her, my people, so that you will not participate in her sins and receive of her plagues; for her sins have piled up as high as heaven, and God has remembered her iniquities." (Revelation 18:1–5)

It is very probable the people of John's day would have understood the command of verse 4 (Come out of her, my people) in light of the teaching of Jesus in Matthew 24:15–18. In that passage Jesus tells the disciples, "When you see the Abomination of Desolation standing in the Holy Place, flee to the mountains."

We know from extra-biblical sources that when the Roman army surrounded Jerusalem, the Christian believers fled to the mountains. The Jews secluded themselves in the city. More than two million people were trapped in the city of Jerusalem and were under siege for two years.

Jesus continues His condemnation of Jerusalem in Revelation 18:7–10:

To the degree that she (Babylon the great) glorified herself and lived sensuously, to the same degree give her torment and mourning; for she says in her heart, "I SIT *as* A QUEEN AND I AM NOT A WIDOW, and will never see mourning." For this reason in one day her plagues will come, pestilence and mourning and famine, and she will be burned up with fire; for the Lord God who judges her is strong. And the kings of the earth, who committed *acts of* immorality and lived sensuously with her, will weep and lament over her

when they see the smoke of her burning, standing at a distance because of the fear of her torment, saying, "Woe, woe, the great city, Babylon,
the strong city! For in one hour your judgment
has come."

The prophecies of pestilence and mourning and famine against
the "great city, Babylon" came very true in the two-year siege of
Jerusalem. Toward the end of the siege food was so scarce that, as the
Jewish historian Josephus tells us, the people were eating straw swept
up from the street and eating the leather of their shoes and shields.
They were also eating even their own children. The bodies of those
killed by the three factions of the city were literally piled high in the
streets and this resulted in severe pestilence.

Further evidence that the great city, Babylon, is actually the
city of Jerusalem is provided in Revelation 18:15–16. The merchants
who have become rich from her stand at a distance, "saying, 'Woe,
woe, the great city, she who was clothed in fine linen and purple and
scarlet, and adorned with gold and precious stones and pearls; for in
one hour such great wealth has been laid waste!'"

Again, the city is described in terms of a woman who is clothed
in purple and scarlet and adorned with gold and precious stones.
This is a description that the people of John's day would have understood referred to the robes of the high priest. The Old Testament
church of the Jewish nation is apostate and is being condemned by
God. Rather than focus on taking the Word of God to the nations,
the apostate leadership of Israel had instead focused on bringing the
wealth of the nations into Jerusalem.

Finally, the strong angel proclaims against apostate Jerusalem,

Rejoice over her, O heaven, and you saints
and apostles and prophets, because God has pronounced judgment for you against her.

Then a strong angel took up a stone like a great millstone and threw it into the sea, saying,

> So will Babylon, the great city, be thrown down with violence, and will not be found any longer.

While today we see the city of Jerusalem still standing, we should remember the words of Josephus who, after the Roman army had destroyed the city, wrote "it was so thoroughly laid even with the ground by those that dug it up to the foundation, that there was left nothing to make those that came thither believe it had ever been inhabited."

The destruction prophesied by Jesus was not simply the physical destruction of the city but the destruction of spiritual Jerusalem as the peculiar people of God. Because of their continued breaking of the covenant of God, He finally brings His promised judgment upon the people and divorces apostate Jerusalem. While the physical city of Jerusalem was rebuilt, the spiritual Jerusalem has been replaced by the new bride of Christ, the New Testament church.

CHAPTER 31

The Millennium

Then I saw an angel coming down from heaven, holding the key of the abyss and a great chain in his hand. And he laid hold of the dragon, the serpent of old, who is the devil and Satan, and bound him for a thousand years; and he threw him into the abyss, and shut *it* and sealed *it* over him, so that he would not deceive the nations any longer, until the thousand years were completed; after these things he must be released for a short time. Then I saw thrones, and they sat on them, and judgment was given to them. And I *saw* the souls of those who had been beheaded because of their testimony of Jesus and because of the word of God, and those who had not worshiped the beast or his image, and had not received the mark on their forehead and on their hand; and they came to life and reigned with Christ for a thousand years." The rest of the dead did not come to life until the thousand years were completed. This is the first resurrection. Blessed and holy is the one who has a part in the first resurrection; over these the second death has no power, but they will be priests of God and of Christ and will reign with Him for a thousand years. When the thousand years are completed, Satan will be released from his prison. (Revelation 20:1–7)

Before we look at the answer to the question of "What is the millennium?" we should look at the overall context of the Revelation. As previously stated, I believe the Revelation is, first, a letter of comfort to the people of God who were shortly to come under intense persecution by the Jews and by the Romans. Another focus of Revelation is the sovereignty and judgment of God against the false state (Rome) and the false church (apostate Israel). Finally, the overall context is, as Dr. Dennis Johnson titled his commentary on Revelation, *The Triumph of the Lamb.*

Jesus Christ, the Lion of Judah, the Lamb of God, will triumph over all creation and will judge the wicked through His bride, the New Testament church.

Jude, the brother of James and therefore a brother of Jesus, writes in Jude 14–15:

> Enoch, *in* the seventh *generation* from Adam, prophesied, saying, "Behold, the Lord came with many thousands of His holy ones (saints), to execute judgment upon all, and to convict all the ungodly of all their ungodly deeds which they have done in an ungodly way, and of all the harsh things which ungodly sinners have spoken against Him."

The Apostle Paul writes to the church in Corinth (and to us), 1 Corinthians 6:2,

> Or do you not know that the saints will judge the world? If the world is judged by you, are you not competent *to constitute* the smallest law courts?

Since judgment is given to Jesus Christ, since we as Christians are in Christ, since the church is His body, His bride, we will judge the ungodly.

The question that many have is, "When does that judgment occur?" Virtually, all commentators and Christians believe the judgment will occur after the Second Coming or Advent of Jesus Christ, the Great White Throne judgment of Revelation 20:11–15, which will be addressed in a subsequent chapter.

However, there are many questions about how that Second Coming relates to the one thousand years, or the millennium, of Revelation 20.

First, we need to answer the question: "What is the meaning of the millennium?"

Many believe it is a literal one thousand earthly years during which the martyrs who have been beheaded for their testimony will reign with Christ on the earth.

However, nothing in the passage is said about a reign *on the earth*. The passage literally says the martyrs "lived and reigned with Christ for a thousand years." Where they are reigning is not indicated.

The New American Commentary states,

> Because of the frequent reference (six times) to a period of 1,000 years, this passage has become the most extensively debated of the entire book. The Latin terms for 1,000 years are combined in the word "millennium." From this designation, interpreters have divided themselves into three major categories with numerous variations. Futurists or premillennialists believe the parousia or return of Christ precedes and inaugurates a thousand-year reign of peace. Postmillennialists insist that the reign of Christ is through his church and that Christ returns at the close of the victorious age. Amillennialists take seriously the reign of Christ but generally believe that the explicit language of 1,000 years should

be allegorically or spiritually understood. Many contemporary interpreters who advance this position prefer some other designation, believing that "amillennial" is not an accurate description of their view.

As the commentary points out, there are three major views of the thousand years mentioned in Revelation 20.

The *amillennial* view sees the millennium as spiritual and symbolic and therefore not a definite period of time. Many who hold this view are not comfortable with the term *amillennial* since the Greek prefix *a*—means "not" and therefore technically the term means "no millennium." Clearly, there is a millennium (one thousand years) in Revelation 20.

The *postmillennial* position is held by those who believe Christ will return after (post) the one thousand years of Revelation 20. They also tend to believe that Christ will return to a more or less Christian world.

The most popular position is the *premillennial* view. Those who hold this view believe that Christ will return before (pre) the millennium. There are two major versions of this view. The first is the *historic premillennial* view. This understanding of the one thousand years has been held by many in the church for centuries. The second major version is the *premillennial dispensational* view. This particular point of view was unknown in the early church and did not exist prior to the late 1800s. It was promoted by John Nelson Darby, a minister in the Anglican Church of Ireland, who left the Anglican church and founded the Plymouth Brethren. His views were further popularized by C. I. Schofield, who promoted them through his publication of the *Schofield Reference Bible*.

A fourth view (and the one to which I hold) is becoming more popular as Revelation is studied. That position is known as the *realized millennial*, or *orthodox preterist* view. Those who hold this position believe we are in the millennium. As Christians, we are presently reigning with Christ.

So what is the millennium? Is it a literal one thousand years, or is it symbolic?

Since the one thousand years is mentioned six times in the first seven verses of Revelation 20, it is clearly important. The question is whether the one thousand years is a literal period of time, as many see it, or whether it is symbolic. Since the nature of the Revelation is symbolic (John states that God gave it to Jesus to *sign* by His angel to His bond servant John—verse 1), I believe the one thousand years is symbolic.

We need to understand, as the readers of John's letter would have understood, that in Scripture, numbers have meaning. The number 3 denotes divine perfection, as in the fact that we have a Triune God of perfection: God the Father, God the Son, and God the Holy Spirit. The number 10 denotes divine completeness of order. God gave us Ten Commandments, His divinely complete Law as to how man should serve Him. Therefore, 10 × 10 × 10 (ten multiplied three times or cubed), or one thousand, indicates God's perfectly complete order.

Lorraine Boettner, in *The Millennium*, quotes B. B. Warfield, who writes,

> It is quite certain that the number 1000 represents in Bible symbolism absolute perfection and completeness... When the seer [uses]... The sacred number seven in combination with the equally sacred number three [it] forms the number of holy perfection, ten, and when the ten is cubed into a thousand the seer [John] has said all he could say to convey to our minds the idea of absolute completeness.

Milton Terry, in his commentary, *Biblical Apocalyptics* writes,

> The thousand years is to be understood as a symbolical number, denoting a long period. It... stands for an indefinite period...whose duration

> it would be a folly to attempt to compute... It is
> the same period as that required for the stone of
> Daniel's prophecy (Dan. 2:35) to fill the earth;
> and the mustard seed of Jesus' prophecy to con-
> summate its world-wide growth (Matt. 13:31–
> 32) How long the King of kings will continue
> His battle against evil and defer the last decisive
> blow, when Satan shall be "loosed for a little
> time," no man can even approximately judge.

Then what does it mean that Satan is bound for one thousand years? Is the binding of Satan a literal event as many commentators state, or is it symbolic? If it is literal, how can Satan, a spiritual being, be confined by a chain?

The New American Commentary states,

> While a literal event is portrayed, the pre-
> cise nature of the chain that binds Satan remains
> unknown.

Although the commentary states that "a literal event is portrayed," there is nothing in the passage to show that it is a in fact a
literal event. That is assumed by those who want to believe the events
are literal rather than symbolic.

Herman Hoeksema, in his commentary, *Behold, He Cometh*, writes,

> It is very evident that in these words the Seer
> of Patmos describes not what he saw happening
> historically, but what he beheld in a vision. A
> strictly literal interpretation of the text, therefore,
> is not in harmony with the nature of the passage.
> Nor is it possible. No one thinks of the possibil-
> ity of a literal interpretation when in Revelation
> 13:1 the prophet tells us that "he stood upon the
> sand of the sea and saw a beast rise up out of

the sea, having seven heads and ten horns, and upon his horns ten crowns, and upon his heads the name of blasphemy." It is understood without difficulty that all this was seen by John in a vision.

If the events of Revelation 20 are symbolic, what does it mean that Satan is bound? When did or when will this binding occur?

Jesus tells the crowd in Matthew 12:28–29:

But if I cast out demons by the Spirit of God, then the kingdom of God has come upon you. "Or how can anyone enter the strong man's house and carry off his property, unless he first binds the strong *man?* And then he will plunder his house.

What we should understand is that Jesus is teaching the kingdom of God has already come. Since He casts out demons by the Spirit of God, He has already bound the strong man (Satan). Therefore, the binding of Satan has already occurred. Jesus is plundering his house by bringing to Himself all those under the power of Satan whom God will save.

Notice that the purpose of the binding of Satan is "so that he should not deceive the nations any longer, until the thousand years were completed."

If Satan has been bound, why is it that there is so much evil in the world? David Chilton, in his commentary, *The Days of Vengeance*, gives a succinct answer.

That Satan has been bound does not mean that all his activity has ceased. The New Testament tells us specifically that the demons have been disarmed and bound (Col. 2:15; 2 Pet. 2:4; Jude 6)—yet they are still active. It is just that their activity is restricted.

What we should understand is that Revelation 20 is the fulfillment of the prophecy of Daniel 7:21–27. In that passage, Daniel states that in his vision,

> [He] kept looking, and that horn was waging war with the saints and overpowering them until the Ancient of Days came and judgment was passed in favor of the saints of the Highest One, and the time arrived when the saints took possession of the kingdom... "Then the sovereignty, the dominion and the greatness of *all* the kingdoms under the whole heaven will be given to the people of the saints of the Highest One; His kingdom *will be* an everlasting kingdom, and all the dominions will serve and obey Him."

All authority in heaven and on earth has been given to Jesus Christ. Because of His perfect work and sacrificial death, He sits at the right hand of God the Father. From there He will come to judge the living and the dead.

As Christians who are His body, His bride, the church, we are seated at the right hand of God the Father with Him (Ephesians 2:6). Since we are in Christ, we will judge the wicked with Him.

CHAPTER 32

The Great White Throne Judgment

The First Resurrection

Then I saw thrones, and they sat on them, and judgment was given to them. And I *saw* the souls of those who had been beheaded because of their testimony of Jesus and because of the word of God, and those who had not worshiped the beast or his image, and had not received the mark on their forehead and on their hand; and they came to life [literally, they lived] and reigned with Christ for a thousand years. The rest of the dead did not come to life [live] until the thousand years were completed. This is the first resurrection. Blessed and holy is the one who has a part in the first resurrection; over these the second death has no power, but they will be priests of God and of Christ and will reign with Him for a thousand years. (Revelation 20:4–6)

In this part of his vision, John sees "the souls of those who had been beheaded because of the testimony of Jesus and because of the word of God."

While we tend to read this passage and combine the phrase "the souls of those who had been beheaded [the martyrs]" with "those who had not worshipped the beast or his image and had not received [his] mark," I believe John is speaking of two groups of souls. In addition to seeing the souls of the martyrs, he also sees the souls of those who had not worshipped the beast or his image and had not received the mark of the beast. John sees that both groups, the martyrs and those who had not worshipped the beast or received his mark, lived and reigned with Christ for the thousand years.

The rest of the dead of whom John speaks, therefore, must mean the ungodly—those who are dead in their trespasses and sins (Ephesians 2:1) and who, because they are ungodly, cannot reign with Christ during the thousand years. They will not live (be resurrected to their immortal eternal state) until the thousand years are completed.

The first resurrection in this passage, therefore, must be speaking of the resurrection of the saints who are raised up together (resurrected) with Christ (Ephesians 2:5–6). As that passage states the saints are presently seated together with Him. Therefore, they must be presently reigning with Christ, and they will reign with Him during the thousand years.

In regard to the first resurrection the *Bible Knowledge Commentary* states,

> It should be obvious, however, that in no sense could this be the number-one resurrection chronologically because historically Christ was the first to rise from the dead with a transformed, resurrected body. There was also the resurrection "of many" (Matt. 27:52–53) which took place when Christ died. In what sense then can this resurrection in Revelation 20:5 be "first"?

As the context which follows indicates, "the first resurrection" (vv. 5–6) contrasts with the last resurrection (vv. 12–13), which is followed by "the second death" (vv. 6, 14). It is first in the sense of before. All the righteous, regardless of when they are raised, take part in the resurrection which is first or before the final resurrection (of the wicked dead) at the end of the Millennium.

In Matthew 22:31–33, Jesus teaches the crowds,

> But regarding the resurrection of the dead, have you not read what was spoken to you by God: "I am the God of Abraham, and the God of Isaac, and the God of Jacob"? He is not the God of the dead but of the living. When the crowds heard *this,* they were astonished at His teaching.

What we should understand from the teaching of Jesus is that those who are saved by God are not dead but are living. Although their mortal bodies may die, they have been "born again." They are a "new creation." They are alive in Christ. They have also died to sin. Therefore, as Jesus taught in John 5:24,

> He who hears My words, and believes Him who sent Me, has eternal life, and does not come into judgment, but has passed out of death into life.

Those of us who believe in Jesus have died to sin and have been resurrected to eternal life in Christ.

God is not the God of those who remain dead in their trespasses and sins, those who have not been saved. He is the God of those whom He has elected from before the foundation of the world (Ephesians 1:4) to salvation through faith alone, in Christ alone.

Those who are His do not come into judgment but have passed out of death into life eternal.

1 Peter 1:3 teaches,

> Blessed be the God and Father of our Lord Jesus Christ, who according to His great mercy has caused us to be born again to a living hope through the resurrection of Jesus Christ from the dead.

In John 11:21–26, after the death of Lazarus, we read,

> Martha then said to Jesus, "Lord, if You had been here, my brother would not have died. "Even now I know that whatever You ask of God, God will give You." Jesus said to her, "Your brother will rise again." Martha said to Him, "I know that he will rise again in the resurrection on the last day." Jesus said to her, "I am the resurrection and the life; he who believes in Me will live even if he dies, and everyone who lives and believes in Me will never die. Do you believe this?"

Jesus very clearly teaches that the one who believes in Him will never die. Although our mortal bodies will cease to function, what we call death, the believer will live eternally. Because we have been made alive together with Christ, raised up together with Him, and seated together with Him in the heavenlies (Ephesians 2:5–6), we will reign together with Him, not just for the thousand years, but eternally.

In John 5:25–29, Jesus states,

> Truly, truly, I say to you, an hour is coming and now is, when the dead will hear the voice of the Son of God, and those who hear will live. For just as the Father has life in Himself, even so

> He gave to the Son also to have life in Himself;
> and He gave Him authority to execute judgment,
> because He is *the* Son of Man. Do not marvel at
> this; for an hour is coming, in which all who are
> in the tombs will hear His voice, and will come
> forth; those who did the good *deeds* to a resurrec-
> tion of life, those who committed the evil *deeds*
> to a resurrection of judgment.

In this verse, Jesus teaches that the final (or second) resurrection of the saved (godly) and the (first or final) resurrection of the repro-bate (ungodly) happen at the same hour. The saved are resurrected to eternal life. The unsaved are resurrected to eternal judgment. The dead in the passage obviously includes all those who are dead in the grave whether righteous or unrighteous. It also includes those who are dead in their trespasses and sins. Those who are saved (those who did the good deeds which God prepared beforehand—Ephesians 2:10) will be resurrected to eternal life. Those who are unsaved (those who committed the evil deeds of their own works) will "live" and be resurrected to eternal judgment.

In Matthew 25:31–46, Jesus states,

> But when the Son of Man comes in His
> glory, and all the angels with Him, then He will
> sit on His glorious throne. All the nations will be
> gathered before Him; and He will separate them
> from one another, as the shepherd separates the
> sheep from the goats; and He will put the sheep
> on His right, and the goats on the left... These
> (the goats or unsaved) will go away into eternal
> punishment, but the righteous into eternal life.

When the thousand years are completed, Christ will return. Then there will be a final resurrection of the saved (the sheep) to their eternal state of glory. At that same time (Scripture teaches both occur "at the same hour"), there will also be a resurrection of the unsaved who are still dead in their sins, and they will suffer a resurrection to the eternal judgment of the wrath of God against their sins.

At the final resurrection, Jesus will separate the saved (sheep) from the unsaved (goats). The saved will be resurrected to eternal life and the unsaved will be resurrected to eternal judgment or punishment.

The Second Death

Scripture clearly teaches there is a second death. Revelation 2:11 states,

> He who has an ear, let him hear what the Spirit says to the churches. He who overcomes will not be hurt by the second death.

In Revelation 20:14–15, John writes,

> Then death and Hades were thrown into the lake of fire. This is the second death, the lake of fire. And if anyone's name was not found written in the book of life, he was thrown into the lake of fire.

In Revelation 21:8, we are told,

> But for the cowardly and unbelieving and abominable and murderers and immoral persons and sorcerers and idolaters and all liars, their part *will be* in the lake that burns with fire and brimstone, which is the second death.

The fact that there is a "second death" clearly implies there is a first death. What does Scripture teach us about the nature of that first death?

First, the Bible teaches that all men born since the sin of Adam are born in trespasses and sins and are, therefore, spiritually dead in the eyes of God. King David, after his sin with Bathsheba, after he is confronted by the prophet Nathan, writes in Psalm 51:1–5,

> Be gracious to me, O God, according to Your lovingkindness; According to the greatness of Your compassion blot out my transgressions. Wash me thoroughly from my iniquity And cleanse me from my sin. For I know my transgressions, And my sin is ever before me. Against You, You only, I have sinned And done what is evil in Your sight, So that You are justified when You speak And blameless when You judge. Behold, I was brought forth in iniquity, And in sin my mother conceived me.

David acknowledges he has been conceived in sin and brought forth (born) in iniquity. He also acknowledges that although he sinned against both Bathsheba and her husband, Uriah, his sin is really only against God. His actions were evil in the sight of God because he had broken the commandments of God.

In Ephesians 2:1–6, the Apostle Paul writes,

> And you were dead in your trespasses and sins, in which you formerly walked according to the course of this world, according to the prince of the power of the air, of the spirit that is now working in the sons of disobedience. Among them we too all formerly lived in the lusts of our flesh, indulging the desires of the flesh and of the mind, and were by nature children of wrath, even as the rest. But God, being rich in mercy, because of His great love with which He loved us, even when we were dead in our transgressions, made us alive together with Christ (by grace you

have been saved), and raised us up with Him,
and seated us with Him in the heavenly *places* in
Christ Jesus.

Notice that the apostle includes himself in the number of those
who were dead as a result of being sinful. He states that before God
saved us, we all "lived in the lusts of our flesh, indulging the desires of
the flesh and of the mind, and were by nature children of wrath, even
as the rest." Because, like David, we all have broken the commandments of God, we all deserve His wrath against our sin.

Also, Paul writes in Colossians 2:13,

You were dead in your transgressions and
the uncircumcision of your flesh.

While he was writing specifically to the Christians in the church
at Colossae, his message is for all of us. Since we all were born in sin,
since we all are rebellious and do not want to obey God, since we all
want to decide for ourselves what is good and evil (Genesis 3:5), we
are all under the just condemnation of the wrath of God.

Although Scripture teaches that all men are born "dead in their
trespasses and sins," that is not the first death.

The Word of God teaches that in His mercy and love, we who
are the elect of God are chosen by Him to die to sin. That is the first
death.

In Romans 6:3–8, the Apostle Paul writes to the church,

Or do you not know that all of us who have
been baptized into Christ Jesus have been baptized into His death? Therefore we have been
buried with Him through baptism into death, so
that as Christ was raised from the dead through
the glory of the Father, so we too might walk in
newness of life. For if we have become united
with *Him* in the likeness of His death, certainly
we shall also be *in the likeness* of His resurrection,

> knowing this, that our old self was crucified with
> *Him*, in order that our body of sin might be done
> away with, so that we would no longer be slaves
> to sin; for he who has died is freed from sin. Now
> if we have died with Christ, we believe that we
> shall also live with Him…

Even though we were dead in our trespasses and sins, even though we were dead in our transgressions and the uncircumcision of our flesh, God made us as believers to die to sin through the crucifixion of Jesus Christ. God in His glory united us together with Christ in the likeness of His death. God also made us alive together with Christ, raised us up together with Him, and seated us together with Him in the heavenlies. God has "caused us to be born again to a living hope through the resurrection of Jesus Christ from the dead" (1 Peter 1:3).

In correcting the Sadducees about their wrong belief that there was no resurrection, Jesus teaches in Luke 20:35–36:

> But those who are considered worthy to
> attain to that age and the resurrection from the
> dead, neither marry nor are given in marriage; for
> they cannot even die anymore, because they are
> like angels, and are sons of God, being sons of the
> resurrection.

Because those who believe in Jesus have been born again, resurrected together with Him (Ephesians 2:5–6), "they cannot even die anymore." They have already died to sin and been resurrected with Christ. Therefore, they are "sons of the resurrection."

It is only the unsaved, together with the devil, the beast, and the false prophet (Revelation 20:10), Death and Hades (Revelation 20:14), who suffer the second death of the lake of fire. Only those whose names have not been written in the book of life are thrown into the lake of fire, which is the second death (Revelation 20:15).

Are Christians Judged at the Great White Throne?

Many Christians ask, "What about the great white throne judgment? Are not Christians also judged at the end of time?"

My answer is that Scripture teaches, "Yes and no."

Revelation 20:11–13 states,

> Then I saw a great white throne and Him who sat upon it, from whose presence earth and heaven fled away, and no place was found for them. And I saw the dead, the great and the small, standing before the throne, and books were opened; and another book was opened, which is *the book* of life; and the dead were judged from the things which were written in the books, according to their deeds. And the sea gave up the dead which were in it, and death and Hades gave up the dead which were in them; and they were judged, every one *of them* according to their deeds.

What is important to remember in this passage is not what we have been led to believe by erroneous teaching. What is important to believe is what the passage, taken together with other passages of Scripture, actually teaches.

It is true that the dead, those who are dead in their trespasses and sins, will be judged by their deeds or works. They will be judged by God because all their works are as filthy rags before God. All the works done "in the flesh" are done for the wrong reason. They are done contrary to the glory of God. It is not true that the living, those who are alive in Christ will be judged (in regard to salvation) for their deeds or works.

It should be noted that the Apostle Paul writes to the church in Rome (and to us) in Romans 8:1–11,

> Therefore there is now no condemnation
> for those who are in Christ Jesus. For the law of

the Spirit of life in Christ Jesus has set you free from the law of sin and of death. For what the Law could not do, weak as it was through the flesh, God *did:* sending His own Son in the likeness of sinful flesh and *as an offering* for sin, He condemned sin in the flesh, so that the requirement of the Law might be fulfilled in us, who do not walk according to the flesh but according to the Spirit... If Christ is in you, though the body is dead because of sin, yet the spirit is alive because of righteousness. But if the Spirit of Him who raised Jesus from the dead dwells in you, He who raised Christ Jesus from the dead will also give life to your mortal bodies through His Spirit who dwells in you.

The clear teaching of the apostle is that there is *now* (present tense) no condemnation for those who are in Christ Jesus. God punished His Son for all the sins, past, present, and future of those whom He would save. Therefore, He would be unjust to punish us for our sins after pouring out His wrath for those sins upon His own Son.

What then do we make of verses that speak of Christians being judged by their deeds?

In John 5:28–29, the apostle quotes Jesus as saying,

Do not marvel at this; for an hour is coming, in which all who are in the tombs will hear His voice, and will come forth; those who did the good *deeds* to a resurrection of life, those who committed the evil *deeds* to a resurrection of judgment.

The Apostle Paul teaches in 2 Corinthians 5:10,

For we must all appear before the judgment seat of Christ, so that each one may be recompensed for his deeds in the body, according to what he has done, whether good or bad.

In the Gospel of Matthew 25:31–46, we are taught,

> But when the Son of Man comes in His glory, and all the angels with Him, then He will sit on His glorious throne. All the nations will be gathered before Him; and He will separate them from one another, as the shepherd separates the sheep from the goats; and He will put the sheep on His right, and the goats on the left. Then the King will say to those on His right, "Come, you who are blessed of My Father, inherit the kingdom prepared for you from the foundation of the world. For I was hungry, and you gave Me *something* to eat; I was thirsty, and you gave Me *something* to drink; I was a stranger, and you invited Me in; naked, and you clothed Me; I was sick, and you visited Me; I was in prison, and you came to Me." Then the righteous will answer Him, "Lord, when did we see You hungry, and feed You, or thirsty, and give You *something* to drink? And when did we see You a stranger, and invite You in, or naked, and clothe You? When did we see You sick, or in prison, and come to You?" The King will answer and say to them, "Truly I say to you, to the extent that you did it to one of these brothers of Mine, *even* the least *of them,* you did it to Me." Then He will also say to those on His left, "Depart from Me, accursed ones, into the eternal fire which has been prepared for the devil and his angels; for I was hungry, and you gave Me *nothing* to eat; I was thirsty, and you gave Me nothing to drink; I was a stranger, and you did not invite Me in; naked, and you did not

clothe Me; sick, and in prison, and you did not visit Me." Then they themselves also will answer, "Lord, when did we see You hungry, or thirsty, or a stranger, or naked, or sick, or in prison, and did not take care of You?" Then He will answer them, "Truly I say to you, to the extent that you did not do it to one of the least of these, you did not do it to Me." These will go away into eternal punishment, but the righteous into eternal life.

In Romans 2:5–8, Scripture teaches,

But because of your stubbornness and unrepentant heart you are storing up wrath for yourself in the day of wrath and revelation of the righteous judgment of God, who WILL RENDER TO EACH PERSON ACCORDING TO HIS DEEDS: to those who by perseverance in doing good seek for glory and honor and immortality, eternal life; but to those who are selfishly ambitious and do not obey the truth, but obey unrighteousness, wrath and indignation.

Clearly these passages speak of Christians being judged for the deeds they have done in the body. In the passage in Matthew, the only difference between the sheep and the goats appears to be the deeds they have done.

Yet the clear teaching of the whole of scripture is that we are not saved by our works. In fact, as Isaiah teaches in Isaiah 64:6,

All of us have become like one who is unclean, And all our righteous deeds are like a filthy garment; And all of us wither like a leaf, And our iniquities, like the wind, take us away.

The words of the Apostle Paul to the church in Galatians 2:16 apply equally to those of us in the church today:

> Nevertheless knowing that a man is not justified by the works of the Law but through faith in Christ Jesus, even we have believed in Christ Jesus, so that we may be justified by faith in Christ and not by the works of the Law; since by the works of the Law no flesh will be justified.

And the words of Paul in his letter to the church at Rome also apply to us.

> For we maintain that a man is justified by faith apart from works of the Law. (Romans 3:28)

We are justified (made right with God) only by faith alone, in Christ alone. None of the works we do (no matter how good they may appear to us or to others) can bring about our salvation. A perfect God requires perfection in obedience to His Law. In the Sermon on the Mount, Jesus teaches in Matthew 5:48,

> Therefore you are to be perfect, as your heavenly Father is perfect.

None of us can accomplish that perfection. Only Jesus Christ perfectly completed the work of salvation as required by God. What then are we to do? Scripture gives us the clear answer. Ephesians 2:8–19 teaches,

> For by grace you have been saved through faith; and that not of yourselves, *it is* the gift of God; not as a result of works, so that no one may boast.

We are not saved by our works. If it were true that our works were the ground of our salvation, we could boast that we were better than those who had not been saved. We are saved only by the grace of God who gives us His gift of faith (Romans 12:3) in the perfectly accomplished work of His Son, our Lord, Jesus Christ.

What then are the good works by which Christians are judged? Paul explains in Ephesians 2:10,

> For we are His workmanship, created in Christ Jesus for good works, which God prepared beforehand so that we would walk in them.

Any good works which the Christian accomplishes are works which God has prepared beforehand that we should walk in them.

Those works which He has prepared for us and which we do to the glory of God will earn us rewards or crowns. The Apostle Paul writes to his protégé, Timothy, in 2 Timothy 4:7–8,

> I have fought the good fight, I have finished the course, I have kept the faith; in the future there is laid up for me the crown of righteousness, which the Lord, the righteous Judge, will award to me on that day; and not only to me, but also to all who have loved His appearing.

James, the brother of Jesus, writes in James 1:12,

> Blessed is a man who perseveres under trial; for once he has been approved, he will receive the crown of life which *the Lord* has promised to those who love Him.

In 1 Peter 5:4, Peter writes to the church,

> And when the Chief Shepherd appears, you will receive the unfading crown of glory.

We should remember, however, that any crown we receive is a blessing of grace given by God and is not a blessing we deserve. I believe that is why John writes in Revelation 4:10–11 that he sees

> the twenty-four elders…fall down before Him who sits on the throne, and…worship Him who lives forever and ever and…cast their crowns before the throne, saying, "Worthy are You, our Lord and our God, to receive glory and honor and power; for You created all things, and because of Your will they existed, and were created."

The elders understand (as we also should), only God is worthy to receive glory and honor and power. Therefore, they cast their crowns before the throne in acknowledgment that the honor belongs only to God. Any reward any of us has is a direct result of the grace of God given to us.

CHAPTER 33

Marriage Supper of the Lamb

In Revelation, chapter 18, John sees in his vision, the destruction of apostate Jerusalem, the great city, Babylon the Great. In Revelation 18:4, John hears "another voice from heaven" that commands the people of God to "come out of her [Babylon the Great]" that they might not participate in her sins and receive of her plagues. After prophesying what is to happen to apostate Jerusalem in verses 7 through 19, in Revelation 18:20 the voice commands,

> Rejoice over her, O heaven, and you saints
> and apostles and prophets, because God has pro-
> nounced judgment for you against her.

Literally, the passage states that "God has judged your judgment on her." In response to the prayers of His people, the Lord judges apostate Israel and the city of Jerusalem is laid waste by the Roman army. All heaven, the saints and apostles and prophets are commanded to rejoice at the judgment of God against those who disobey Him.

Revelation 19:1–9 states,

> After these things I heard something like a
> loud voice of a great multitude in heaven, say-
> ing, "Hallelujah! Salvation and glory and power

belong to our God; BECAUSE HIS JUDGMENTS ARE TRUE AND RIGHTEOUS; for He has judged the great harlot who was corrupting the earth with her immorality, and HE HAS AVENGED THE BLOOD OF HIS BOND-SERVANTS ON HER." And a second time they said, "Hallelujah! HER SMOKE RISES UP FOREVER AND EVER." And the twenty-four elders and the four living creatures fell down and worshiped God who sits on the throne saying, "Amen. Hallelujah!" And a voice came from the throne, saying, "Give praise to our God, all you His bond-servants, you who fear Him, the small and the great." Then I heard *something* like the voice of a great multitude and like the sound of many waters and like the sound of mighty peals of thunder, saying, "Hallelujah! For the Lord our God, the Almighty, reigns. Let us rejoice and be glad and give the glory to Him, for the marriage of the Lamb has come and His bride has made herself ready." It was given to her to clothe herself in fine linen, bright *and* clean; for the fine linen is the righteous acts of the saints. Then he said to me, "Write, 'Blessed are those who are invited to the marriage supper of the Lamb.'" And he said to me, "These are true words of God."

John hears a fourfold "Hallelujah"—a term that comes from the Hebrew word for praise "*hallel*" and the short form of the name of YHWH, "*Yah*," in other words, "Praise YHWH."

The first hallelujah praises God because His judgments are true and righteous, and He has rendered true judgment against the apostate leadership of Israel as the great harlot who is corrupting the earth. The second hallelujah gives praise to God because the punishment of the harlot is eternal. Her smoke rises up forever and ever. The third hallelujah is a shout of praise to God by the twenty-four elders and the four living creatures as they worship God. The fourth hallelujah is a tremendous sound like many waters and peals of thunder and like a great multitude who shout to give glory to God because He reigns and because the marriage of the Lamb has come and His bride has made herself ready.

What we should see in this passage is that God has divorced apostate Israel for her adultery and has cast her down by destroying Jerusalem and the corrupt temple. God then turns to His new bride, the church, those who believe in Jesus Christ as Lord and Savior.

The Lord gives His bride her wedding clothes, "fine linen, bright and clean." We should remember that the righteous acts of the saints are not our acts. Our works are as filthy rags. It is only the perfect acts of Jesus Christ that are righteous in any sense. Any good works we do are only those works which "God prepared beforehand, that we should walk in them" (Ephesians 2:10).

Note also the fine linen which is the righteous acts of the saints is given to the bride. Jesus Christ took upon Himself the punishment for our sin.

> [God] made Him who knew no sin *to be* sin on our behalf, so that we might become the righteousness of God in Him. (2 Corinthians 5:21)

God poured out His wrath for our sins upon His own Son that He might pour out the righteousness of Jesus Christ upon those whom He would save. When we stand before God, we will not stand in the filthy rags of our own works. We will stand dressed in the righteous robes of the perfect work of Jesus, our Savior.

John is then told to write,

> Blessed are those who are invited to the marriage supper of the Lamb.

All of us as believers are blessed in that we are invited to the marriage supper of the Lamb. Since all Christians are part of the church, we are His bride, and therefore we will be guests of honor at the marriage supper of the Lamb.

Our sacrament of the Lord's Supper, or Communion, looks forward to that meal. It is an amazing fact that at the Last Supper, Jesus never finished the meal. He arrested the supper.

In the Jewish Passover celebration in the time of Jesus, there were four cups of wine that were served during the meal. The first cup, served at the beginning of the Passover, was the cup of sanctification, or bringing out. That cup represented the deliverance of Israel as God sanctified or separated them and brought them out of bondage in Egypt. The second cup was the cup of deliverance or judgment. That cup represented the deliverance or salvation of Israel when God parted the Red Sea and allowed them to escape the pursuing Egyptian army. It also represented the final judgment of Egypt by their destruction as God caused the waters to overwhelm them. The third cup was the cup of redemption and was taken after the meal.

It is this cup that Jesus was speaking of in all three of the synoptic gospels. In Matthew 26:26, we read,

> While they were eating, Jesus took *some* bread, and after a blessing, He broke *it* and gave *it* to the disciples, and said, "Take, eat; this is My body." And when He had taken a cup and given thanks, He gave *it* to them, saying, "Drink from it, all of you; for this is My blood of the covenant, which is poured out for many for forgiveness of sins. "But I say to you, I will not drink of this fruit of the vine from now on until that day when I drink it new with you in My Father's kingdom."

It is clear that the third cup is the one in view because the gospel writers tell us Jesus took the cup "while they were eating." It was at this point that Jesus says of the cup,

> This is My blood of the covenant, which is poured out for many for forgiveness of sins. But I say to you, I will not drink of this fruit of the vine

from now on until that day when I drink it new
with you in My Father's kingdom.

The words of Jesus are almost exactly the same in the gospel of
Mark and are very similar in the gospel of Luke. Jesus says, He will
not drink of the fruit of the vine until He drinks it new in the kingdom of heaven. Jesus never drank the fourth cup that was normally
part of the Passover. That fourth cup was the cup of *hallel*, or praise.
That cup represents the promise of God to "take you as My people."

Why does Jesus say, "I will not drink of this fruit of the vine
from now on until that day when I drink it *new* with you in My
Father's kingdom"? I believe He is referring to the fact that *all* things
will be new in the new heavens and new earth. There will be no pol-
lution of anything in God's new creation.

That cup looked forward to God gathering His people to
Himself. Those of us whom God has chosen in love from before the
foundation of the world (Ephesians 1:4) have been adopted into His
family through our salvation in Christ. We who are blessed by being
invited to the marriage supper of the Lamb will finish that meal in
heaven with Jesus and lift the cup of praise to Him for His perfect
work of salvation.

CHAPTER 34

The New Jerusalem

John writes in Revelation 21:1–11,

> Then I saw a new heaven and a new earth; for the first heaven and the first earth passed away, and there is no longer *any* sea. And I saw the holy city, new Jerusalem, coming down out of heaven from God, made ready as a bride adorned for her husband. And I heard a loud voice from the throne, saying, "Behold, the tabernacle of God is among men, and He will dwell among them, and they shall be His people, and God Himself will be among them, and He will wipe away every tear from their eyes; and there will no longer be *any* death; there will no longer be *any* mourning, or crying, or pain; the first things have passed away." And He who sits on the throne said, "Behold, I am making all things new." And He said, "Write, for these words are faithful and true." Then He said to me, "It is done. I am the Alpha and the Omega, the beginning and the end. I will give to the one who thirsts from the spring of the water of life without cost. He who overcomes will inherit these things, and I will be his God

and he will be My son. "But for the cowardly and unbelieving and abominable and murderers and immoral persons and sorcerers and idolaters and all liars, their part *will be* in the lake that burns with fire and brimstone, which is the second death." Then one of the seven angels who had the seven bowls full of the seven last plagues came and spoke with me, saying, "Come here, I will show you the bride, the wife of the Lamb." And he carried me away in the Spirit to a great and high mountain, and showed me the holy city, Jerusalem, coming down out of heaven from God, having the glory of God. Her brilliance was like a very costly stone, as a stone of crystal-clear jasper.

Most people in the church today focus on John's description of the city in verses 12 through 27 of chapter 21. They are truly amazed by how magnificent his description of the city is. Songs are written about walking the streets of gold. Our imaginations are overwhelmed by the incredible beauty and the sheer size of the city that John describes.

John writes,

> The city is laid out as a square, and its length is as great as the width; and (the angel) measured the city with the rod, 12,000 stadia; its length and width and height are equal.

Most translations convert the Greek word *stadia* into modern measurements. The New American Standard Bible (NASB) points out that a "stadion" was approximately 600 feet. Using that standard, the city would be a cube of 1,500 *miles* in length and width and height. That works out to a cubic volume of 3,375,000,000 *cubic miles*!

We should remember, however, that the Revelation is a letter to the churches written in signs or symbols (Revelation 1:1).

David Chilton writes,

> Each side of the City—length, breath, and height—measures twelve thousand stadia... The absurdity of "literalism" is embarrassingly evident when it attempts to deal with these measurements. The numbers are obviously symbolic, the multiples of twelve being a reference to the majesty, vastness, and perfection of the Church.

Herman Hoeksema, in his commentary *Behold, He Cometh* writes,

> Now it is of the utmost importance to understand that what John beholds in not a literal city, but a symbolic and visionary city. It is, in fact, very difficult to avoid thinking of a literal city when we contemplate this passage. Yet we make a very serious mistake if we do so, a mistake which could cause us to miss the thrust of the entire passage, and one which would also involve us in impossible difficulties as far as the interpretation of this graphic and detailed description of the city is concerned.

In the context of the passage, we are told that John sees "the holy city coming down out of heaven from God" (verse 2), and we are told in verse 9 and 10 one of the seven angels says to John,

> Come here, I shall show you the bride, the wife of the Lamb. And he carried me away in the Spirit...and showed me the holy city, Jerusalem, coming down out of heaven from God.

THE REVELATION OF JESUS CHRIST

Clearly, what John sees is not a literal city. What he sees is symbolic of the church, the bride, the wife of the Lamb.

John's description should not be understood as a literal depiction of a future celestial city. He is telling us about the incredible perfection and beauty of the church of Jesus Christ.

We should also remember that John states,

> Then I saw a new heaven and a new earth; for the first heaven and the first earth passed away.

In the new heavens and the new earth which God will create,

> There will no longer be *any* death; there will no longer be *any* mourning, or crying, or pain; the first things have passed away.

As David Chilton points out in *The Days of Vengeance,*

> We can look forward to the absolute and perfect fulfillment of this promise at the Last Day, when the last enemy is destroyed. But, in principle, it is true already. Jesus said: "I am the Resurrection and the Life; he who believes in Me shall live even if he dies, and everyone who lives and believes in Me shall never die" (John 11:25–26). God has wiped away our tears, for we are partakers of His First Resurrection.

In the new heavens and the new earth, as Augustine wrote, we will not be able to sin. The new creation will be without the corruption of Adam's sin and will be perfectly righteous due to the finished work of Jesus Christ. That is why John writes of the city,

> Nothing unclean and no one who practices abomination and lying, shall ever come into it,

but only those whose names are written in the
Lamb's book of life.

Those whose names have not been written in the Lamb's book
of life,

> The cowardly and unbelieving and abom-
> inable and murderers and immoral persons and
> sorcerers and idolaters and all liars, their part *will
> be* in the lake that burns with fire and brimstone,
> which is the second death.

There are only two biblical possibilities for the eternal state of
all men. Those whose names have been written in the book of life
from before the foundation of the world will be with God in the
new heavens and the new earth for eternity. They will experience the
incredible grace of God forever. Those whose names are not written
in the book of life will suffer eternal condemnation in the lake of fire
with the devil, the beast, and the false prophet (Revelation 20:10).

CHAPTER 35

The Eternal State

Then he showed me a river of the water of life, clear as crystal, coming from the throne of God and of the Lamb, in the middle of its street. On either side of the river was the tree of life, bearing twelve *kinds of* fruit, yielding its fruit every month; and the leaves of the tree were for the healing of the nations. There will no longer be any curse; and the throne of God and of the Lamb will be in it, and His bond-servants will serve Him; they will see His face, and His name *will be* on their foreheads. And there will no longer be *any* night; and they will not have need of the light of a lamp nor the light of the sun, because the Lord God will illumine them; and they will reign forever and ever. And he said to me, "These words are faithful and true"; and the Lord, the God of the spirits of the prophets, sent His angel to show to His bond-servants the things which must soon take place. "And behold, I am coming quickly. Blessed is he who heeds the words of the prophecy of this book." I, John, am the one who heard and saw these things. And when I heard and saw, I fell down to worship at the feet of the angel who showed me these things. But he said to me, "Do not do that. I am a fellow servant of yours and of your brethren the prophets and of those who heed the words of this book. Worship God." And he said to me, "Do not seal up the words of the prophecy of this book, for the time is near. Let the one who does wrong, still do wrong; and the one who is filthy, still be filthy; and let the one who is righteous, still practice righteousness; and the one who is holy, still keep himself holy. "Behold, I am coming quickly, and My reward *is* with Me, to render to every man according to what he has done. I am the Alpha and the Omega, the first and the last, the beginning and the end." Blessed are those who wash their robes, so that they may have the right to the tree of life, and may enter by the gates into the city. Outside are the dogs and the sorcerers and the immoral persons and the murderers and the idolaters, and everyone who loves and practices lying. (Revelation 22:1–15)

The *he* in verse 1 refers back to Revelation 21:9–10:

> One of the seven angels who had the seven bowls full of the seven last plagues [who] came and spoke with [John], saying, "Come here, I will show you the bride, the wife of the Lamb." And he carried me away in the Spirit to a great and high mountain, and showed me the holy city, Jerusalem, coming down out of heaven from God…

The angel continues with his description of the "bride, the wife of the Lamb…the holy city, Jerusalem."

While most in the church today understand these words of John in Revelation 22 as pertaining to a future state that has not yet occurred, we must also remember that in Revelation 21, John is describing the church, the bride of Christ. Therefore, God is telling us through the words of the Apostle John, what is the present and future state of the true church of God.

God has divorced apostate Israel for their adultery, and He is about to destroy the unholy temple (in AD 70) that the unbelieving Jews had polluted. He has made ready "the holy city, new Jerusalem... as a bride...for her husband."

There is no temple in the new Jerusalem, the bride of Christ, for Revelation 21:22 tells us, "the Lord God the Almighty and the Lamb are its temple." The city of the New Jerusalem which God is creating in the church "has no need of the sun or of the moon to shine upon it, for the glory of God has illumined it, and its lamp is the Lamb." In the new Jerusalem church that God is preparing, "nothing unclean and no one who practices abomination and lying, shall ever come into it, but only those whose names are written in the Lamb's book of life."

This tells us that only those who are "in Christ" can be in the true church. We may see many in the visible church who appear to be Christians, but they are not "those whose names are written in the Lamb's book of life."

It is only those whom God has chosen from before the foundation of the world (Ephesians 1:4) who will be adopted as sons and daughters of God and be born again to live in His new creation. They will live by the True Light of Jesus Christ.

In the gospel written by John, he tells us about the True Light of Jesus Christ in John 1:1–5.

> In the beginning was the Word, and the Word was with God, and the Word was God. He was in the beginning with God. All things came into being through Him, and apart from Him nothing came into being that has come into being. In Him was life, and the life was the Light

of men. The Light shines in the darkness, and the
darkness did not comprehend it.

John clearly teaches that Jesus Christ is the Word that was with
God in the beginning as Creator and He is the light that shines in the
darkness to give to those who believe in Him the light of life.

It is Jesus Christ Who shines in the darkness of our sinful life
to change our hearts and enlighten our minds to understand He is
the Light of the World and the only way into the state of eternal life.

John states in John 1:6–13,

> There came a man sent from God, whose
> name was John (the Baptizer). He came as a wit-
> ness, to testify about the Light, so that all might
> believe through him. (John the Baptizer) was not
> the Light, but he came to testify about the Light.
> There was the true Light which, coming into
> the world, enlightens every man. He was in the
> world, and the world was made through Him,
> and the world did not know Him. He came to
> His own, and those who were His own did not
> receive Him. But as many as received Him, to
> them He gave the right to become children of
> God, even to those who believe in His name,
> who were born, not of blood nor of the will of
> the flesh nor of the will of man, but of God.

By the way, in the Bible, John is not called "the Baptist" even
though most translations refer to him by that title. The actual Greek
indicates that he is referred to as "the one baptizing." Particularly in
the gospel of Mark the word we translate "Baptist" is a participle,
which means "the one baptizing." In the other gospels the word is a
noun but has the sense of "one who baptizes."

John the Baptizer was sent by God to testify about Jesus Christ,
the Light of the World. Jesus is the True Light that enlightens every
man and gives eternal life to those who believe in Him. To those

who "received Him, to them He gave the right to become children of God, even to those who believe in His name, who were born, not of blood nor of the will of the flesh nor of the will of man, but of God."

The Apostle Paul writes to the church in Corinth (and to us) in 1 Corinthians 6:19–20,

> Or do you not know that your body is a temple of the Holy Spirit who is in you, whom you have from God, and that you are not your own? For you have been bought with a price: therefore glorify God in your body.

All true Christians are part of the body of Christ, His bride. We are the temple of God the Holy Spirit, whom God the Son sent to be with us eternally.

In Ephesians 2:5–6, we are taught,

> Even when we were dead in our transgressions [God] made us alive together with Christ (by grace you have been saved), and raised us up with Him, and seated us with Him in the heavenly *places* in Christ Jesus…

The form of the original language means that when Jesus Christ was made alive, God made us alive together with Him. When Jesus Christ was raised up from the tomb, we were raised up together with Him. When Jesus Christ was seated at the right hand of God the Father, we were seated together with Him and we will always be there.

Jesus Christ is reigning now, and we who believe in Him are reigning with Him. While we do not see that reality yet, that is the reality that God has reserved and kept for us.

Revelation 22 describes the eternal state of the true church by referring John's readers (and us) to Ezekiel 47:1–12 and Ezekiel's vision of the new temple. That passage reads,

Then he brought me back to the door of the house; and behold, water was flowing from under the threshold of the house toward the east, for the house faced east. And the water was flowing down from under, from the right side of the house, from south of the altar. He brought me out by way of the north gate and led me around on the outside to the outer gate by way of *the gate* that faces east. And behold, water was trickling from the south side. When the man went out toward the east with a line in his hand, he measured a thousand cubits, and he led me through the water, water *reaching* the ankles. Again he measured a thousand and led me through the water, water *reaching* the knees. Again he measured a thousand and led me through *the water,* water *reaching* the loins. Again he measured a thousand; *and it was* a river that I could not ford, for the water had risen, *enough* water to swim in, a river that could not be forded. He said to me, "Son of man, have you seen *this?*" Then he brought me back to the bank of the river. Now when I had returned, behold, on the bank of the river there *were* very many trees on the one side and on the other. Then he said to me, "These waters go out toward the eastern region and go down into the Arabah; then they go toward the sea, being made to flow into the sea, and the waters *of the sea* become fresh. It will come about that every living creature which swarms in every place where the river goes, will live. And there will be very many fish, for these waters go there and *the others* become fresh; so everything will live where the river goes. And it will come about that fishermen will stand beside it; from Engedi to Eneglaim there will be a place for the spreading of nets. Their fish will be according to their kinds, like the fish of the Great Sea, very many. But its swamps and marshes will not become fresh; they will be left for salt. By the river on its bank, on one side and on the other, will grow all *kinds of* trees for food. Their leaves will not wither and their fruit will not fail. They will bear every month because their water flows from the sanctuary, and their fruit will be for food and their leaves for healing.

Clearly Ezekiel and John are describing the same vision of the restoration of creation to its former sinless state. In the new heavens and new earth that God will create, those who are chosen by God from before the foundation of the world will be living in the new paradise of God, a restored Eden.

The New American Commentary points out,

That the source of this river had its origin at the threshold of the sanctuary is a most significant fact. Symbolically it presents a beautiful picture of God as the Source of life for a world that thirsts for spiritual truth, including forgiveness and salvation (John 4:14; 7:37–38). The correspondence of language, symbols, and figures between Ezek 47:1–12 and Rev 22:1ff. is more than coincidental. The answer to this phenomenon is not to be found in borrowing but is evidence that there are two independent witnesses each with its vision describing the same area. Ezekiel's vision has been a common source of rituals associated with Sukkoth among Jews and with water baptism among Christians. The root meaning of these symbolic applications is expressed in the truth Ezekiel saw that God is the source of life-giving and healing waters, which flowed from his sanctuary (vv. 1–2).

The commentary continues,

> The sufficiency of this life-giving water from the throne of God is portrayed in language reminiscent of the garden of Eden and is similar to that of Rev 22:1–4. It also is another expression of the idea presented in [Ezekiel] 36:35 regarding the restoration of Eden... As Ezekiel walked with the angel-guide along the banks of the river, the guide asked, "Do you see this?" (v. 6). Ezekiel saw numerous evergreens on both banks (v. 7) that bore fruit every month (v. 12). The fruit of the trees was good for food, and the leaves of the trees had healing properties. Thus both the elements of the tree of life concept from Gen 3:22 and the restoration of the tree of life with healing and salvation of John's vision in Revelation are found in Ezekiel's vision of the healing waters of the river.

From Genesis to Revelation, the Word of God reminds us that God has provided a way to return to the sinless perfection of His new creation of the true Eden. That way is through the living water provided by God the Son, Jesus Christ. The way of salvation is only through faith in the finished work of our Lord, the Light of the World.

Revelation 22:17 reminds us,

> The Spirit and the bride say, "Come." And let the one who hears say, "Come." And let the one who is thirsty come; let the one who wishes take the water of life without cost.

The Spirit of God is speaking through those of us in the true church. As His bride, we should be speaking to all the nations and saying, "Come. Take of the water of salvation without cost. Jesus has paid the cost in full."

May the grace of God be with you all. Amen. (Revelation 22:21)

Bibliography

Adams, Jay E., *The Time is at Hand: Prophecy and the Book of Revelation*. Woodruff, SC; 2000.

Barnhouse, Donald Grey. *Revelation*. Grand Rapids, MI: Zondervan Publishing House, 1971.

Bass, Ralph Jr. E. *Back to the Future: A Study in the Book of Revelation*. Greenville, SC: Living Hope Press, 2004.

Beale, G. K., *The Book of Revelation: A Commentary on the Greek Text*. Grand Rapids, MI: William B. Eerdmans Publishing Co., 1999.

Chilton, David. *The Days of Vengeance: An Exposition of the Book of Revelation*. Horn Lake, MS: Dominion Press, 2006.

Clark, David S. *The Message from Patmos: A Postmillennial Commentary on the Book of Revelation*. Grand Rapids, MI: Baker Book House, 1989.

Hendriksen, William. *More Than Conquerors: An Interpretation of the Book of Revelation*. Grand Rapids, MI: Baker Book House, 1983.

Hoeksema, Herman. *Behold, He Cometh!: An Exposition of the Book of Revelation*. Grand Rapids, MI: Reformed Free Publishing Association, 1980.

Johnson, Dennis E. *Triumph of the Lamb: A Commentary on Revelation*. Phillipsburg, NJ: P&R Publishing, 2001.

Lenski, R. C. H. *The Interpretation of St. John's Revelation*. Minneapolis, MN: Augsburg Publishing House, 1963.

Mounce, Robert H. *The Book of Revelation*. Grand Rapids, MI: Wm. B. Eerdmans Publishing Co., 1977.

Russell, J. Stuart. *The Parousia: A Study of the New Testament Doctrine of Our Lord's Second Coming.* Grand Rapids, MI: Baker Book House, 1990.

Sproul, R. C. *The Last Days According to Jesus.* Grand Rapids, MI: Baker Book House, 1998.

Thomas, Derek. *Let's Study Revelation.* Edinburgh, UK: The Banner of Truth Trust, 2003.

Wilcock, Michael. *The Message of Revelation.* Downers Grove, IL: Inter-Varsity Press, 1975.

About the Author

Pastor David Crenshaw is a veteran of twenty years in the US Navy Submarine Force. After retirement from the Navy, he graduated from Chaminade University in Hawaii with an undergraduate degree in psychology. He then attended Westminster Theological Seminary in California at Escondido and earned both a Master of Arts in Religion and a Master of Divinity degree in a three-year program. He was ordained by the Pacific Presbytery of the Presbyterian Church in America (PCA) in January 1987 and served churches in California, Virginia, and Florida in his more than thirty years of ministry. He was honorably retired by the Gulf Coast Presbytery of the PCA in 2014. He has been active in a teaching ministry to pastors in Russia and Africa. He is coauthor (with Gordon Lunsford) of *Calvinism—Is It Biblical?: Two Sides to the Issue* and is the author of *What Is…?: Short Answers to Biblical Issues*. He and his wife, Jan, have been married since 1981. Dave enjoys teaching theology, sailing, and painting in acrylics.